AROMATHERAPY

BLENDS FOR LIFE

OTHER BOOKS BY JUDITH WHITE

Aromatherapy for Scentual Awareness

Aromatherapy for Lovers and Dreamers

Aromatherapy for Men

Aromatherapy for Natural Health

Aromatherapy for Scents and Sensuality

Make Up Make Over Make Love

AROMATHERAPY
BLENDS FOR LIFE

JUDITH WHITE

Aromatherapy is a natural therapy and a form of complementary medicine, however, it is strongly recommended that one should always consult a doctor before replacing any existing medication with an aromatherapeutic treatment. If you have any doubts about your health, consult your doctor before you embark on any treatment.

This book is not intended as a medical reference book. The information it contains is general, not specific to individuals. Do not attempt self-treatment for serious or long-term problems without consulting a qualified practitioner.

The authors and publishers disclaim all responsibility for any adverse reaction caused by inappropriate use, or poor quality essential oils.

First Published in December 1999 by
Blends for Life Pty Ltd
5 Peel Street, Collingwood VIC 3066
Ph: (03) 9416 4444 Fax: (03) 9415 9208

ISBN 0-9577710-0-2

Design by *Eli Nacson*

Front Cover Photo by *Steve Satushek, The Image Bank*

Editing by *Pat Princi-Jones*

Printed and Bound in Australia by *Mcpherson's Printing Group*

Thank you to my dear friend Leon
who inspired me to encapsulate
my aromatherapy journey in these pages,
and to the most exquisite range of
pure essential oils, In Essence.

– JUDITH WHITE

ACKNOWLEDGEMENTS

I'D LIKE TO THANK MY DEAR FRIEND AND colleague Pat Princi-Jones for taking charge of the project and ensuring that it stayed on track.

Richard Young, my highly esteemed business partner, for his friendship and encouragement.

A special thanks to Deepak Chopra for continuing to inspire and encourage me.

CONTENTS

FOREWORD

BY DEEPAK CHOPRA

As a medical practitioner and endocrinologist I have always been interested in health and wellbeing. It is this motivation that brought me also to the study of Ayurveda, the ancient Indian tradition of healing through harmony of the self and the elements within the universe. I encourage the reader of Judith's work to embrace the art of aromatherapy as a compliment to Ayurvedic practice.

With the gentle guidance of *Aromatherapy Blends For Life* you can personally experience greater wellbeing. You will find that your habits can change for the better, you can begin to make more evolutionary decisions in your life, you can assuredly make correct changes that will bring you and others joy, and you can experience the magic of the miraculous—a gift available to all.

In my own search for self-knowledge I have been opened to the realms of consciousness that have vitally transformed and enlightened my life. In Chapter 10 you will be introduced to different modes of meditation that will give you an insight into some of the methods taught thousands of years ago that are still being practised today. The technique I personally rediscovered is Primordial Sound Meditation (PSM) which is also discussed in this chapter.

Meditation is indeed a powerful force that can change our lives. I can think of nothing more important or effective in bringing about peace and prosperity to us as individuals and to the rest of our world. And as more and more people meditate, the collective consciousness of humanity will evolve with greater connection to spirit and greater conceptuality of principles which foster compassion, nurturing and abundance. Combined with the graceful art of aromatherapy, an ancient modality that has complementing qualities including healing, relaxation, creative stimulation, inspiration and many more, meditation will open for you a universe of infinite possibilities.

CHAPTER ONE

The Gift of Nature

My FIRST EXPERIENCE WITH THE HEALING POWER of essential oils came during my childhood when I was growing up in the country in Maffra, Gippsland, Victoria.

My father would wander around the garden digging the soil, tending all the plants putting in all the new seedlings. He'd wander up to the fruit trees with their new blossoms, pick some, rub them between his hands, and take a deep breath inhaling the aromatic vapours.

Then he'd put his hands to my nose and tell me to breathe in too. The glow on his face, the sparkle in his eyes, the energy he emanated taught me about the connection between fragrance, nature and healing.

Essential oils taken from plant parts can be used on their own or in combination with other essential oils to create a change in the state of the mind or the body. Essential oils offer a safe and simple alternative to conventional medicine. It is important to note however, that any natural alternative that's used to change a presenting condition, either physically, mentally, emotionally or spiritually, should not be regarded as a fix it or cure all on its own. Ultimately we are the ones who heal ourselves, and the resources we call on to assist us to heal our body and tend our mind, whether these resources are natural or otherwise, are merely supporting catalysts for change. It is the intention in how we use these substances that ultimately determines the results that we achieve. Essential oils can address physical, emotional and mental conditions. This we know because science has verified their efficacy, not only in skin care and therapeutic use but also in the pyscho-aromatherapeutic arena. The beauty of essential oils is that we can use them when we're well or unwell. They are ultimately the greatest change makers within the alternative medical industry.

Throughout the Ages

I would love to wind the clock back some 2000 years and sit with the father of medicine, Hippocrates himself to have a conversation about the value of plants and the role they play in healing both the body and the mind. I know that if we were in a dialogue certain words and phrases would be recognised and understood by both of us. Words such as aromatic bath, scented massage, restoring, healing, unguent and environmental fragrancing to name but a few. The scriptures also depict the healing power of plants. In the Bible it is written that Moses was directed to prepare a healing potion from flowering mer, sweet cinnamon, calymus, cassia and olive oil. Today myrrh is still used as an effective antiseptic for open wounds and ulcers. Why? Because scientists have validated the chemical composition of myrrh as being able to address these symptoms. Throughout the ages men and women from all walks of life have continued to explore and test the diverse ways in which natural remedies taken from plants can be used. Essential oils, heralded as one of the greatest natural plant extracts, today are used by qualified aromatherapists to address physical and mental disease.

So what are essential oils? How do they fit in to what has become a highly profiled natural remedy called aromatherapy?

Aromatherapy simply means a therapy using aromas. The aromatic part of the therapy relates to the essential oils which have been extracted from plants. All different plants from around the world. They have been extracted from flowers, roots, leaves, resins, woods, barks the list goes on. The most common method to extract essential oils from plants is steam distillation. The steam carries the essential oil molecules from the plant and undergoes a specific process, at the end delivering a distinctive fragrance. To a greater or lesser degree this has an antiseptic, antiviral and/or antibacterial nature, the degree depends on the chemical composition of the essential oil.

The aromatic essences are volatile, oily and fragrant, highly sensitive to both heat and light. The volatility of each oil varies depending on the molecular structure of the oil. Very often the essential oils are present in such small quantities within the plant, that stringent measures are taken to extract the precious yield.

Considerations include the time of day that the plant is picked; the time taken to move the plant from the source to the distillation area and, in particular, the distillation process and time of processing. These considerations determine the quality and quantity of the essential oil that's extracted.

In general essential oils pre-exist in plants. There are some which form only in the presence of water. Each one varies in colour, some appearing completely colourless. While others are distinctly coloured. They can be yellow or a reddish colour, as in cinnamon. They can be blue or green, as chamomile or bergamot. Other essential oils can appear quite dark brown. Their viscosity is determined by their natural chemical composition. Because the essential oils evaporate they aren't true oils. In fact they are soluble in alcohol, ether and fixed oils. Nevertheless, they are insoluble in water, which shows them to be, by definition an essential oil.

Essential oils undergo many different testing methods to verify their authenticity and quality. The most common methods of testing are by a liquid gas chromatograph and a mass spectrometer which identifies the active ingredients of each extract. It is the fragrance of an essential oil that is most appealing to our sense of smell. Ultimately, it is the fragrance that creates a change in the way we feel and think. Our emotions respond either favourably or not, depending on the particular aroma.

Essential oils, once tested and verified for their chemical composition, can be assessed for efficacy in, or the role they play on, our body and our mind. They can relax us, stimulate us, sedate us and they can make our blood vessels dilate or constrict. They have the capacity to do all this and more.

Most importantly, they exist to serve us and support our vitality, our health and well being. Because essential oils are so potent, it is said 70 times more potent than the plant or herb from which they are extracted, it is important to dilute them. There are hundreds of different essential oils in the world available to us for use. Scientists have declared and verified the essential oils which are unsafe or unwise to use in the arena of health and healing.

Authentic Essential Oils

It is important when you work with essential oils to choose the ones which have undergone specific testing methods to verify their authenticity; those that have followed government guidelines and procedures to protect us and enable us to choose essential oils to self prescribe for our health and well being.

The Australian Government has specified clear guidelines under the Therapeutic Goods Administration Act and has endorsed essential oils that have passed stringent testing methods. They have issued each essential oil with an identifying Aust L (Australian Listed) number on the front of the packaging. This number lets you know that the essential oil you're considering is what is says it is and is therefore safe.

The Application of Essential Oils

Today essential oils are used in a variety of ways. They're used in the food and flavouring industry. They're used in the cosmetic industry. They're used by natural therapists and by medical practitioners. There are three main methods to use essential oils: by external application, by inhalation or by internal application. For those of you who are wanting to pursue the internal application of essential oils I recommend you read Dr Danielle Penoel's work on aromatherapy. The two other applications, external and inhalation, will be explored in the following chapters.

The methods of use for these applications include massage, vaporisation, compressing, bathing, sitz baths, hand and foot baths, hair rinses, inhalation, perfumes, room sprays- to name a few. When we use essential oils on the skin they are absorbed by the hair follicle.

Once absorbed by the skin they disperse around the body and are excreted through the urine, the faeces, perspiration and exhalation. It takes between three and fourteen hours to expel essential oils from the body once they've entered. A healthy body will expel essential oils much more quickly than a diseased body. When using essential oils on children it's important to have a responsible adult administer the drops. It is vital to ensure that the correct dosage is administered (halve the number of drops for children as the oils are highly concentrated and children may be very sensitive). There are special directions in the Methods of Use Chapter, which highlight specific dosage guidelines for children. The important point to remember when using essential oils is that less is best.

Essential oils can help us maintain a healthier way of living. They generally improve our vitality, increase our confidence and self-esteem. All these elements form the basis of good health. Remember that essential oils are supporting catalysts for change. They can't maintain our health and well being on their own. We need to support them by re-evaluating the foods and liquids that we put into our bodies. Are they natural? Are they organic or bio-dynamic? Are they still rich in their essential fatty acids, vitamins and minerals? Do we take in sufficient fresh air, sunlight and exercise regularly? Are we resting and sleeping, giving our bodies time to regenerate and revitalise? Sleep and rest are vital components with any alternative therapy.

CHAPTER TWO

Blends for Life

OVER THE LAST 15 YEARS, I HAVE BEEN USING essential oils on a daily basis. My compendium has varied marginally during this time. It's interesting that, for more than a decade and with all the choices available within the aromatherapy industry, I still choose the essential oils which have had the greatest effect, physically, mentally, emotionally and spiritually.

This compendium of essential oils, which I call, Blends for Life, contains the blends that I use in my life. I offer them to you from experience. I trust that you will enjoy them as much as I have. These essential oils have formed the basis of my skincare. They have helped me heal my most turbulent emotional states, and supported my husband and children through sickness and in health. They are the 40 heroes of the essential oil spectrum and will help support you too in your ever-changing existence. For those of you who have read my previous work, you will see familiar words and phrases, those that are generic to the art of aromatherapy and each of the oils. However, this compilation is an endeavour to go one step further and express my new phase of aromatherapy and how to use essential oils. Thus I seek to give you something fresh and new all in one book. It's a little bit like an encyclopedia of recipes and oils and methods of use. It's condensing something from the past into something new and current, filled with fresh possibilities. I have included new recipes and revised others to give you over a thousand and one combinations, so as to speak!

There is also, a new component that I have included. This is the cultural, energetic presence that I have contemplated is inherent within each essential oil. Just as we are beings made up of a soul and spirit, so too is nature the sum total of the seen and the unseen.

Elements of this can be recognised in the work of Rudolf Steiner. Likewise, Rosemary Steel's work with Kirlian photographs indicates that plants have an energy, an aura as do all living things. I believe this unseen force or, energy that emanates from the plant is embodied in the essential oil and captured too is all the impression of the culture and the geography from which it originates. I have included a brief impression, a brush stroke, of the culture of the country of origin for several of the following forty oils. This endeavour is two-fold. Firstly, it celebrates the rich and diverse cultural mass on this planet and secondly it provides a background for what I call the energetic force present within each of the oils in question.

I trust this will deepen your appreciation of each oil as you consider the impact of the energetic presence in your life.

The snapshot of cultures that I have included in this chapter are Austria (Juniper), Tunisia (Neroli), Morocco (Cedarwood), Russia (Clary Sage), Germany (German Chamomile), Bulgaria (Rose Otto), Egypt (Basil), Africa (Frankincense) and Australia (Eucalyptus). These countries do not indicate the optimum growing conditions nor do they signify the historical origins of each of the oils in question. This concept will be given status in my next book which will contemplate the historical origins of the Blends for Life oil.

This idea is also considered in my recent publication, Make Up, Make Over Make Love which further contemplates essential oils and their energetic presence in greater depth

It is noted that essential oils are very valuable as antiseptics because their aggression towards germs is matched by their total harmlessness to tissue. It is most important when treating disease in the body to know that the essential oil can go to work on the microbes without assaulting the healthy tissue.

Basil

BOTANICAL NAME: *Ocimum basilicum*
COUNTRY OF ORIGIN: *Egypt, India*
Derived from the herb flower

Basil is an oil for enthusiasm. When sudden doubts occur or confusion reigns, use Basil to reflect. This oil will help you to get in touch with your intuition and assist the decision making process. It is extremely effective for relieving mental fatigue and has a clarifying effect on the brain. A vaporiser is the ideal way to emit Basil for concentration and clarity.

Physically, Basil is an appetite stimulant and digestive aid. Emotionally, it can be used to activate an appetite for life. Purpose and focus are valued qualities brought about by this herbaceous oil.

Basil is excellent as a chest rub for all kinds of respiratory ailments such as bronchitis, coughs and colds. Use Basil in a compress application to relieve migraines. It is an excellent all-round nerve tonic, bringing energy and strength.

Still today in India, Basil is grown in households at the front entrance to ward off unfortunate destinies and evil spirits, and to ensure immortality.

An ideal choice if you're just about to conduct or attend a business conference, or for any environment where you are wanting the participants to be more focused when receiving important data that is to be remembered. An ideal choice to centre your focus during the mantra meditation.

CULTURE

Egypt, the land of the Pharaohs spans from the pyramids to the Valley of Kings, from the crowded streets of Cairo to the remote oasis of the desert. The Nile River is lined with date palms, and fruit and vines grow abundantly in the fertile Delta. The sea is a brilliant turquoise blue and deserted bays and sandy beaches line its shores. Cairo, the capital, is a city of temples and mosques. It is a multi-cultural melting-pot, a modern day metropolis and a magnificent oriental bazaar. The great port of Alexandria, once the centre of trade and education, is where Euclid and other scholars took inspiration. Egypt is the ancient city of Thebes, it is symbolised by the great pyramids built of granite and limestone, by marble statues representing deities and Tutankhamen's solid gold portrait mask which has triumphed and defied the ravages of time.

THE ENERGETIC PRESENCE

The energetic presence of Basil is survival, precision and contentment. It is for those who seek to be in touch with all that has been, all that is and all that will be. Basil brings about clarity especially in the heat of the moment. Basil facilitates contrast, focus and contemplation - useful resources when making decisions and considering the impact that they will have in the world.

VIRTUES

Basil is efficacious for situations involving apprehension, confusion, nervous exhaustion, lethargy, depression, loss of memory, irregular periods, spasmodic coughing, headaches and migraines, indigestion, wasp stings, snake bites (first aid only), mosquito repellant.

FUNCTIONS

Mind and Emotions: To focus thoughts, promote clear thinking. For decision making. Restorative.

Body: Anti-spasmodic, assists digestion, to induce and regulate menstruation.

Skin Care: Stimulating tonic for congested skins (use sparingly). Improves hair lustre.

PRECAUTIONS

Avoid topical use during pregnancy.

Bergamot

BOTANICAL NAME: ***Citrus aurantium s. bergamia***
COUNTRY OF ORIGIN: ***Italy and Ivory Coast***
Derived from the peel of the fruit

Bergamot delights the senses. When spontaneity and light heartedness is called for vaporise Bergamot into the environment or soak in an aromatic bath. Consider as an essentially cooling oil which quells anxiety and promotes the flow of energy throughout the body. When things seem stuck, this is the oil to bring movement and flow. With its refreshing qualities, it is great for melancholy and depression. It encourages a feeling of letting go.

When you have nervous butterflies, inhale a few drops before embracing the situation to disperse pent up emotions and concerns.

The citrussy aroma makes this oil extremely versatile. It blends well with other oils and will often enhance the bouquet of their fragrance. It was documented in Italian folk medicine as an antiseptic. As a facial oil it is an excellent acne treatment when blended in Jojoba. It is also good for oily skin problems. Use it in a compress and for the treatment of dermatitis.

If you are a teacher, presenter of facilitator of information to an audience, simply breathe in the aromatic vapours to disperse those pre-presentation jitters. This oil elevates the spirit when practising visualisations.

VIRTUES

Bergamot is useful in dealing with anorexia nervosa, loss of appetite due to nervous conditions, stressful states, nervous anxiety, melancholy, depression, nervous butterflies. Skin disorders—eczema, dermatitis, wounds and sores, acne. Intestinal parasites, adult colic, urinary infection and cramps.

FUNCTIONS

Mind and Emotions: To disperse nervous anxiety, uplifting, refreshing, balancing. Promotes energy flow and a positive outlook.

Body: Stimulates appetite, antiseptic. Relieving. Supports general wellbeing.

Skin Care: Assists healing (especially eczema and dermatitis), highly antiseptic, cleansing.

PRECAUTIONS

Bergamot is photosensitive. Not to be used externally in the presence of ultra-violet light, ie sunbaking or sunbeds, for up to twelve hours following applications.

Black Pepper

BOTANICAL NAME: ***Piper nigrum***
COUNTRY OF ORIGIN: ***India, Indonesia***
Derived from the fruit

Black Pepper is an energising oil great for endurance. This oil brings warmth and activity to both body and mind, especially when you feel you can't go on, as it stimulates mental faculties and energises the body.

Improving our performance in these very demanding times often needs high energy levels to be maintained. Black Pepper is the oil for stamina and direction.

Change can sometimes bring a deep sense of uncertainty. Black Pepper can help promote steadfastness during life changes. It will be especially beneficial to build self-esteem and confidence, giving a new sense of direction.

A great body oil for physical activities, before – to bring confidence mentally, and after – to prevent stiffness occurring physically. With its stimulating and mobilising qualities, it can be used to assist in weight loss when massaged in a blend over the area of concern. Assists in the maintenance of peripheral circulation and healthy digestive function.

VIRTUES

Use Back Pepper to aid you in dealing with the following: Fatigue–physical and emotional, for dramatic life changes, mental exhaustion, disorientation, debilitation.

Arthritis, poor muscle tone, sprains and strains, muscle stiffness.

Constipation and sluggish conditions, heartburn and flatulence. Obesity.

FUNCTIONS

Mind and Emotions: Improves endurance levels and motivation. Uplifts despondent moods. Recharges the batteries. Strengthens the nervous system.

Body: Eases muscular aches and pains, or stiffness after physical exertion. Warms and stimulates the body functions. Add to any weight loss blend.

Skin Care: Cleansing to cuts and wounds–use highly diluted. Assists to head bruising and chilblains.

Cardamon

BOTANICAL NAME: ***Elettaria cardomomum***
COUNTRY OF ORIGIN: ***Ecuador, Guatamala***
Derived from the seeds

Fortitude and courage are just two of the attributes of this spicy oil. Cardamon can bring purpose and inspiration, especially when you are feeling stretched. This is an oil to assist our resolve when we are burdened by worries and concerns. Cardamom brings balance to the situation.

Used for digestion, it is particularly helpful for nervous digestive disorders and helps to settle vomiting, heartburn, indigestion and colic. Warms the body during the colder months. Protects against coughs and colds and will break down mucous congestion. This is an excellent oil for those with an addictive nature. Cardamon helps to break the addictive pattern.

Extensively used as a domestic spice for its purging qualities. Cardamon has been around for 3,000 years in Chinese and Indian medicine. Still today, it is included in modern herbal texts (pharmacopoeia), with many having confirmed its known aphrodisiac qualities. Experience the fragrance of Cardamon during Zazen meditation.

VIRTUES

Cardamon is helpful when dealing with: Apathy, inflexibility. Lack of focus or direction. Impatience. Impotence and frigidity. Indigestion and gastritis. Anorexia, diarrhoea, dyspepsia. Chest congestion, bronchitis, coughs, colds and flu. PMS. Sciatica.

FUNCTIONS

Mind and Emotions: Helps to expand perspectives in any situation. Invigorating and stabilising as it counteracts stress. Relieves mental exhaustion. Warming, uplifting.

Body: Relieves indigestion, flatulence, vomiting. Assists in poor digestion, especially where dairy products are concerned. Stimulates peripheral circulation. Excellent as a tonic for the immune system.

Skin Care: Particularly good on the internal processes of the body and is therefore effective on the sub-cutis layer of the skin which acts as the skin's digestive system.

Cedarwood

BOTANICAL NAME: ***Juniperus virginiana***
COUNTRY OF ORIGIN: ***North America, Morocco, France***
Derived from the wood

One of the oldest know essential oils, Cedarwood can bring a quality of certainty and reassurance. It has a stabilising and grounding influence on the mind and emotions. With these qualities it encourages the will and gives the power to be steadfast during times of trauma or crisis.

Throughout the Middle East in ancient times, it was used extensively to build places of worship including temples and tombs. Used in the construction of King Solomon's temple, it symbolically represented abundance, bringing with it fertility and inner strength. A great oil for life's journey.

It is often used in men's toiletries due to its popular woody fragrance. Many men will enjoy its fragrant attributes. It carries a sense of dignity and power.

Cedarwood when used in a vaporiser or inhaled, greatly assists chest complaints such as catarrh and bronchitis: it decongests and strengthens. With its restorative powers it can support the cleansing of the body via the lymphatic system. Therefore it is of value during weight loss programs. Used in conjunction with Rosemary, it can assist in restoring hair growth.

CULTURE

With its long Atlantic seaboard, soaring Atlas mountains and lush desert oases, Morocco is a strikingly beautiful country. It represents an exotic brew of rich Arab and Berber culture with a strong French influence. A country where elegantly groomed townswomen jostle with Jabali tribeswomen and where tradition and modernity comfortably coexist. One is entranced by this country of striking contrasts where handsome, swathed horsemen fire muskets and the air is charged with the smell of jasmine scented courtyards. Where outcrops of palms and white-domed Kolibbas lift the many shades of pink, ginger and brown. Scratch the newest surface of this ancient kingdom and you will find the astonishing world of Scheherazade, where strange deeds and magic prevail.

THE ENERGETIC PRESENCE

The energetic presence is one of preservation, longevity and invincibility. For those who wish to deepen their appreciation of life and draw the breath of colourful experience into the lungs of the soul. Moroccan Cedarwood is for those who wish to deepen their appreciation of life, to draw the breath of individualism into the lungs of the soul and those who seek to feel triumphant over life's obstacles.

VIRTUES

Consider using Cedarwood when confronting or dealing with the following: Nervous debility, emotional instability. Mental strain. Chronic anxiety and tension. Sense of being overwhelmed.

Alopecia (hair loss), skin conditions where flakiness occurs–dermatitis, eczema, dandruff, psoriasis, seborrhoea of the scalp.

Chest conditions such as catarrh, bronchial cough, congestion.

Genito-urinary infections.

FUNCTIONS

Mind and Emotions: Relaxing, regenerating, stabilising and strengthening. For persistence and dignity. Restorative.

Body: Restorative as a general tonic. Promotes longevity. Relieves congestion. Promotes cleansing activity in the body. Fortifying mildly diuretic.

Skin Care: Preserving, regenerating, hair restorer. Improving the quality of the skin.

Chamomile (GERMAN)

BOTANICAL NAME: ***Matricaria chamomilla***
COUNTRY OF ORIGIN: ***Germany, France, Egypt***
Derived from the flowers

German Chamomile is at work to balance one of the most important energy centres of the body–the solar plexus. This vital point can be the core of pent up frustrations and conflicts. German Chamomile can dissipate tension and promote a sense of ease and inner-peace. This allows us to dismiss old resentments and move on.

With its calming influence, German Chamomile is an oil for bedtime, to help carry you off into a deep sleep.

As a result, you will feel more deeply rested with a greater sense of inner contentment.

The most anti-inflammatory of all the essential oils, German Chamomile possesses wonderful healing qualities and is particularly good for applying on inflamed areas of the body.

In ancient Egypt, Chamomile was used as a significant part of the medicine system. It was used to call upon the sun god Ra who played an important part in restoring the body's health. In fact, it was said to have the power to restore a sense of connectedness with the inner-self.

CULTURE

Germany is a country of diversity, variety and contradictions. It has elements of Baroque style and Prussian splendour and boasts a dramatically successful industrialisation with a highly disciplined and regimented work force. Its struggle and glory are epitomised in its capital, Berlin, a city which has long been the collision point of Eastern and Western Europe. Here, bohemia and opulence, the oppressed and liberated, the insecure and the extrovert, mix. The country is also reminiscent of a wonderful panorama of woods and forests, farmhouses with crumbling Prussian moldings and lakes where herons and kingfishers suddenly rise from the surface of the water.

THE ENERGETIC PRESENCE

The energetic presence is one of stature, a serious earnest approach to structure and form. Inner strength and solidarity temper inflammatory issues. German Chamomile is useful for those who with to tame and consolidate an over whimsical approach to life and living.

VIRTUES

German Chamomile's positive energy can help in dealing with the following: Anger at self and others, frustration and irritability. Nervous tension. Unexpressed emotions and upsets. Bitterness and deep seated resentment. For conditions in the body: bursitis, laryngitis, tonsillitis, cystitis, neuritis, dermatitis, bronchitis. Hayfever, eczema, neuralgia, thrush, abscesses. Burns, skin irritation, psoriasis and acne.

FUNCTIONS

Mind and Emotions: Inner calm, gently sedating, fulfilment. Brings comfort during times of stress or nervous anxiety.

Body: Anti-inflammatory, bronchitis, laryngitis, tonsillitis. An antibacterial wash for wounds. Assists to relieve pain and inflammation.

Skin Care: Relieves discomfort and irritation of allergies. Soothes dermal inflammation. Calming.

Chamomile (Roman)

Botanical name: ***Anthemis nobilis***
Country of origin: ***England, France, Egypt***
Derived from the flowers

Roman Chamomile is a truly great essential oil. While it is closely related to German Chamomile, it is another of the Chamomile species but its qualities are marginally different. It is cooling and calming to any agitated or emotional state and is great for deepened states of relaxation and meditation. It has a calming, soothing effect on both the body and mind.

Chamomile and Lavender have some properties in common. The nurturing properties bring serenity and calm.

Roman Chamomile has particular qualities which can balance the female reproductive organs, especially when applied in a massage blend to the abdominal area. It assists to regulate the menstrual cycle.

Hippocrates used Chamomile for fevers, whilst others have used it for the treatment of young children because of its known gentle calming properties. Both species have long been part of herbal medicine texts. Chamomile herbal tea is a wonderful beverage when made with the flowers and ideal to sip before retiring to bed. With its calming and sleep-inducing effect, you can sleep like a babe.

VIRTUES

Roman Chamomile's gentle supportive presence can assist with: Nervousness, hypersensitivity, unstable emotions, irritability. Being unreasonable and difficult. Anger and fear. PMT, rheumatism, gout, flatulence, conjunctivitis, allergies, dermatitis. Irritated skin. Irritable bowel, gastric discomfort. Anaemia, loss of appetite, flatulence.

FUNCTIONS

Mind and Emotions: Soothing, calming, releasing. Encourages patience and serenity.

Body: Regulates menstruation, relieves painful menstrual cramps, balances female reproductive system. Soothing to irritated conditions.

Skin Care: Deodorising. Relieves and soothes. Lightening to fair hair.

Clary Sage

BOTANICAL NAME: ***Salvia sclarea***
COUNTRY OF ORIGIN: ***Austria, Russia, China***
Derived from the flowers

This is the most euphoric of all essential oils. It is particularly effective in the type of stress-related problems where tension is experienced in the mind and the body. In states of fatigue, even the most despondent person can feel they have taken a revival tonic.

The Latin botanical name for this oil means *clear* and still today, as in ancient times, it is renowned for this medicinal quality. It can restore clarity to both body and mind as it dispels nervous anxiety and confusion, and simultaneously relieves the body of tension. As a result our insight and intuitive forces are restored.

Clary Sage will be of great benefit to young girls. It assists in the transition into adolescence, when both emotional and physical changes are dramatic. Then during the menopausal phase of a woman's life Clary Sage is there to support the transition; these are times when sensitivity is needed.

For the relief of menstrual cramping apply a few drops neat, using friction massage to the abdominal area. Use a compress or massage blend to relieve PMS. It restores a sense of equilibrium, especially for women. Used to increase self-awareness during Vipassana meditation.

CULTURE ***(Russia)***

The excitement of this monumental country is the excitement of change clashing with tradition. Russia has survived Tartar hordes, Polish occupation and the rise of

Soviet domination. The Kremlin marks the reign of the Tsars during which time Moscow flourished as one of the most cultured cities in the world. Now it is faced with the inequalities caused by economic freedom and tourists are viewed with interest in this vast isolated country. The traditional street image of Moscow is grey waves of fur-hatted, booted citizens, struggling through deep snow. The babushkas (elderly ladies) still shout and point if your head is not adequately covered and the marble halls and stained glass panels within the Metro seem incongruous with the recent prosaic tower blocks that loom over the capital.

THE ENERGETIC PRESENCE

The energetic presence is one of leadership and self-expression brought about through change. Poise and resilience and the ability to raise oneself beyond limitation are also contained within this oil. Ideal for those moving beyond the entrapment of the mundane and seeking a sophisticated wisdom.

VIRTUES

Because it brings clarity and is an adjunct to transitional phases in life, Clary Sage helps deal with: Depression, postnatal depression, oversensitivity. Uncontrollable emotions, paranoia and nightmares, despondency. Irregular and absent menstruation, abdominal cramps, PMT, menopausal hot flushes, frigidity. Tired, aching legs. Stomach and kidney disorders. Vertigo. Sore throats. Oily skin and hair. Cellulite.

FUNCTIONS

Mind and Emotions: Euphoric, uplifting, promotes communication, harmonises. Reduces tension, especially PMS. Inspiring.

Body: Regulates menstruation–heavy or painful periods. Relieving. Soothing to sore throats. Assists in maintaining healthy digestive function.

Skin Care: Cell regeneration, especially for ageing skin. Assist to regulate production of sebum.

PRECAUTIONS

Avoid topical application during pregnancy.

Cypress

BOTANICAL NAME: *Cupressus sempervirens*
COUNTRY OF ORIGIN: *Spain, France*
Derived from the leaves and twigs

This oil helps to disperse nervous tension. It makes a wonderful blend with Cedarwood as a treatment for those who feel they have lost touch with life. In ancient times it was said to be a cure for a grieving heart and to be associated with the immortality of the soul, thus it is often found growing near cemeteries.

With its reassuring qualities, it can be of value in times of change when deep wisdom and patience is needed. The Cypress trees with its lofty peaks and slender form serves to remind us of our own majestic qualities. This, in turn, helps us to move forward when transition and change are required.

Throughout ancient civilisations, Cypress was highly valued as a medicine and an incense. Cypress may help to prevent asthma attacks and treat whooping cough and croup, especially if they are wet type conditions. It is also useful in treating all conditions where excess fluid is a problem, and to tonify the body during weight loss programs. This highly astringent oil is ideal for treating oily skin.

VIRTUES

Cypress' gentle supportive essence helps alleviate some of the strains in times of transition. Use it in dealing with any of the following: Feeling discontented. Impatient. Weariness. Grief. Bereavement. Haemorrhoids, varicose veins, fluid retention. Loss of voice, whooping cough, colds, acute and chronic bronchitis. Sweaty palms and feet. Rheumatism and osteoarthritis.

FUNCTIONS

Mind and Emotions: To disperse nervous anxiety, to relieve concern and worry. Assists us to make dramatic transition in life, moving from one phase to another. Comforting.

Body: Astringent, antibacterial, vein tonic – helps to strengthen veins. Eases painful periods. Sweat regulator. Venous decongestant – helps to move the flow of blood.

Skin Care: For oily skin as a tonic. Anti-perspirant, deodorant. Detoxifying.

PRECAUTIONS

Avoid topical application during pregnancy.

Eucalyptus

BOTANICAL NAME: ***Eucalyptus globulus***
COUNTRY OF ORIGIN: ***China, Australia, Spain***
Derived from the leaves

Eucalyptus has a cleansing effect on the mind and body. Eucalyptus brings energy and vitality to any circumstance or situation that seems stagnant. Inhale the cleansing vapours of Eucalyptus to clear the head and bring rational thoughts to the task at hand. It is refreshing and invigorating. An oil to motivate and get things started.

It is one of the most antiviral essential oils and works miracles as an inhalant for coughs, colds and flu. It will clear the sinuses. In a massage blend as a chest rub, it will decongest and be effective for all respiratory conditions. Anti-catarrhal and anti-infectious, it can be used in any hospital or first aid environment to disinfect. As a general body tonic it can enhance the function of breathing and promote oxygen uptake thoughout the body.

CULTURE *(Australia)*

Australia's paradox lies in the fact that it is one of the oldest and one of the youngest continents at the same time. Some 50,000 years ago, Aborigines crossed from Asia Minor to settle in Terra Australis yet it was only 200 years ago that the First Fleet landed in New South Wales. Now, it is a vibrant country with a cosmopolitan population and an international perspective. The cities sprawl endlessly and the heat in summer rises off the bitumen to form a delicate, shimmering haze. The endless kilometres of white sand and blue ocean form a coastline of scalloped and sheltered beaches. The wilderness is captured in the vast display of eucalyptus trees from which emanates a greyish-blue aura. It is the country where the amber fluid and Aussie Rules dominate.

THE ENERGETIC PRESENCE

The energetic presence is one of daring optimism. This oil engenders a pioneering spirit which resonates with opportunity and adventure. The courage and resilience are also charismatic at the same time. Ideal for those wishing to open up, go with the flow and thrive.

VIRTUES

With its up-lifting, invigorating and energising presence use Eucalyptus for dealing with: Melancholic moods, exhaustion, lack of concentration, irrational behaviour. All respiratory disorders, coughs, colds and flu. Sinusitis, bronchitis and catarrh. To clear infection. Relieves muscular aches and pains. High temperature and fevers, rheumatism and arthritis.

FUNCTIONS

Mind and Emotions: Invigorating, clarifying, opening and clearing, energising. Restores vitality to the thinking process.

Body: Decongestant, stimulating and activating. Promotes oxygen uptake, anti-viral. Stimulates circulation. Promotes wellbeing. Strengthens the immune system. An energising tonic.

Skin Care: Promotes oxygen exchange. Decongesting to sluggish skin. A great tonic to revitalise.

PRECAUTIONS

Avoid topical application during pregnancy.

Fennel

BOTANICAL NAME: ***Fonneculum vulgare***
COUNTRY OR ORIGIN: ***Spain***
Derived from the crushed seeds

This oil has a warm aniseed bouquet and is perfect for encouraging communication. For those engaged in projects when new ideas need to be generated, Fennel can expand the creative process. This is the oil to support productive and talented people express themselves more fully. This is certainly an oil to promote self-expression, bringing confidence and clarity to communication.

The seeds were said to be eaten by Olympic athletes in ancient times to enhance their performance. Fennel can act as a tonic in physical situations where endurance and fortitude are needed. Long seen as an oil which conveys strength, courage and longevity. The ancient Greeks discovered the worth of Fennel as a diuretic and an aid to weight loss. It is a potent digestive aid, especially working in the lower intestinal area. It relieves nausea, morning sickness, travel sickness, colic and flatulence. It helps to increase the flow of digestive juices. For nursing mothers it will increase the flow of milk and also assist to balance out excess fluids and fatty tissue retained in the body after pregnancy.

During menstruation, Fennel can be used as an invaluable aid in the treatment of irregular and painful periods. Due to its detoxifying function which acts upon the liver, Fennel is an extremely beneficial oil as a hangover remedy.

VIRTUES

Because of its fortifying and detoxifying properties, Fennel can assist in: Emotional need and mental blockages. Lack of creativity. Nervous anxiety, feelings of insecurity. Fear of failure. Digestive problems such as nausea, colic, flatulence, constipation. Menopausal problems, PMS, irregular periods. Aids weight loss programs for obesity and bloating. Catarrh and chest congestion. Sluggish digestion and lymphatic system.

FUNCTIONS

Mind and Emotions: Calming and warming. Encourages communication and brings a productive energy. Strengthens. Self expression.

Body: Digestive support to the stomach, liver and intestines. Balances oestrogen levels in the body. Excellent during PMS, menstruation and menopause. A tonic to cleanse and purge the body.

Skin Care: Tonifies open pored skin. An excellent astringent for cleansing and purifying the skin.

PRECAUTIONS

Avoid topically on hypersensitive, diseased or damaged skin. Avoid topical application during pregnancy.

Frankincense

BOTANICAL NAME: ***Boswellia thurifera***
COUNTRY OF ORIGIN: ***Persia, Arabia***
Derived from the gum of the tree

This is an oil that instills tranquility. Frankincense affects us at the deepest level, setting our spirit free. By using Frankincense in a vaporiser we can enhance the blissful state of meditation. Throughout history, Frankincense has been used for its spiritual and religious qualities – to dismiss negative energies, to hold at bay evil spirits. It was often used as incense to expand consciousness and awaken the spirit within. We use it in its essential oil form for these qualities.

Frankincense will bring courage and strength to all occasions. It will fortify and comfort at all levels. The resin from which Frankincense is distilled has been burnt on altars for centuries and continues to be held as a sacred remedy. It can be used to dispel fear, paranoia and nightmares because it puts us in touch with an inner peace and truth.

It promotes a peaceful state of mind while meditating.

Due to its rejuvenating qualities, it can be used as a skin tonic – especially for mature skins – to revitalise and regenerate. For the body and the mind it will heal old wounds.

CULTURE *(Africa)*

Africa is a formidable country of staggering beauty and contrasts. It is a country of wild life safaris and peaceful beaches, of fertile plantations and barren deserts, of sheer mountains and dense forests and of remote villages and sophisticated towns. Its people originate from nomadic herder immigrants from Ethiopia who brought livestock into Kenya. Africa has also had a strong Arab influence followed by colonial rule and now faces the ultimate struggle for freedom. The country is depicted by the rare sable antelope, the spectacular views down the Gorges Valley and the shallow soda lake of Bogoria where gazelles and impalas migrate annually.

THE ENERGETIC PRESENCE

The energetic presence is one of agility, fortitude, exploration and survival. African Frankincense connects us with our immortal nature and conjures the courage to surmount obstacles. Ideal for those who choose to surpass fear and limitation.

VIRTUES

Because of its use in spiritual traditions, Frankincense is ideal for healing. Used for old emotional wounds, emotional or mental anguish, paranoia, nightmares and irrational fears. Sores, wounds, stress conditions in the body, especially where operative practices have occurred or repair is needed. Aggravated joints. Ulcerated skin, ulcers. Diarrhoea, fluid retention and excessive watery type conditions in the body. Old injuries or wounds. Injured tissue. Bronchial irritation. For weight loss regimes.

FUNCTIONS

Mind and Emotions: To reflect inwardly. Meditative. Rejuvenating, comforting and fortifying. For tranquility in quiet moments – to still the mind. Healing the past.

Body: Deeply relaxing. Heals both the superficial and deeper layers of the body. Will assist in repair. Relieves irritation and will act as a mild expectorant. A mild diuretic to assist in tonifying the body.

Skin Care: Helps rejuvenate mature skin. Repairing and healing to the superficial layers.

PRECAUTIONS

Avoid topically on hypersensitive, diseased or damaged skin.

Geranium

BOTANICAL NAME: ***Pelargonium graveolens, Macfaden***
COUNTRY OF ORIGIN: ***Egypt, China, Morocco***
Derived from the herb

This is certainly an oil that takes care of both the physical and emotional. This is the oil to balance the highs and lows. Bringing a certain sense of calm and assuredness, you are left feeling more stable and comforted.

In times of rapid change and uncertainty, Geranium will promote and assist you to regain your emotional composure and respond with sensitivity and ease. This oil nourishes the feminine spirit and restores harmony.

Geranium balances the body during dramatic hormonal changes, i.e. during menopause and puberty. It regulates excessive blood flow and it encourages the natural rhythms of circulation to return to the body. On a physical and emotional level, it is an excellent choice for postnatal women.

Experience Geranium during your Primordial Sound Meditation.

VIRTUES

Due to its ability to balance use Geranium at the following times: Emotional extremes, feeling overwhelmed, inflexibility, insensitivity, mood swings. Nervous tension and anxiety. PMT, menopause. Irregular menstrual cycle. Used to treat the symptoms of eczema, shingles and chaffed skin. Bruising and congested skin types. For rheumatism and lymphatic congestion. Neuralgia.

FUNCTIONS

Mind and Emotions: Provides consolation during emotional extremes. Soothes, stablises and balances. Brings comfort. To support the nervous system. To encourage a sense of ease.

Body: Balancing to hormonal irregularities and functions. Excellent to support during menopause and menstruation, Analgesic, antispasmodic, astringent.

Skin Care: Promotes healing, normalises sebum production, antiseptic and astringent.

PRECAUTIONS

Do not use topically on inflamed or damaged skin.

Ginger

BOTANICAL NAME: ***Zingiber officinalis***
COUNTRY OF ORIGIN: ***China, West Indies***
Derived from the root

This oil restores a sense of optimism, energy and goodwill to plans that have been thwarted or delayed. When things are at their lowest ebb, use Ginger to restore confidence and vitality. An excellent tonic for the mind and the body.

This widely appreciated oil has, for centuries, been used for its digestive properties. It can help to assimilate food or to relieve nausea and indigestion. This makes Ginger an ideal travelling companion for those who experience motion sickness or digestive disorders.

In the cold of winter, protect and warm your body by adding Ginger to your massage blend, especially in temperature extremes, to aid the flow of blood to the hands and feet. With its energetic qualities it would be wise to use this oil when feeling cold and vulnerable, physically and emotionally.

Vaporise to further enhance the environment during Transcendental Meditation.

VIRTUES

Because Ginger imbues a situation with its stimulating warmth use it in the following situations: Poor memory, tiredness, nervous exhaustion, lethargy, resignation. Swollen glands, sore throat, colds, flu, poor circulation, especially to extremities, i.e. to hands and feet.

Varicose veins or where physical injury has occurred–sprains or strains. Constipation, headaches, frigidity and loss of appetite, nausea, gastric conditions, bacterial infections affecting digestive system.

FUNCTIONS

Mind and Emotions: Warming, encouraging. To replenish yourself. Acts to sharpen the senses. Stimulating and grounding during times of stress and change.

Body: Expectorant action on the lungs. Stimulates circulation due to its warming qualities.

Skin Care: Clearing to the skin. Regulates moisture content of the skin. Tonifying.

PRECAUTIONS

Avoid topically during pregnancy.

Grapefruit

BOTANICAL NAME: ***Citrus paradisi***
COUNTRY OF ORIGIN: ***Israel, California, South Africa***
Derived from the peel of the fruit

This popular citrus oil promotes alertness and sharpens the senses. Its bright and refreshing nature will boost confidence, bringing with it a certain sense of reassurance. Use this oil to promote spontaneity and light heartedness especially when feeling overwhelmed.

Grapefruit will serve you well during any weight loss program. Use this oil to settle anxiety and comfort when food cravings occur.

It assists in activating functions of the liver, especially in the production of bile, therefore aiding the digestive process. It has mild diuretic properties and can assist to break down fats in the body. An excellent support in the treatment of obesity and cellulite.

Grapefruit's refreshing and antiseptic qualities make it a great aid to cleanse any office or home environment.

VIRTUES

Grapefruit's bright and lively qualities make it ideal for dealing with: Lethargy. Negative thinking. Despondency. Dependency. Depression. Anxiety and self doubt. Anorexia. Bulimia. Sluggish lymphatic system. Muscle fatigue, colds and flu. Alcohol and drug withdrawal. Athlete's Foot. Hair loss. Obesity. Cellulite. Oily skin.

FUNCTIONS

Mind and Emotions: Brings spontaneity and euphoria. Brings reassurance and comfort. Confidence booster. Purifies.

Body: Stimulates gall bladder, liver tonic. Can be used effectively to activate the lymphatic system and peripheral circulation. Assists to regulate body weight, a healthy digestive function and general wellbeing.

Skin Care: Promotes activity in circulation. Cleanses and purifies the skin. An excellent tonic to tighten and tone the skin. Aids hair growth.

PRECAUTIONS

Grapefruit is photosensitive. Not to be used topically in the presence of ultra violet light, ie sunbaking or sunbeds, for up to twelve hours following application.

Jasmine

BOTANICAL NAME: ***Jasminum officinale***
COUNTRY OF ORIGIN: ***India, France***
Derived from the flower

This sensual and exotic aroma with its renowned aphrodisiac qualities has the ability to arouse the senses and warm the heart. For those who suffer from nervous exhaustion, pessimism or difficulty in communicating, this is the oil to open conversation more positively.

It has been celebrated for its ability to arouse and intoxicate. It is an intoxicating oil which appeals to both men and women. On a physical and emotional level, Jasmine will bring balance.

It can assist balance disorders of the reproductive organs. It is indicated for frigidity and impotence and is an excellent aid in the treatment of menopause. Its potent balancing qualities can be of great value during labour to ease the pain and enhance the joy of the experience.

VIRTUES

Because of its uplifting and buoyant qualities, Jasmine is useful for the following situations: Irrational fears, nervous anxiety. Vulnerability. Pessimism. Low self-esteem and guilt. For frigidity and impotence. Labour pains, PMS, menopausal highs and lows, painful periods. Eases muscular aches and pains including painful abdominal cramps. Headaches. Bacterial infections, dermatitis and catarrhal conditions.

FUNCTIONS

Mind and Emotions: Euphoric, sensual. Boosts confidence and dispels fear. A mender of the heart. Especially good to bring optimism and a sense of renewed self expression and openness. Awakens passion.

Body: To soothe and calm. For general wellbeing. To promote sensual awareness. To arouse and sharpen sensitivity. Antiseptic.

Skin Care: To soften and soothe irritated skin. Can be used to assist in the healing of stretch marks.

Juniper

BOTANICAL NAME: *Juniperus communis*
COUNTRY OF ORIGIN: *Austria, France, Yugoslavia*
Derived from the fruit

Juniper works on the mind to help clear unwanted emotions, thereby relieving tension. With its purging qualities, Juniper can bring a sense of resolve and movement to situations that have been stagnant and restricted, releasing the burden of worry and concern.

The Chinese have for centuries revered this tree as possessing immortal qualities for spiritual purification. It is distilled from the ripe berries of the tree and has an exquisite fresh aroma.

As a purifying agent in the body it brings aid to fluid retention and rids the body of other toxic wastes. Excellent as a decongestant to the lymphatic system. This is an oil with activating properties to cleanse and mobilise, and can assist to relieve the symptoms of arthritic or rheumatic conditions. Due to its cleansing and purifying properties, it can clear the tissue of bruising or where wounds have damaged the tissue. Excellent as a joint rub in your massage blend to relieve the symptoms of joint injury or muscle tear. It is a liver tonic and can be used as a remedy for hangovers or excessive alcohol intake.

CULTURE *(Austria)*

Austria is a country where perpetual charm lies in the gradually evolving harmony between architecture and landscape. The treasures that arrest the onlooker are from Celtic and Roman generations. It is a country of exquisite panorama and of dignified houses. Baroque churches, defiant castles and lofty spires rise above the roof-tops; at every glimpse one encounters elegance and sophistication. Austria is also characterised by dwarf pine forests and bare rocks and lakes scoured out by glaciers.

THE ENERGETIC PRESENCE

The energetic presence is one of clarity, verification, freshness and untamed natural forces which respond to the will of Mother Nature. Austrian Juniper is ideal for those who chose to further attune themselves to the whispers of their soul, purify the spirit, and bring inspiration and creativity to thought.

VIRTUES

Juniper's purifying qualities make it an ideal choice for: Stagnation. Nervous exhaustion. Lethargy. Loneliness and lack of self worth. Weepy, teary, irrational states. Arthritis, rheumatism, gout. Urinary infections. Joint injury or breaks. Bruising. For recurring injuries.

Fluid retention, swelling, bloating. Liver problems, obesity, urinary infections and general debility.

FUNCTIONS

Mind and Emotions: Purifying, cleansing, restores self worth, wisdom.

Body: Detoxifying, promotes cleansing. Acts to tonify the body and purify the blood. Repairing to injured joints and tissue.

Skin Care: Weepy, fluid type conditions in the body. Cleanses the skin. Diuretic. Has a drying up and purifying effect.

Lavender

BOTANICAL NAME: ***Lavandula augustifolia, Lavandula officinalis***
COUNTRY OF ORIGIN: ***Bulgaria, France, Tasmania, England***
Derived from the flowering tops

Lavender has psycho-therapeutic qualities which focus on soothing the heart, allaying nervous anxiety and panic. It can be of great value during trauma and times of crisis. It can help to release restrained emotions and restore equilibrium.

Lavender's properties range from being anti-bacterial and cell-stimulating to a sedative and an insect repellent. It may be used in a vaporiser, inhaled, applied neat on a small area or in dilution in a massage blend over a large area, depending on the treatment required.

At night, a highly active or restless child can often be calmed with just a few drops on a pillow. With its powerful quality as an anti-inflammatory agent, it can cool and heal any type of burn, sunburn, scalds, skin inflammation and/or infection.

The analgesic properties of Lavender will disperse the pain of headaches and migraines and settle sensations of dizziness often associated with these conditions. An excellent oil as a general tonic or during convalescence as it nurtures, heals and strengthens.

VIRTUES

Lavender's soothing and uplifting qualities make it ideal for: Impatience, irritability. Mood swings. Anger. Hysteria. Oversensitivity and insecurity. Heart conditions–palpitations. Stress, anxiety. Infectious diseases, states of debility. Rheumatic pain and discomfort. During convalescence.

For skin repair–scar tissue, eczema, psoriasis, dermatitis, mosquito and insect bites.

FUNCTIONS

Mind and Emotions: Healing the heart. Gently sedating. Nurturing. Comforting and soothing. Promotes peace of mind.

Body: An excellent tonic during convalescence. Activates the immune defence system. Excellent for first aid. Promotes recovery. Repairs the body.

Skin Care: Cell rejuvenating, healing. Soothing to any irritation and injury.

Lemon

BOTANICAL NAME: ***Citrus limonum***
COUNTRY OF ORIGIN: ***Spain, Italy, Israel, USA***
Derived from peel of the fruit

The light, clear, refreshing fragrance of Lemon uplifts the spirit and cleanses the mind. When doubt and confusion reign, Lemon can bring focus and clarity. A mind weighed down with uncertainty can be uplifted and positively energised. An excellent oil for the home or office when concentration and alertness is needed. Light your vaporiser and add Lemon, Basil and Rosemary as an aid to produce focused results.

Lemon oil helps the body defend itself against infections, especially respiratory conditions where there is catarrh. Lemon is excellent to cleanse healing environments such as nursing homes or hospitals. In areas like these Lemon blends well with Eucalyptus and Sage.

It aids circulation, assist purification and is especially useful in the treatment of oily, or congested skin, when used topically on the body or in a compress.

VIRTUES

With its light refreshing qualities try Lemon when confronted by the following: Irritability, indecision, lethargy, tiredness. Liver congestion, flatulence, gall stones, kidney stones. Respiratory disorders such as colds and flu, bronchitis. Broken capillaries, weakened nails and hair, oily skin, warts.

FUNCTIONS

Mind and Emotions: Brings direction and focus, mental alertness. Enlivens. For concentration. Stimulating to the mind.

Body: Antiseptic in respiratory remedies. Vein tonic, blood purifier, stimulating, diuretic, anti-infectious. Helps to maintain a healthy digestive function. Assists to stimulate the lymphatic system and clear toxicity. Activates the body.

Skin Care: Astringent, tonifying, cleansing. Strengthens connective tissue. Excellent as a toner or astringent for oily skin. Improves circulation.

PRECAUTIONS

Lemon is photosensitive. Not to be used topically in the presence of ultra violet light, ie sunbaking or sunbeds, for up to twelve hours following application.

Lemongrass

BOTANICAL NAME: ***Cymbopogon flexuosus***
COUNTRY OF ORIGIN: ***India, Florida, Guatamala***
Derived from the leaf

Lemongrass carries a strength and vitality in its sweet and herbaceous aroma. It encourages flexibility and movement in the most robust of personalities. It is a fortifying oil for the nervous system, especially for those who persevere regardless of feeling stretched. Lemongrass disperses the underlying tension and anxiety.

Lemongrass oil is tonifying and cleansing for the whole body. It is a powerful wellbeing tonic and has the capacity to revive and revitalise a weary body.

Its ability to move and activate can reduce lactic acid after physical activity as well as tone connective tissue, making it a great oil for weight loss, post-exercise and fluid retention. Lemongrass has anti-microbial properties and can act as a potent disinfectant in any environment. It is indicated to treat bacterial infections.

VIRTUES

Lemongrass qualities make it useful when used to deal with the following: Hypertension. Over demanding. Overwhelmed. Chronic anxiety. Fluid retention, flatulence, obesity. Promotes weight loss. Stimulates milk supply in nursing mothers. Muscular aches and pains, joint stiffness. Lymphatic congestion. Oily skin, congested acne skin, bruising.

FUNCTIONS

Mind and Emotions: For acuity. A nerve tonic, fortifying, purifies emotions. Releasing and focusing.

Body: Assists to cleanse and detoxify. Tonifies the muscles. Antiseptic. Aids circulation and digestion. Prevents muscular aches and pains.

Skin Care: Stimulates lymphatic system, reduces puffiness, tones the skin, astringent, strengthens connective tissue. Deodorises, detoxifies.

PRECAUTIONS

Avoid topically on hypersensitive or damaged skin. Avoid topical application during pregnancy.

Lime

BOTANICAL NAME: *Citrus aurantifolia*
COUNTRY OF ORIGIN: *Peru, Mexico, Ivory Coast*
Derived from the peel of the fruit

As a citrus oil, Lime can bring its refreshing qualities to uplift and revitalise. This oil has the ability to activate a positive outlook, especially for those who are a little melancholic. In terms of its stimulating qualities, Lime promotes assertiveness when the intention is high yet the spirit is low. When attention is flagging, use Lime to bring back alertness, waking you up to engage fully once again and be totally present.

An excellent oil for the elderly who tend to feel their ability to recall things is slipping away. Lime can assist activating the mind and engaging the intellect.

Lime with its antibacterial properties serves to cleanse the body. Used in a massage blend, it can assist in eliminating fluid retention due to its diuretic properties, making this an excellent oil in any weight loss program. An anti-viral oil of great benefit when the immune system is lower during the winter months.

VIRTUES

Lime's fresh uplifting qualities may aid in dealing with: Negativity. Melancholy. Apathy. Anxiety. Loss of self worth. Lack of concentration. Used for the treatment of dementia. Chest and cold conditions – asthma, bronchitis, congestion, flu. Muscle spasms, stomach cramps. Lymphatic congestion, fluid retention, flatulence. Obesity.

FUNCTIONS

Mind and Emotions: Stimulates mental responsiveness. Refreshing to a tired mind. Uplifting to despondent attitudes. Stimulates focus and clarity.

Body: A muscle tonic for post and pre training to help prevent injury. An antiviral oil. Antibacterial, excellent for the chest. Assists poor digestion. Appetite stimulant.

Skin Care: As a deodorant to cleanse and purify. Acts as an astringent to tighten and tonify the skin.

PRECAUTIONS

Avoid topically on hypersensitive or damaged skin. Avoid topical application during pregnancy.

Lime is photosensitive. Not to be used topically in the presence of ultra violet light, ie sunbaking or sunbeds, for up to twelve hours following application.

Mandarin

BOTANICAL NAME: *Citrus reticulata*
COUNTRY OF ORIGIN: *Italy, Israel, Spain*
Derived from the peel of the fruit

This oil is a favourite to ease restlessness and uncertainty. It soothes worry and tension to bring joy and light-heartedness. The sweetness of this oil can ignite an inner quality of caring and childlike innocence. Therefore, it is of great benefit to those with compulsive or excessive behaviour. Mandarin blends well with Cardamon.

Used in a vaporiser before going to sleep, or in an essential oil bath, it can bring a restful and deep sleep, especially when combined with Lavender and Marjoram. Mandarin is excellent for digestive disorders and intestinal discomfort when massaged onto the abdominal area in a clockwise direction. Note that this oil is also safe and beneficial during pregnancy for dispelling anxiety;

physically apply it to prevent stretch marks. Many children and young people are drawn to this oil.

Mandarin is a great choice when practising Zazen Meditation.

VIRTUES

Mandarin's uplifting quality makes it an ideal choice for handling the following: Amnesia. Shock and hysteria. Grief. Depression. Narrow mindedness. Muscular spasms, constipation, abdominal cramps during PMS. Hiccups. Stretch marks, congested and oily skin.

FUNCTIONS

Mind and Emotions: Inspiring, calming. Soothing to an overactive mind. Promotes calm and serenity. For open communication.

Body: Supportive to the respiratory system, especially in cases of restrictive breathing. Aids lymph flow and circulation. Maintains great wellbeing.

Skin Care: Cleansing to acne skin. A tonic which moisturises and softens as it helps to strengthen the skin.

PRECAUTIONS

Mandarin is photosensitive. Not to be used topically in the presence of ultra violet light, ie sunbaking or sunbeds, for up to twelve hours following application.

Marjoram

BOTANICAL NAME: ***Origanum marjorana***
COUNTRY OF ORIGIN: ***Egypt, France***
Derived from the herb

The warm, penetrating aroma of Marjoram works to lessen hyperactivity and extreme emotional responses. It brings a steadfast calming quality that somehow puts things back into perspective. The nourishing aspects of this oil will relax at the deepest level, restoring our capacity to be generous with ourselves and with others – an inner contentment will always result.

In ancient Greece, Marjoram was known as a funeral herb to ease the journey of the departed spirit. It is a great companion with Cypress during times of bereavement.

Marjoram offers comfort to those suffering grief or a deep loss. The sedating qualities of Marjoram promote a deep and restful sleep.

Due to its analgesic and antispasmodic properties it makes an excellent massage oil for injured and strained muscles. Marjoram works well to relax and relieve tension and pent up stress in the body. As a sedative in a warm bath before retiring, it blends well with Lavender. It is said to be an anti-aphrodisiac and may assist to calm excessive sexual urges.

VIRTUES

Due to its warming but calming spirit Marjoram can assist with: Grief, hostility, anger, hyper-anxiety, emotional extremes, apprehension, nervous tension. Muscle stiffness, palpitations. Cramps and spasms. Bronchitis, coughs, chronic coughing. Long-term insomnia, high blood pressure. It moderates excessive sexual desire.

FUNCTIONS

Mind and Emotions: Encouraging. To promote nobility. Pacifying, deeply relaxing. Comforting, warming. For perseverance.

Body: Deeply sedating, relaxes muscles. Anti-aphrodisiac, balancing. Analgesic, antispasmodic.

Skin Care: Soothes and nourishes the skin.

PRECAUTIONS

Avoid topical application during pregnancy or with those with low blood pressure. Do not use during stages of deep depression.

Myrrh

BOTANICAL NAME: ***Commiphora myrrha***
COUNTRY OF ORIGIN: ***East Africa, France***
Derived from the gum

There are often marathons in life, not always of the physical kind. This oil is renowned for promoting endurance and support for demanding physical and emotional performance. Myrrh has been considered precious since ancient times. As it brings forth strength and fortitude it promotes a deep connection to spirit. As with its companion, Frankincense, Myrrh has the ability to bring a quiet calm to the hustle and bustle of life, connecting us to an inner silence and tranquility. This makes Myrrh an ideal oil for quiet moments of reflection and repose.

A thick resinous oil, Myrrh is an excellent expectorant, helping with all kinds of cough, colds and catarrh. It may be used for gum disorders and quickly heals ulcers in the mouth. Ideal for healing wounds both physically and emotionally.

Create an aromatic environment for your Transcendental Meditation with the resonating fragrance of Myrrh.

VIRTUES

The virtues of Myrrh enable us to deal with: Apathy. Lethargy, despondency. Lack of energy or will to go on. Loss of purpose and direction. Throat infections, respiratory disorders, mouth ulcers, inflammation, bronchial congestion, bronchitis. In the intestinal area–flatulence, diarrhoea. Excess discharge of body fluids–weeping, eczema, loss of appetite, vaginal discharge.

FUNCTIONS

Mind and Emotions: For a positive outlook. Inspiring. Warming. Fortifying. For seeking life's direction. For endurance.

Body: Antiseptic, anti-infectious, an expectorant, strengthening to the lungs, soothing to ulcerated tissue.

Skin Care: Cooling to wounds. Rejuvenating to aged skin. Astringent. Use as a tonic for a skin pick me up.

Neroli

BOTANICAL NAME: *Citrus aurantium, amara*
COUNTRY OF ORIGIN: *Tunisia*
Derived from the flower

There are times when emotional poise and discernment are needed and this is the oil to evoke these qualities. Especially useful in reducing states of anxiety Neroli allays worry and concern. It has a tendency to arouse the senses and promote euphoria, making it an excellent oil to release frigidity both emotionally and physically.

The seductive sweetness of this oil can disperse emotional intensity and bring reassurance and security during stressful times. Combined with Lavender it is an excellent rescue remedy to treat shock or hysteria.

It has regenerating qualities which can act to heal the body quickly. By stimulating new cell growth, it is useful in skin care, especially for dry skin. It is also excellent as a vein tonic, assisting to treat varicose veins and broken capillaries as it strengthens the tissue. It has a restorative effect on natural body functions, rhythms and desires.

CULTURE *(Tunisia)*

Tunisia is a richly diverse and multi layered Mediterranean nation. The ancient city of Carthage was once the greatest maritime and commercial power in the region. The result of successive invasions has made the culture a heady and exotic mix of Roman, Arab, Ottoman Turk overlaid with French sophistication. Tunisia is reminiscent of thick aromatic coffee in tiny cups, honey soaked pastries in shop windows and the sound of hubble bubble pipes in the air. One is captivated by the endless panorama of stark white domes, gorgeous patterned tiles and rows of olive groves. A land where talcum powder fine sand is fringed by palm trees and camel charging displays of horsemanship are seen at festival time.

THE ENERGETIC PRESENCE

The energetic presence is one of humility, community, peace and fulfillment. From a meandering and simplified existence where custom permeates modernisation, Tunisian Neroli is ideal for those desiring a greater quality of life, relaxed behaviour and a deepening sensory pleasure.

VIRTUES

Neroli's ability to bring poise and discernment make it useful for dealing with: Depression. Emotional frigidity.

Anxiety. Hysteria. Apprehension. Nervous butterflies. Insomnia and exhaustion. Nervous tension from overwork. Muscular cramps and spasms, especially in the intestinal tract. PMS, palpitations. Inflamed and dry skin, broken capillaries, sensitive skin, menopause.

FUNCTIONS

Mind and Emotions: Steadying, reassuring, restorative, agelessness. Settling, sensual. Emotional poise.

Body: Tonic for the heart. Steadying during hormonal disturbances. Intestinal carminative. Anti-spasmodic, restores rhythm to the body.

Skin Care: Vein tonic, strengthens capillaries, cell regenerating, soothing.

Orange

BOTANICAL NAME: ***Citrus aurantium, sinensis***
COUNTRY OF ORIGIN: ***Brazil, China, Israel, USA***
Derived from the peel of the fruit

This is the oil of exuberance. It has an energetic, refreshing fragrance. Orange oil promotes joyful communication and is used to embrace new ideas and perspectives, especially when working in a creative environment.

When working with a team it brings union and a harmonising effect, instilling compatibility. Orange used in a vaporiser is excellent for setting the mood for entertainment and parties, especially when combined with Bergamot and Clary Sage. It is an extremely popular oil with children.

Promotes a more positive approach to difficult and confronting tasks. It is excellent when used in meetings to move the conversation forward, and for brainstorming and generating new possibilities.

It can help relieve acute headaches or mild insomnia. In skin care it is useful for cleansing oily skin. Distilled from the outer peel, this refreshing and uplifting oil blends well with all other essential oils. With its gentle qualities it is said to reduce the needs or cravings for the tobacco plant.

Broaden your imagination with Orange to enhance your creative visualisations.

VIRTUES

Orange's exuberant quality combined with its calming qualities make it ideal for the following: Uneasiness. Worry. Negativity. Pessimism. Inflexibility. Depression. Nervous anxiety. Constipation, abdominal cramps from poor digestion, flatulence, irritable bowel, muscular spasms, all acute conditions. Weak epidermis, open pores, dry skin. Cellulite.

FUNCTIONS

Mind and Emotions: To promote adaptability. Optimism. For joyful communication, exuberance. Refreshing and uplifting.

Body: Supports general wellbeing. Carminative properties to aid the intestinal tract. Aids the digestive process.

Skin Care: Addresses open pores. Softens hardened or cracked skin, allowing it to be cleansed. Smoker's skin.

PRECAUTIONS

Orange is photosensitive. Not to be used topically in the presence of ultra violet light, i.e. sunbaking or sunbeds, for up to twelve hours following application.

Palmarosa

BOTANICAL NAME: *Cymbopogon martini*
COUNTRY OF ORIGIN: *India, Brazil, Madagascar*
Derived from the herb

Palmarosa has the ability to activate your mind when feeling fatigued. It will quieten and calm any frantic thoughts, or when your mind feels overactive.

The nourishing qualities of Palmarosa mobilse and encourage an inner sense of security. With a new sense of certainty the ability to accomplish a task will prevail, enabling you to adapt and move forward in any situation. As a relaxant, it can provide an excellent remedy for nervous tension and concerns in matters of the heart.

For physical conditions it is a cardiac tonic and a generally good pick-me-up. With its ability to counteract infections and inflammation, it can be of great value as a first aid tool, especially for genito-urinary disorders.

Ideal choice for aromatic mediation- savouring those quiet moments that you spend with yourself.

VIRTUES

With its sweetness and calmative qualities Palmarosa helps us deal with the following situations: Irritability. Fatigue. Insecurity. Sense of failure. Viral infections, sinusitis. Bronchial irritation. Thrush. Vaginitis. Acne, scars and wrinkles, skin disruptions, dehydration, undernourished skin, boils, shingles. To ease childbirth/labour. Muscle fatigue.

FUNCTIONS

Mind and Emotions: Settling, mobilising, stabilising. Activates the mind and body from states of fatigue. Known to have aphrodisiac qualities.

Body: Antiseptic, antiviral. Assists detoxification. Maintains a healthy digestive function. A tonic for the heart. Aid during labour.

Skin Care: Hydrating to the skin. Assists to regulate natural cell function. Treats scars and wrinkles, skin regenerator.

Patchouli

BOTANICAL NAME: ***Pogostemon cablin***
COUNTRY OF ORIGIN: ***Indonesia, Brazil,Malaysia***
Derived from the leaf

This oil has a rich Eastern aroma which can relieve anxiety and uplift despondent moods. Patchouli is renowned for its exotic and provocative aroma and was used in ancient India as an aphrodisiac.

It tends to connect the physical and the spiritual, especially in a sexual expression of intimacy. Throughout the 1960's it was used as perfume to expand consciousness and evoke freedom in sexual expression.

It works well as an antiseptic to heal chaffed or broken skin and fungal infections, including Athlete's Foot. In old herbal texts from the East, it was said to be of great benefit to stimulate the immune system. Old scar tissue responds well to a blend of Patchouli and Lavender.

This fragrance is a superb anchor for your Primordial Sound Meditation.

VIRTUES

Given its sensual aroma and its lifting quality Patchouli can assist with: Apathy, frigidity, indifference, emotional suppression, depression, anxiety. Open wounds, psoriasis, eczema, dermatitis, acne, dry skin, Athlete's Foot, dandruff, healing wounds and scars. Diarrhoea, colonic disorders, prolapsed colon. Fungal infections.

FUNCTIONS

Mind and Emotions: Certainty, tenacity, striving. Brings relief to anxious states, nervous tension. Lifts despondent moods, can enhance sexuality, harmonising for sexual expression.

Body: General antiseptic, anti-inflammatory, soothing to grazed and chaffed skin. Provides a strengthening effect on tissue. Contributes to general wellbeing. Diuretic.

Skin Care: Regulates oil secretion. Can be used to bring tone to slackened skin. Repairs scar tissue. Used to treat disruptions of the skin.

Peppermint

BOTANICAL NAME: *Mentha piperita*
COUNTRY OF ORIGIN: *USA, England, France*
Derived from the leaf

This is an oil for recovery. The fresh fragrance of Peppermint stimulates the mind and body to wakeful activity. Peppermint promotes clear thinking and stimulates the brain. It is a renowned digestive aid, working both on the digestive tract and to help assimilate new ideas. When feeling a little stagnant use Peppermint to mobilise the intellect and process new ideas and concepts. It is an oil to promote concentration and keep you alert.

Peppermint is engergising to the body when used as a massage blend. It cools and warms simultaneously. Peppermint has antispasmodic and analgesic qualities which relieve nerve pain, i.e. sciatica, toothache.

Inhaled directly from the bottle, it brings alertness, clears the head and is an effective treatment for travel sickness, nausea and sinusitis. As a mild expectorant and antispasmodic, it will benefit both chest and intestinal disorders. In steam inhalation, Peppermint can bring immediate relief to sinus congestion, clearing the head and nasal passages.

Just inhale the enlivening vapour and your mind clears while your body naturally engages in deep slow breathing.

VIRTUES

Peppermint's fresh qualities make it ideal for: Fatigue, lethargy. Feeling stuck. Loss of focus. Loss of concentration. Indigestion, travel sickness, nausea, menstrual cramps. Asthma, bronchitis, sinusitis, colds, coughs, flu, fever. Relief from the pain of sciatica. Menstrual cramps. Neuralgia and nerve pain.

FUNCTIONS

Mind and Emotions: To activate intuition, fearlessness. Stimulates the mind. Energising, invigorating.

Body: The classic stomach remedy stimulates digestion, settles upset tummies, antispasmodic. An excellent inhalant.

Skin Care: Cooling. Decongestant, especially for acne. Rehydrating.

PRECAUTIONS

Use in moderation due to the menthol content. Avoid topical application during pregnancy. Not to be used topically by those who suffer from epilepsy or convulsions.

Petitgrain

BOTANICAL NAME: ***Citrus aurantium amara***
COUNTRY OF ORIGIN: ***Paraguay, Italy***
Derived from the leaf

With its fortifying qualities, Petitgrain is heartening and uplifting, especially when expectations are unfulfilled. It can encourage new communication from a place of strength. Its fresh yet strong fragrance is a tonic for the nervous system, especially when recovering from stress related conditions. Petitgrain eases confusion when in the midst of disruptive forces.

With antispasmodic and anti-inflammatory qualities, Petitgrain is similar in its benefits to Neroli yet not quite as active. It can assist to balance the body quickly and be helpful for gastric type discomfort. It has great value as a digestive aid when used in a massage blend on the abdominal area.

Due to its versatility it blends well with almost any other oil and has a most pleasant fragrance.

VIRTUES

Its heartening qualities make Petitgrain ideal for when we encounter the following: For the highly strung. Tension. Anxiety. Moodiness. Mental anguish. Nervous asthma, respiratory conditions where rhythm is affected in the body. Sleeplessness. Indigestion, hepatitis, low immune system. Excessive perspiration, acne, dry skin, infections caused by excessive sebum or sweat, weepy skin conditions.

FUNCTIONS

Mind and Emotions: Regulating to the nervous system. Has strength and tends to ground flighty people. An aid in times of panic or hysteria. Use during times of change and transformation for flexibility.

Body: Eases constrictive breathing. A respiratory aid. Eases joint discomfort. Tonifying to the digestive system. A good tonic for the whole body. Antispasmodic.

Skin Care: A great cell regenerator, astringent, brings balance to excess secretions, cleansing.

Pine

BOTANICAL NAME: ***Abies siberica***
COUNTRY OF ORIGIN: ***Siberia, Russia, Austria, France***
Derived from the leaf

Pine is the oil for inspiration. Imagine for a moment the loftiness of the pine tree, the strength of pine needles, the embracing freshness of the aroma- these qualities are captured in the oil. Invigorating and refreshing, Pine can bring a new lease of life to any project.

Inhalations of Pine are excellent for relieving colds and catarrhal conditions. A massage blend will free the chest and bronchials as it promotes oxygen uptake in the body, making it an excellent remedy for any stifled environments or respiratory complaints.

Pine has a stimulating effect on the circulation, making it a useful aid in pre and post exercise. It has a fresh aroma popular with most people, especially if working in air-conditioned or stuffy environments.

It helps improve breathing techniques.

VIRTUES

Pine's inspirational qualities help in dealing with the following conditions: Helplessness. Loss of will. Lack of vitality. Pessimism. Respiratory tract infections, colds, catarrh. Poor circulation, pulmonary conditions, chest infections, chills and colds, physical exhaustion, fatigue, rheumatism. Clogged pores and sluggish conditions.

FUNCTIONS

Mind and Emotions: Vibrancy. Fortifying. Refreshing. Brings inspiration and restores self-esteem. Clearing to the mind. Revives creative forces.

Body: Stimulates circulation and oxygen exchange. Antiseptic, expectorant, promotes a healthy digestive function.

Skin Care: Purifying, promotes oxygen uptake. Excellent cleanse for smoker's skin. Cleansing.

PRECAUTIONS

Not to be used topically on hypersensitive, diseased or damaged skin.

Rose

BOTANICAL NAME: *Rosa damascena*
COUNTRY OF ORIGIN: *Bulgaria, Morocco*
Derived from the flower.

This nurturing oil can assist to mend emotional wounds and restore compassion and forgiveness where resentment once resided.

The very nature of Rose touches the deepest chords within to trust again and have faith.

Rose soothes inflamed conditions and helps release toxins, especially in the liver. Rose can balance the reproductive organs and is an excellent choice for treating many disorders unique to women. It can also support the reproductive organs in the body.

Rose is one of the least toxic of all essential oils and will promote a healthy glow and vital appearance to the skin. The true Bulgarian rose comprises natural waxes that turn it solid in cold temperatures. It is one of the most superior ingredients used in fine perfumery.

Use the essence of Rose to nurture your spirit and heighten your awareness.

CULTURE ***(Bulgaria)***

Bulgaria spans from the rugged Balkan mountain chains to the plains of Bulgaria. The very name of the country is a Turkik verb meaning to mix and this reflects the various marauding tribes that have invaded the region and created a rich and diverse culture. The country inherits its vibrant colours of woven braids from this period as well as the folklore and festivals which capture the struggle against the Sultan's domination. Bulgaria is a land of nomadic people where traditional subsistence was structured around agriculture and herding. Despite the impact of modernisation, the horse and cart and wine barrel are still featured in this land. Its prosperity is captured in the commercial production of rose oil in the Rose Valley.

THE ENERGETIC PRESENCE

The energetic presence is characterised by sensory stimulation, beauty and movement. Seekers of rich experience wandering spirits search for vital natural resources that heal and regenerate the body and soul. Bulgarian Rose is ideal for those who seek the courage to search the chambers of the heart and to heal the wounds of the soul. It reminds us of the beauty contained in small things.

VIRTUES

As Queen of the essential oils, Rose's gentle dignified presence gives us the courage to deal with: Broken hearts. Depression. Anxiety. Jealousy. Resentment. Anger. Grief.

Liver disorders- hangovers. For inflammation, circulatory disturbances.

Use during menopause, frigidity, uterine imbalance, painful periods, excessive bleeding.

Broken capillaries, rashes, boils, dry and dehydrated skin.

FUNCTIONS

Mind and Emotions: Brings emotional poise. Heartening. Restorative. Passionate. Rejuvenating, comforting. Contributes to emotional wellbeing.

Body: Promotes circulation. Strengthens the liver. Aids detoxification. Menstrual symptoms.

Skin Care: Cell regenerator, rehydrator, strengthens capillaries, soothes the skin. Excellent for mature skins.

PRECAUTIONS

Avoid topical application during pregnancy.

Rosemary

BOTANICAL NAME: ***Rosmarinus officinalis***
COUNTRY OF ORIGIN: ***Spain, Tunisia***
Derived from the herb

In ancient times Rosemary was used for remembrance and is still known today as one of the most stimulating and awakening essential oils. Its strongest effect is on the nervous system; it can act as a brain stimulant. This is an oil for over-thinkers to heighten sensory perception and stimulate recall. Simply inhale a few drops of Rosemary to keep you focused on the task at hand and allay those external or extraneous worries.

It is an oil to strengthen confidence. For those with low esteem, it can stimulate and strengthen a healthy ego.

Rosemary is a good oil to use in massage, helping tired or injured muscles to recuperate. As a muscle tonic it can be used pre-or post-training as it stimulates and promotes circulation and arterial blood flow. Due to its qualities and effect on the circulatory system, use this oil for rheumatic cramps and on any areas of the body that lacks mobility. With its stimulating effect it will assist to cleanse the body and alleviate liver congestion.

Radiant hair with a glowing lustre is certainly the result achieved by using Rosemary in your hair care. Add a few drops of Rosemary to the final rinse or as a scalp rub. Rosemary will stimulate hair growth.

VIRTUES

Rosemary's bracing stimulus lends itself to deal with matters like: Lack of will, lack of concentration. Being distracted. Over-thinking. Mental fatigue, tiredness, poor memory. Lethargy, drowsiness. Poor circulation. Back pain. Muscular aches and pains. Chest congestion, rheumatic cramps, gout, sprains. Obesity, liver congestion. Alopecia, baldness. Headaches, poor circulation.

FUNCTIONS

Mind and Emotions: Strengthening. Memory activator. Enlivening, stimulating. Exhilarating. Boosts confidence. Great for study and focus.

Body: Enlivening to the nervous system. Promotes circulation, stimulates metabolism, contributes to the maintenance of peripheral circulation. A body and muscle tonic.

Skin Care: Activating, cell regenerating. Stimulates hair growth. Adds lustre to hair.

PRECAUTIONS

To be used with extreme caution on those who have epilepsy and high blood pressure. Avoid topically during pregnancy.

Rosewood

BOTANICAL NAME: ***Aniba roseaodora***
COUNTRY OF ORIGIN: ***Brazil***
Derived from the wood

This is a wonderful oil for quiet moments, to instil centredness and be left with a sense of wholeness. Rosewood will evoke a sense of wellbeing and restfulness as it eases the mind. Especially beneficial during times of grief and bereavement as it brings emotional healing. Rosewood can warm the body, restoring a sense of connectedness to loved ones. Use this oil to embrace and restore intimacy.

Rosewood helps to release tension, especially for those who suffer headaches due to concentrated activity. It brings a sense of ease as it releases tension and stress from the body and mind. By soaking in an aromatic bath at the end of the day, Rosewood can assist to sustain your energy levels. Rosewood blends with most other oils to create the perfect end to a stressful day.

With its antibacterial properties, Rosewood promotes the body's own natural defence system, therefore making it a general tonic to maintain balance for the mind, body and emotions. On the chest, Rosewood helps bring relief to spasmodic coughing and eases it during times of flu and colds. Rosewood is a cell regenerator – add one drop to your daily beauty regime.

VIRTUES

By virtue of its restful and embracing qualities Rosewood is there for: Emotional extremes. Stress and tension. Headaches. Restless mind. Uneasiness. Infection, parasites, flu, coughs, sore throats, nausea, bronchial disorders. Aged and tired skin, dry skin. Jetlag, weariness, lack of energy.

FUNCTIONS

Mind and Emotions: To maintain balance, calming to the central nervous system, relaxing, centering, emotionally healing, evokes wellbeing.

Body: A general tonic to sustain balance, aphrodisiac, strengthening to the chest and respiratory system, warming, embracing.

Skin Care: Soothes. Supports. Heals. Restores elasticity at the deepest level. Rejuvenating to tired skin.

Sage

BOTANICAL NAME: ***Salvia officinalis***
COUNTRY OF ORIGIN: ***Albania, France, Italy, Turkey, Yugoslavia, Spain***
Derived from the leaf

With its clean and imposing fragrance, Sage cleanses both body and mind. When mentally strained or exhausted from overwork, Sage can assist you to regain your ability to respond and engage quickly in the task at hand. It activates memory and clears negativity.

The hearty plant brings this very quality to our body as it fortifies and strengthens, especially for women during times of vulnerability. Sage protects us from bacteria and fungal infections while strengthening reproductive organs.

Sage regulates fluids in the body, i.e. excess secretions such as sweaty palms and perspiration, or fluids retained by the body. It has an expectorant quality and is a great remedy for respiratory disorders.

This oil is reputedly a regulator and rebalancer. Its characteristics specifically work in areas to do with the genital area. As its action predisposes itself to balancing and improving the blood flow Sage is particularly helpful for amenorrhoea and dysmenorrhoea. Indians also use it to cleanse the spirit during meditation.

VIRTUES

Sage's cleansing ability makes it useful for dealing with: Mental strain and exhaustion. Lack of sensitivity. Anxiety. Worry. Thinking negatively. For kidney dysfunction, fluid retention, excessive perspiration, catarrhal conditions, coughs and colds, toxic lymphatic system. Painful muscles, stiffness. Sprains and strains, rheumatism. Excessive bleeding, dysmenorrhoea, amenorrhoea. Bacterial infections, tinea, puffiness, acne, excessively oily skin.

FUNCTIONS

Mind and Emotions: Responsiveness, sharpens the senses, activates inner wisdom, cleansing to thoughts, refreshing.

Body: Antiseptic, protecting, cleansing, detoxifying, strengthening. Activates cleansing of catarrh.

Skin Care: Cleansing, astringent, purifying, tonifying.

PRECAUTIONS

Warning: Do not use topically during pregnancy. Do not use if you suffer from epilepsy or convulsions.

Sandalwood

BOTANICAL NAME: *Santalum album*
COUNTRY OF ORIGIN: INDIA- *Eastern District*
Derived from the twig

Sandalwood is a strengthening oil which provides courage and releases irrational fears. It can have a stabilising influence during dramatic life changes. Sandalwood has long been used in prayer, meditation and ritual because it brings harmony to mind, body and spirit.

For those who have become dependent, feeling insecure when faced with being alone, this oil can alleviate a sense of isolation as it stills a worrying and fearful mind. This is the oil for genito-urinary disorders as it cools and heals. In Ayurvedic practices, its anti-inflammatory and anti-infectious properties have been used to treat heated conditions in the body such as inflammation, irritation and infection. It is one of the oldest known perfume materials with a history of 4,000 years of use.

Sandalwood aids the skin as well as giving a pleasant aroma liked by both men and women.

VIRTUES

Sandalwood's courageous and strengthening qualities make it ideal when facing: Isolation. Aggressive behaviour. Obsessive nature. Insecurity. Possessiveness. Nightmares. Fears, depression. Genito-urinary problems-cystitis, urinary tract infections, kidney disorders.

Cracked and dry skin, itchy skin. Inflamed conditions – eczema, psoriasis.

FUNCTIONS

Mind and Emotions: Acceptance. Tranquility. Peace of mind. Strengthening. Brings courage, centredness. Stabilises.

Body: Balances adrenals. Strengthens the immune system. Protective, strengthening.

Skin Care: Promotes elasticity. Soothing, strengthening, anti-inflammatory. A topical astringent to soothe and heal the skin.

Tea Tree

BOTANICAL NAME: *Melaleuca alternifolia*
COUNTRY OF ORIGIN: *Australia*
Derived from the leaves

When feeling despondent or low in morale, we can become vulnerable to infections. Tea Tree will act as a pick-me-up while building resistance and protection. A booster physically and emotionally.

Well known to Australians, Tea Tree oil has many uses and is unique in its action against bacteria, viruses and fungi. So when the body is threatened, Tea Tree increases its ability to respond and resist. It was traditionally used in the outback as a medicine for coughs and colds.

Diffuse Tea Tree to disinfect any environment and fortify immunity. This oil will act quickly to eradicate harmful organisms in the body and prevent further infection.

Tea Tree oil can assist in the removal or warts and is effective in relieving the discomfort of bites, stings, boils, thrush, sore throats, sinusitis, cuts and grazes- truly first aid in a bottle. An excellent skin toner, Tea Tree works especially well on oily or infected skin to cleanse and disinfect.

VIRTUES

Tea Tree's pick me up quality helps with: Victimisation. Deep depression. Low morale. Fatigue, feeling thwarted. Antifungal- thrush, Athlete's Foot, ringworm, Herpes Simplex, cold sores. Respiratory disorders- asthma, coughs, colds, flu. Viruses. Cysts, boils, acne. Open wounds. Bacterial infections. Low resistance, chronic ill health, recurring infections, poor circulation.

FUNCTIONS

Mind and Emotions: Strengthening. Protecting. Tonifying. Boosts morale. Fortifying.

Body: Antiseptic, antiviral, antifungal. Improves resistance. Anti-infectious, disinfectant.

Skin Care: Cleansing, disinfecting, antifungal, antibacterial, astringent.

PRECAUTIONS

Keep away from eyes, keep away from children, avoid topically during pregnancy.

Thyme

BOTANICAL NAME: *Thymus vulgaris*
COUNTRY OF ORIGIN: *Spain, Morocco, France*
Derived from the herb

Invigorating and enlivening as it stimulates and energises, Thyme can dissolve depression and initiate drive. Healthy activity and enthusiasm will be restored. This fragrant culinary herb has been used for its antibacterial qualities for thousands of years. It was originally picked as a food additive for its purging and detoxifying effect on the body.

Thyme is an excellent aid for addressing respiratory disorders- it must be applied externally and blended in a massage base oil as it is a highly potent essential oil. It works to stimulate the body's natural defence system, strengthening our resistance to disease. Thyme's refreshing, herbaceous fragrance blends well with other oils to restore physical strength and encourage decisive action. Blends especially well with Lemon, Eucalyptus and Tea Tree.

Use Thyme to clear the mind for Vipassana meditation.

VIRTUES

Thyme's invigorating qualities are ideal for: Apprehension. Despondency. Debilitation. Chronic nervous anxiety. Lethargy. Bacterial infections- colds, coughs, flu, chest complaints. Whooping cough. Physical exhaustion. Toxic conditions, sluggish lymphatic system. Prematurely aged skin. Dry dehydrated, wrinkled skin. Bacterial infections of the skin- acne.

FUNCTIONS

Mind and Emotions: Fortifying. Encouraging. Decisive. Stimulates awareness. Energising, activating.

Body: Energising, antiseptic, detoxifying, strengthens the immune system, purging, stimulates sluggish digestion.

Skin Care: Cleansing, antibacterial. Purifying. Rejuvenating. Anti-ageing.

PRECAUTIONS

A mucous membrane irritant. Avoid topically during pregnancy. Avoid contact with the mouth and genital areas. Do not use topically on hypersensitive, diseased or damaged skin. Use with caution.

Vetiver

BOTANICAL NAME: ***Vetiveria zizanoides***
COUNTRY OF ORIGIN: ***Java, China, India***
Derived from the root

Vetiver is a deeply relaxing oil with a strengthening influence. It can steady and deepen a sense of security and certainty from within. It serves to release anger at ourselves and others. Vetiver has a deep, pungent aroma which brings strength and promotes new opportunities. As a root oil its very nature involves drawing nourishment from the earth. When it is vaporised into the environment it has the potential of drawing new possibilities into one's life.

At the end of the day, Vetiver in an aromatic bath will restore balance. Its steadying qualities can replenish the body and mind.

Where any weakness occurs in the body, Vetiver can be used to strengthen and fortify. As a tonic for the skin, it can encourage utilisation of nutrients in undernourished skin. It can also be used as an aid for mature skin for it strengthens at the deepest layer. Vetiver has the ability to cool, nourish and replenish simultaneously.

This is the perfect oil to include in your morning meditation.

VIRTUES

Vetiver's strengthening and deepening attributes make it an ideal adjunct for dealing with: Nervousness, Disorientation. Exhaustion. Intestinal disorders- indigestion, nervous dyspepsia, constipation. Hormonal imbalances, particularly for emotional upheavals. Antirheumatic, especially for inflamed joints and arthritis, anaemia, constipation. Prematurely aged skin. Loss of skin tone. Antiwrinkle. Skin irritations. Slackened skin.

FUNCTIONS

Mind and Emotions: Steadying. Nourishing. Promotes self-esteem. Draws opportunities for abundance. Relaxing.

Body: Assists colonic action. Promotes metabolism of food. Promotes circulation. Anti-inflammatory.

Skin Care: Regenerating at the deepest level. Soothing, anti-irritant. Rejuvenating. Replenishing. Restorative.

Ylang Ylang

BOTANICAL NAME: *Cananga odorata*
COUNTRY OF ORIGIN: *Madagascar, Philippines, Comoro Islands (off the coast of North Africa)*
Derived from the flower

The exotic aroma of Ylang Ylang uplifts the spirit and dissolves resentment. It has warming qualities which promote a scentual awareness, encouraging openness and physical expression. It has the capacity to dismiss emotional frigidity and encourage warm communication, instilling confidence.

With the stresses and strains of everyday life, tiredness, lethargy, complacency and despondency can sometimes set into relationships. Wherever there is withdrawal from sexual expression or emotional intimacy use Ylang Ylang to release the barriers to bring a calming and supportive energy to the heart. If feeling alienated, soak in an aromatic bath of Ylang Ylang combined with other oils to please and arouse your senses. This is an oil that helps to unify both the masculine and feminine expressions of us in the world. From ancient times this oil has been considered a potent aphrodisiac to arouse the senses and stimulate the body.

It has the ability to calm and support. Where there is hyperactivity, palpitations and blood pressure, Ylang Ylang can soothe and quieten.

It is distinctive in its ability to act as a powerful psychological agent, bringing forth its anti-depressant qualities, and is extremely effective in the treatment of anxiety, anger and hysterical states.

VIRTUES

Ylang Ylang's distinctive enveloping and uplifting qualities are there for use when we face: Emotional frigidity, depression, anxiety, frustration, anger, guilt, jealousy, resentment. Heart irregularities – tachycardia, racing heart, palpitations, hypertension. Physical frigidity. Muscular cramps and spasms. Oily and combination skin.

FUNCTIONS

Mind and Emotions: Intimacy, sensual, warming, euphoric, exotic, uplifting. For confidence, enthusiasm.

Body: Aphrodisiac. Cardiac tonic. For general well-being. To restore balance to natural body rhythms.

Skin Care: Balances the skin.

PRECAUTIONS

Can cause headiness in high doses. Do not use topically on inflamed or reddened skin.

CHAPTER THREE

Methods of Use

THIS IS WHERE WE REALLY EXPLORE THE VERSATILITY of aromatherapy. The recommended methods of use are suggestions to stimulate your imagination and evoke your creativity; to experience all the different methods of use and to invent or reinvent expressions of them. There are many ways in which I've used peppermint oil. I've used peppermint oil as a massage blend to rub over my abdominal area when I've been feeling nauseous.

I've used peppermint essential oil when I've had a head cold as an inhalation. Iíve even put one drop of peppermint oil on a small cotton wool square, placed it in a small sealed cellophane bag and guests have opened the sealed cellophane bag, inhaled their delicious after dinner mint and delighted that it's been a calorie free experience. So, when you're experiencing the different methods of use I recommend don't wait to have a cold, don't wait to get sick and don't wait to recuperate

Endeavour to partake of the different methods of use simply as an enhancement to your well being. Try an inhalation to clear your mind before going out and doing the shopping. Try taking an aromatic bath at the start of the day to refresh and energise you. Give an aromatic massage to a friend when they pop around. It might be that you make up an oil blend to massage the hands and feet of a loved one who's undergoing a really stressful time. There are so many different possibilities for essential oils. The variety of ways you can use them to enhance each and every moment of your life is infinite.

Main Methods of Use

MASSAGE

50 drops of essential oil in 100mls massage base oil

(This formula can be modified to create smaller massage blends. The ratio is 2:1. For every drop of essential oil add 2mls of massage base oil).

Once an essential oil has been absorbed, the epidermis acts as a reservoir, where some of the oil will remain for a time before it enters the bloodstream. This period will vary with different essential oil constituents, but is likely to be measured in hours or even days. Essential oil components, then, are gradually "time-released" from the epidermis into the dermis. Once in the dermis, the molecules enter its blood capillaries, and are carried away. The rate of systemic absorption increases due to the effect on blood flow, which is increased by massage. There is evidence that massage enhances the absorption of at least some essential oil constituents.

The aromatic massage can be as professional or as personal as you like. The rubbing action will activate the nerve endings in your body and stimulate the circulation of blood to the surface of the skin – thereby increasing the entry of the oils into your body. Massage has an incredible relaxation response on the body in its own right. And combined with aromatherapy, it becomes a powerful therapeutic tool.

Massage is so important – it promotes circulation, stimulates the release of toxins through the lymphatic system and provides a sense of warmth and well being. I firmly believe that everyone needs to experience and share touching to maintain emotional and physical balance.

As the body is cleansed of toxins, the skin is given a new suppleness and elasticity.

Up to three or four essential oils can be combined with a massage base oil to incorporate the individual expressions of each oil, working together to produce the most effective results.

SELF MASSAGE

Nurturing and caring for yourself will increase your self-esteem and your own sense of worth. It can also make you more attractive to others. The sensory experience of using essential oils enhances self-awareness and will turn a normal, everyday activity into a joyous, aromatic and sensual experience.

The letting go of physical tensions during massage often stimulates the release of emotional tension. The cumulative effects of massage are also very strong, promoting a lasting feeling of well being.

I often take the time to massage my body from top to toe. When you massage your own body start after your shower in the morning. Massage your skin from either your toes up your legs, crossing around your abdomen in a clockwise direction, your chest or breast area, your arms, hands, back up into the back of the neck and face. The back of your body as far as you can comfortably reach, the buttocks and complete. It's good to alternate either starting from the feet, from the hands or the neck and shoulders, just to keep your body guessing, allowing it to continually experience change.

To prepare your massage blend pour 10mls of massage base oil into a glass or ceramic bowl and add 5 drops of essential oil in total. If you're making up a facial skin oil or a children's massage blend, all you need to do is add 1 drop of your chosen essential oil into approximately 10 mls of massage base oil, before applying. Remember, with all massage base oils avoid contact with the eye area, especially with infants. If you're giving them an aromatherapy massage avoid contact with their face and hands so that they don't rub those volatile liquids into their eyes.

To choose your massage base oil simply select one that is cold pressed, still containing all the vital nutrients to feed your skin. Essential oils being soluble in massage base oils enables them to be transported evenly across the surface of the skin. Remember to store them in glass containers and in hot climates it's a great idea to refrigerate them, to prolong the life of the oil. Many of the massage base oils can turn rancid over a period of time. They will usually last between 12-18 months with the exception of macadamia and jojoba oil which can last for up to 8-10 years, providing that they're stored correctly.

MASSAGE BASE OILS

Essential oils in the pure state are too highly concentrated to be used directly on the skin, and you will therefore find references to massage base oils.

The essential oils are diluted in a base oil so that they can be massaged or rubbed onto the skin in the correct dosage.

Massage base oils are vegetable, nut or seed oils, many of which themselves have therapeutic properties. Base oils are obtained from the seeds of plants that grow all over the world. There are several hundred different plants known to have oil-bearing seeds, but only a few have been produced commercially. Base oils are usually produced for food and are therefore good sources of nutrients and energy.

Before I give you a rundown on some of the most commonly used massage base oils, there are some important points to remember when using these oils for your massage blends.

SWEET ALMOND OIL – *Prunus amygdalus*

This is a light, fine, odourless oil ideal for general massage. It is traditionally used to prevent skin from wrinkling and has a high nutritional value. It helps relieve itching, soreness, dryness and inflammation.

APRICOT KERNEL OIL – *Prunus armeniaca*

A fine textured oil rich in vitamins for body and facial massage. It is often used in a warm oil treatment with the addition of essential oils. Apricot Kernel is excellent for dry or sun-baked skin and has long been used by Chinese women to refine the texture of their skin.

OLIVE OIL – *Olea europaea*

This base oil has a wonderful warming effect on the whole body. It is particularly good for children, the elderly and those who feel the cold. It is also a valuable scalp and hair tonic. A wonderful base oil with the addition of essential oils to address cellulite.

EVENING PRIMROSE OIL – *Oenothera biennis*

The ultimate in skin care. Softening to the texture of your skin it relieves sensitivity and the symptoms of allergies. An excellent oil for treating the effects of eczema and psoriasis.

ROSEHIP OIL – *Rosa rubiginosa*

This oil is energising and moisturising to the skin. It is a complete conditioning treatment that softens dry chapped skin, helping to reduce redness. An excellent treatment for the effects of eczema and psoriasis, improving peripheral circulation and general wellbeing.

AVOCADO OIL – *Persea americana*

A highly penetrative oil, used on its own as a luxury base or with Sweet Almond. It is excellent for dehydrated skin types. It is rich in vitamins A and E and ideal for expectant mothers to help prevent stretch marks.

MACADAMIA NUT OIL – *Macadamia integrifolia*

Extremely high in Vitamin A, this true Australian oil with its warm nutty aroma assists rejuvenation. An excellent body oil for daily skin care to nourish and moisturise. It is highly valued for its ant-oxidising properties, making it a valuable addition to your skin care program.

WHEATGERM OIL – *Triticum uulgave*

This oil is high in vitamin E. The addition of 10% of this oil to a massage base such as Sweet Almond will help to preserve your blended oils. An excellent oil for the treatment of eczema or dermatitis it is also very good for healing burns. Wheatgerm oil is rarely used on its own but is a valuable addition to other base oils.

JOJOBA OIL – *Simmondsia californica*

A natural fluid wax, non-greasy and quickly absorbed by the skin. Jojoba acts as a luxurious moisturiser for ageing, dry and hardened skin types. It leaves your skin with a beautiful silky softness and will not turn rancid. This versatile fluid wax is a superb base for massage and hair treatments. Its wax nature predisposes it to go solid in cold temperatures – placing the bottle under a warm tap will return it to its liquid form.

ALOE VERA – *Aloe barbadensis*

Aloe Vera is a smooth, soothing gel-like substance. It is renowned for its anti-rheumatic and anti-inflammatory properties. It is also attributed with digestive virtues and is effective in the treatment of asthma. It also helps to heal burns and ulcers. It is a highly protective, nourishing and moisturising gel.

SAINT JOHNS WORT – *Hypericum perforatum*

Saint Johns Wort is a herbaceous plant with a balsamic scent. It has an aromatic, astringent texture and is renowned for its soothing, anti-inflammatory and analgesic properties. It is used to treat insomnia and other nervous troubles and is recommended in the cases of stomach pains, colic or intestinal disorders. A protective nourishing oil that improves circulation.

NEEM OIL – *Azadirachta indica*

Neem oil comes from a tree native to India. It has a silky feel and is highly moisturising. It is antiseptic and ant-inflammatory and has an anti-bacterial effect. It is also endowed with anti-rheumatic properties. Neem oil relieves itching sensation and heals skin disorders such as eczema. It is very strengthening to nails and hair.

BATHING *(3-5 drops)*

The presence of water has been shown to influence the rate of absorption of some essential oil constituents. Hydration of the skin which happens during a bath or shower, facilitates the penetration of essential oils. Taking a hot bath increases the amount of blood circulating in the dermis, which will enhance the absorption of essential oil. The oiliness of the skin's surface encourages oils to adhere to it, meaning that a high proportion of the bath oil which has not evaporated will come in contact with the skin.

In many of my workshops and seminars I have asked the participants, "who showers?" And of course most of the hands in the audience, if not all, are raised. By contrast when I ask the question, "who takes a bath?" inevitably, a handful of hands flutter up into the air. Proportionately, we tend to shower more than we bathe.

Why? In our ever-busy world bathing seems to be a luxury that is on the low end of the priority list. In fact, it is one of the most luxurious and nurturing treatments that we can give ourselves. I especially recommend taking a bath at the completion of the day. It's a great way to relax and release all that has taken place, lying back in the aromatic water, taking time to reflect on the achievements, the challenges and insights that you've gleaned, whilst your body soaks and absorbs the healing benefits of the essential oils.

Bathing with essential oils can release congestion, promote circulation, dissipate muscle tension and fatigue, stress and tension. It can cleanse the body and help quieten the mind. The choice of essential oils that you sprinkle in the bath can of course redirect the entire experience from a quietening one to an energising one, in a moment.

Let's look at the different way that you can indulge in an aromatic bath. Once again it's the intention that determines the results. If you're taking a quick, energising aromatic bath in the morning, then you simply fill the bath to three quarters full with warm water, then dispense 5 drops of your chosen essential oils. Add them to the drawn bath and agitate the surface to disperse the essential molecules. Once you've done this, climb into the bath, splash over your body. It can be as short as five minutes if you're in a hurry. Sponge your body down, wring out the flannel, place it over your face and inhale the aromatic vapours, wiping over the face. Emerge from the bath, patting dry the skin and venture out into the day.

Another way to take a bath at the end of the day, given that you're preparing for sleep, is to light a candle rather than use the electric light. You might play some relaxing music. Prepare the water, add the essential oils as previously described and climb in. This time, when you're in the water lie back with a rolled towel, supporting your neck. Use your face cloth to slowly stroke your body, moving over each limb in a soft, soothing action with long flowing strokes. Wring out the flannel occasionally drawing it up over the face, drawing in deep breaths. With each exhalation breathe out any worries, tensions or concerns. Stay there for up to 15 minutes until you feel totally relaxed. I know I've taken the opportunity sometimes to have a cry, just to release any further residual tension. Step out of the bath and with a towel pat dry the skin. Climb into bed to have a restful sleep.

A variation on the aromatic bath is an aromatic partner bath. Set up the room in the same way as for a night-time bath. This time choose music that you and your partner both enjoy. It may be something sensually arousing or seductive. You may choose a musical track that is relaxing and sleep inducing for you both. This time you may choose to light several candles. Sit at different ends of the bath and as you become more relaxed, perhaps begin by sharing your day. Blow out one candle at a time until you have only one remaining.

This is an ideal time for each of you to take your partner's foot on your lap and massage the soles of each other's feet. One takes the lead and the other one follows. With your thumbs you simply press and release the soles of the foot and just allow each other to gradually seduce the body into deeper relaxation, by triggering the acupressure points on the soles of the feet. This feels fantastic when you get out of the bath.

Also consider your children. They absolutely love bath time. Roman chamomile, lavender and sandalwood are the preferred oils. Only one drop of essential oil is required in their entire bath. When you're sitting next to them on the edge of the bath simply lift the flannel, bathe their back and wash their face. This is an opportunity to educate our children about how to release their stress. By wringing out the flannel when you wash their face, ask them to inhale a big deep breath. Enact it for them so you breathe in at the same time. Encourage them to follow as they breathe in the aromatic molecules on the flannel, whilst you gently hold it over their face. Many times I've watched my children move from that erratic, active pace to a quiet calmness, and by the time they get into their pyjamas, they are absolutely ready for a good night's sleep.

Oil combinations to consider for the bath:

Bathing Blend 1 (Unwind)
Patchouli – 2 drops *Orange – 1 drop*
Sandalwood – 2 drops

Bathing Blend 2 (Uplift)
Bergamot – 2 drops *Orange – 1 drop*
Ylang Ylang – 2 drops

Bathing Blend 3 (Sleepfullness)
Marjoram – 2 drops *Lavender – 2 drops*
Sandalwood – 1 drop

Bathing Blend 4 (Wakefullness)
Rosemary – 2 drops *Lemon – 1 drop*
Pine – drops

Bathing Blend 5 (Balance)
Geranium – 1 drop *Lavender – 2 drops*
Cedarwood – 2 drops

VAPORISATION (8 drops)

"Aromatherapy invariably results in odoriferous molecules being inhaled. The main stream of inhaled air does not impinge directly on to the olfactory epithelium, but air currents carry odoriferous molecules to it."
— ROBERT TISSERAND

Vaporisation provides the perfect means to permeate the atmosphere with the delightful aromas of pure essential oils. As the droplets evaporate our sensitive olfactory nerves transmit the scent to our brains. The effect on our minds and bodies starts within seconds.

All the forty essential oils are suitable for vaporisation. But it is important that you choose oils that you like, and which are pleasing to the senses. Practice a little caution. You may find there are some oils which have a "dampening" effect on your mood. You will find that by varying the oils and combinations, you will be able to constantly change the atmosphere in your surroundings. You can choose when to relax or stimulate your senses and when to refresh and uplift weary spirits.

Vaporising is so simple. Any vaporising unit will do as long as it's not made from plastic or any other porous material. You simply fill the bowl on top of the unit with water and dispense 8 drops of your chosen essential oils onto the surface of the water. It's now time to light the match, ignite the candle and when it warms the water the heat dispenses the essential molecules into the air as they evaporate.

It's important that you continue to choose oil combinations which please you and the people who share your environment. I remember speaking to a woman who set up her vaporising unit in her workplace. She was thrilled with the pungent aroma of sage, pine and thyme essential oils. However, it set up a negative chain reaction response in all her colleagues who felt that the aroma was overpowering. When you're introducing essential oils into your workplace, where many other people may move in and out of that space, it's wise to start with essential oils such as orange, bergamot, lavender, mandarin, lime and lemon. The sweet floral oils in a very diluted proportion enable people to become accustomed to the fact that there is a new scent in the air. It is perceived as delicate and unintrusive, rather than overpowering and dominating.

I enjoy it when I can set ambience ahead of time. For example, when it's time for me to go to sleep every night I take great pleasure in lighting my vaporiser with oils such as lavender, marjoram, palmarosa, orange and sandalwood. I light my vaporiser so that my bedroom is filled with an aroma that permeates the bedroom well ahead of retiring. I usually do this an hour before I go to sleep at night. When

I open the door to the bedroom all my senses are assailed with the sweet smells and the bedroom environment beckons me to go to sleep and truly have sweet dreams.

INHALATION/FACIAL STEAM ***(3-4 drops)***

Because the lungs have a large surface area, the amount of essential oil which reaches the bloodstream will be increased by deep or rapid breathing.

Inhalation is another way in which vaporisation of essential oils is used to balance physical disorders and to help in the release of emotions. You can take a steel or glass bowl and half fill it with near boiling water. Have ready your chosen oils and a towel. Add 3-4 drops of oil to the water and agitate gently to release the vapours. Close your eyes and breathe deeply at least 20cms away from the bowl with the towel over your head. Continue for up to 10 minutes for maximum benefits.

The very action of this process opens the pores allowing the steam to cleanse the skin and therefore this method of use is ideal in your skincare routine.

COMPRESS ***(3-6 drops)***

There are two specific uses for a compress. For facial skin care, it is useful for softening the skin and promoting cell regeneration. For therapeutic applications, compresses may be used in first aid. They can help to relieve pain and swelling, and will reduce inflammation. Hot compresses are generally used to relieve chronic pain, while cold compresses are ideal for acute pain or injury.

You may also release pent up emotions by inhaling the vapours from a warm aromatic compress. Dispense 3-6 drops of essential oils in 200 mls of water, agitate the water, and then soak a washer in hot or cold water to which the essential oil blend has been added. Make sure the cloth absorbs as much of the oil as possible from the surface of the water.

FACIAL COMPRESS COMBINATIONS

Compress Blend 1 (Mature, Dry Skin)

Frankincense – 1 drop *Sandalwood – 1 drop*

Clary Sage – 1 drop

or

Compress Blend 2 (Oily Skin)

Lemon – 1 drop *Cypress – 2 drops*

Keep compress cloth away from the eye area.

Further Methods of Use

(N.B. Use only 1 drop for all applications for children under 5).

WARM OIL MASK

4 drops of essential oil in 10mls massage base oil.

FOR THE FACE

Once a week you can treat your skin to a warm oil mask. Remember to apply your eye cream for further protection and choose an essential oil combination which is suitable for your skin type. This mask applied weekly will assist to moisturise your skin.

You need a pastry brush, 10mls of Jojoba oil and 4 drops in total of your chosen essential oils. Warm your base oil. Add your chosen essential oils and apply the oil with a pastry brush in a thin layer over the throat and facial area, over the nose, and through to the hairline in long sweeping strokes.

FOR HAIR

This method can also be used on the scalp to treat hair and skin conditions such as psiorisis, eczema, hair loss and dandruff. This treatment will also condition and nourish the hair follicle and can, at the same time, address emotional needs. For instance, if you are feeling depressed and require some comfort, the infusion of essential oils into the scalp, via the hair follicles, ensures quick penetration.

As a warm oil treatment (follow warm oil mask technique above) apply to the root of the hair in sections, as though you were applying a tint to colour the hair. Leave in overnight. The following morning, emulsify your hair with your shampoo before wetting it to cleanse your hair of all the oil.

HAIR RINSE

Add a total of 4 drops of essential oils into 100ml blending bottle filled with warm water. Shake the bottle and pour the blend through the hair before leaving the shower in the morning.

FACIAL MASK/CLAY

2 dessert spoons of natural clay and 2 drops of essential oil. Blend your chosen oils with a fine paste of kaolin powder. Apply the mask with a pastry brush to the skin in long strokes, avoiding the eye area.

SHOWER

3-5 drops on a bath sponge. Wash your body as usual and follow by adding your chosen oils to a sponge or flannel and, with light friction, rub the oils over the entire body. This can replace the use of soap.

SPRITZ

Using a 200 ml glass bottle or stainless steel spray can, fill with distilled or purified water. Add 2 drops of essential oil and agitate. Use as a facial toner and spritz to refresh the skin.

N.B. Never use plastic bottles with essential oils.

FOOT BATH

Dispense 5 drops of essential oil into large bowl of warm to hot water. Agitate the water. For foot massage treatment place a cloth under the water on the bottom of the bowl, drop a few large marbles into water on top of the cloth. Roll the marbles around with the soles of your feet. Take a foot bath at meal times, or late in the evening to help you relax, or after a hard day at work. Soak the feet for a minimum of 15 minutes. Remember your foot bowl is portable so it's easy to ease a stressful day at work, too!

DIRECT (Neat)

Direct application- Apply a few drops neat onto a cotton bud or onto a sterile gauze and apply to the affected area.

SWAB / WASH

Dispense 2-3 drops of essential oil into 200mls of distilled or purified water. Agitate the water. Swab: bathe

the area with aromatic water and cotton wool pad. Wash: sprinkle the solution over the skin with aromatic water.

PERFUME

Apply three drops of essential oil onto the palm of a hand. Rub hands together and quickly rub through the hair. Or add oils to a cotton pad and place hidden in clothing. You can blend 2-3 different oils for your individual scent.

AROMATIC STEAM

10 drops of essential oil to the shower basin. Creating an aromatic steam filled environment addresses any bronchial or breathing disorders. This can be done using the shower in your bathroom. Place a washcloth over the plug-hole in the shower basin. Add 10 drops of your chosen oil to the shower basin. Turn on the hot tap, as the water ruptures the essential oil molecules the healing vapours evaporate with the steam into the air. Make sure all the doors and windows are closed. Spend time deep breathing in through the nose. Or alternatively, in through the mouth and lungs to assist the airways to open and function properly. If you have a small child with croup this is an ideal treatment.

AROMATIC COTTON BALL (adults only)

1-2 drops. Roll the piece of pure cotton wool to the size of a large pea. Dispense 1 or 2 drops of pure essential oil into the piece of cotton wool and quickly blot the excess oil onto an absorbent tissue. Take the infused cotton wool and place it just inside the orifice of the ear for a 30 minute period. This technique is ideal for those who are flying and experience ear pain. It is also ideal for earache associated with colds or flu.

Caution: Do not push the cotton wool down into the ear canal. Do not sleep with cotton wool in the ear. Never use this technique on children.

AROMATIC SNIFF

Dispense 1-3 drops of the chosen essential oil onto a handkerchief or tissue and allow the essential oil vapours to evaporate for 30 seconds before use. Use your aromatic tissue as a means to safely take in the healing vapours of essential oils directly through inhalation. This method of use is ideal to ease mucous membrane irritation associated with hayfever, or to assist breathing when congestion is present with cold and flu symptoms. For migraine headache symptoms which include nausea, this technique can be used as well.

MOUTH WASH

1-2 drops into half a glass of water. Dispense 1-2 drops of your chosen essential oil into half a glass of tepid water. Agitate the water with a stainless steel spoon. You may choose to add a half teaspoon of honey to the mixture. This is an ideal way to produce an antiseptic gargle for gum infection or as a mouthwash and gargle for sore throats.

SITZ BATH

3 drops to 3 litres water. Add 3 drops of essential oil to a large basin of warm water (preferably glass or stainless steel). Agitate the surface of the water to disperse oil molecules. Place basin on the floor and squat down over the surface of the water. Using your hand, splash the aromatic water gently over the genital area to soothe away all irritation.

DOUCHE

3 drops to 1 litre warm water. To facilitate a douche you need to purchase an enema kit from your pharmacist. Instead of using it as directed, insert the apparatus into the opening of the vagina. Dispense 3 drops of essential oil into 1 litre of warm water and fill the bag. Hang the bag over the end of the bath. Sit naked in the bath and fold a towel under your bottom and splay your

legs. Insert the apparatus inside the vagina opening and allow the bag to naturally empty and douche the area. Recommended as a monthly cleansing treatment.

Further Creative Ways of Using Your Oils

AROMATIC LIPSTICK

Dispense half drop of essential oil onto the back of your hand and mix your lipstick with your lip brush with the oil, then apply. You can treat the condition of your lips while enjoying the taste and fragrance.

SAUNA

3 drops per 100mls of water. Add 3 drops of a cleansing, tonifying oil to a 100ml bottle of water and shake. Pour the aromatic water over the hot coals. I suggest using Eucalyptus, Tea Tree, Pine or Lemon.

FLAVOURINGS

Culinary use. Essential oils may be added to food preparations. Remember, these oils are highly concentrated so be sparing. Only 1-2 drops are required, eg: 1 drop of Lemongrass onto a teabag to make a full pot of tea.

CANDLES

1 drop. Light your candle and allow the wax to melt. Dispense 1 drop of oil into the liquid wax. The aroma will begin to rise. The essential oils are extremely volatile so please be careful not to use directly on the naked flame.

LIGHT BULBS

1-2 drops. Add your favourite essential oil to a cool bulb before it is turned on and heated. Then switch on to release the oil molecules.

WOOD FIRES

1-2 drops per log. Any of the woody oils will give a rich aromatic ambience to the warmth of the fire. Allow some time for the oil to penetrate the wood. We suggest using Pine, Cypress, Cedarwood or Sandalwood.

LINGERIE

Place a hanky laced with essential oil into your lingerie drawer for a long-lasting effect. Alternatively, a few drops in the last rinse cycle of your wash will do the trick. A hanky impregnated with oils popped into the dryer with clothing also makes clothes smell fantastic.

Caution: Be careful with the oils which retain their natural colour, eg. Orange and Mandarin.

FRAGRANT SPRAYS

5 drops. Use the above spray method with a combination of 3 essential oils and you can deodorise and freshen your bathroom. Spray several times into the toilet bowl after flushing to cleanse and fragrance.

BED LINEN

Place a potpourri bag with your favourite blend in the linen cupboard. For those special evenings, a few extra drops on satin pillowcases and sheets will set the mood. Essential oils easily wash out of clothing and bed linen, so don't worry about stains.

AROMATIC IRONING

5 drops. Dispense 5 drops of Lavender oil into a small glass, or stainless steel spray can, filled with water. Shake well. Delight yourself and your clothes as your work.

POTPOURRI BOWLS

You can buy unscented potpourri blends at leading department stores to which you can add your favourite blend. Stir the potpourri regularly to keep it fresh and light. Alternatively, save the rose buds your lover sends you and place them in a bowl. Add a few drops of Rose Otto to give them extra fragrance. If you're more the mountain-air type, gather pine cones, clean leaves and woodchips next time you're out walking to make your own nature mix. Just add the appropriate blend to suit your mood.

ROOM SPRAYS

10 drops to 500mls water. Using a glass or stainless steel spray can, add 10 drops of oil blend to 500mls of distilled water. Warm the water before adding the oils. Spray the environment to freshen and cleanse the atmosphere. This spray can also be used on furniture and carpets.

PERSONALISED GIFTS

50 drops. Take your 100ml empty blending bottle and make your friends or loved ones a special aromatic massage blend. Show you care by making blends for birthdays, Mother's Day, Father's Day, Christmas, Easter or any other special occasion.

CHAPTER FOUR

The A-Z of Aromatherapy

PEOPLE TODAY ARE EAGER TO GAIN INFORMATION and knowledge that will ultimately contribute to their health and well being. The availability and right to choose products and services for therapeutic use are considered by both industry and government bodies to further ensure our safety.

This chapter is designed to categorise in alphabetical order the most common ailments encountered in day-to-day life. I have included blends designed to provide temporary relief of the symptoms of such conditions. At the same time I need to stress that people must act responsibly and seek medical advice if the symptoms persist. This chapter provides a greater understanding of minor ailments and equips people with skills and a choice of blends using pure essential oils to self-treat such conditions.

It would be incorrect to assume that all essential oils meet the criteria of the Therapeutic Goods Act which determines the purity of essential oils. The following information has been written with the understanding that only the purest essential oils will suffice for therapeutic purposes.

Each company has the choice to register or list their essential oils as either therapeutic or cosmetic goods. If the manufacturer lists or registers their essential oils, then they must conform to the strict verification system for each oil. This includes strict purchasing requirements to ensure that the essential oils are authentic and unadulterated. They must adhere to specific bottling and packaging guidelines as well as documentation procedures in order to enable them to make therapeutic claims about their products. Each claim must conform to the Therapeutic Goods Media Code.

The system exists to protect us all as consumers and to provide us with the right to simply and safely self prescribe. All therapeutic essential oils can be identified by the packaging. They will have an 'AUST L' (Australian Listed) or 'Aust R' (Australian Registered) number on the front of the label or carton.

The companies who fail to list or register their products, do not comply with the quality control system outlined above. They do not have the right to make therapeutic claims about their essential oils and this places the purity of the oils in question. Therefore, purchase your oils carefully for your health and well being.

Essential oils are potent by nature—less is always best. Please follow chapter three—"Methods of Use"—for each application so that you can adhere to the recommended drops.

Most of all, enjoy the process. Pro-activity and personal responsibility are the perfect accompaniment to successful aromatherapy treatments that nourish our body and soul.

A

ACNE

Acne is usually associated with adolescents and is a common inflammatory disorder of the sebaceous glands, the actual cause is unknown. It involves the face, back and chest and is characterised by the presence of blackheads and pustules.

Essential Oils: Bergamot, Cedarwood, German Chamomile, Geranium, Juniper, Lavender, Lemon, Lemongrass, Palmarosa, Rosewood, Sage, and Tea Tree.

Application: Compress, Warm Oil Mask.

Compress Blend 1

Lavender – 1 drop
Bergamot – 1 drop
Palmarosa – 1 drop
Rosewood – 1 drop

or

Compress Blend 2

Cedarwood – 1 drop
Geranium – 1 drop
Juniper – 1 drop
Lemongrass – 1 drop

or

Compress Blend 3

Chamomile (G) – 1 drop
Chamomile (R) – 1 drop
Sage – 1 drop
Tea Tree – 1 drop

or

Compress Blend 4

Lemon – 1 drop
Lemongrass – 1 drop
Juniper – 1 drop
Sage – 1 drop

Warm Oil Mask Blend 1

Chamomile (R) – 1 drop
Juniper – 1 drop
Lavender – 1 drop
Palmarosa – 1 drop

or

Warm Oil Mask Blend 2

Bergamot – 1 drop
Chamomile (R) – 1 drop
Palmarosa – 1 drop
Rosewood – 1 drop

ALLERGIES

An Allergy is a reaction in which the body becomes hypersensitive to particular antigens that provoke characteristic symptoms whenever they are subsequently inhaled, ingested, injected or otherwise contacted. Allergic reactions are usually first evident on the skin and may be merely local and temporary, e.g. heat rash or contact dermatitis.

Essential Oils: Bergamot, German Chamomile, Roman Chamomile, Lavender, Neroli, Patchouli, Palmarosa, Rose and Sandalwood.

Application: Massage, Bathing.

Massage Blend 1

Chamomile (G) – 10 drops
Geranium – 10 drops
Lavender – 20 drops
Sandalwood – 10 drops

or

Massage Blend 2

Chamomile (R) – 15 drops
Lavender – 10 drops
Palmarosa – 15 drops
Rose – 10 drops

Bathing Blend 1

Bergamot – 2 drops
Neroli – 2 drops
Palmarosa – 1 drop

or

Bathing Blend 2

Chamomile (G) – 1 drop
Chamomile (R) – 2 drops
Lavender – 1 drop
Patchouli – 1 drop

ANOREXIA NERVOSA

Anorexia Nervosa is a complex eating disorder. It is most common in female adolescents, in which the person starves themselves or use other techniques, such as vomiting or taking laxatives to induce weight loss.

Essential Oils: Black Pepper, Cardamon, Eucalyptus, Fennel, Ginger, Grapefruit, Lavender, Orange and Palmarosa.

Application: Massage, Bathing, Vaporisation.

Massage Blend 1

Black Pepper – 10 drops	*Cardamon – 20 drops*
Fennel – 10 drops	*Ginger –10 drops*

or

Massage Blend 2

Grapefruit – 10 drops	*Lavender – 20 drops*
Orange 10 drops	*Palmarosa – 10 drops*

Bathing Blend

Cardamon – 1 drop	*Fennel – 1 drop*
Ginger – 1 drop	*Grapefruit – 2 drops*

Vaporisation Blend 1

Fennel – 1 drop	*Ginger - 2 drops*
Grapefruit – 3 drops	*Eucalyptus – 2 drops*

or

Vaporisation Blend 2

Cardamon – 2 drops	*Lavender – 2 drops*
Orange – 3 drops	*Eucalyptus – 1 drop*

ANXIETY

Anxiety is a condition in which anxiety dominates a person's life. It is the response to the interpretation that one makes of something that happens. Symptoms of anxiety include difficulty in concentration, irritability, tense muscles, aches and pains, nausea, dizziness, breathlessness, sleep problems, dry mouth, decreased or increased appetite can be acute or chronic.

Essential Oils: Basil, Bergamot, Cedarwood, Geranium, Jasmine, Lavender, Lemongrass, Lime, Marjoram, Neroli, Orange, Palmarosa and Sandalwood.

Application: Massage, Bathing, Vaporisation, Inhalation.

Massage Blend 1

Basil – 10 drops
Bergamot – 20 drops
Lavender – 10 drops
Neroli – 10 drops

or

Massage Blend 2

Lemongrass – 10 drops
Lime - 10 drops
Jasmine – 20 drops
Mandarin – 10 drops

or

Massage Blend 3

Cedarwood – 20 drops
Marjoram – 10 drops
Orange – 10 drops
Palmarosa – 10 drops

Bathing Blend 1

Cedarwood – 2 drops
Lavender – 2 drops
Lemongrass – 1 drop

or

Bathing Blend 2

Cedarwood – 2 drops
Neroli – 1 drop
Lime – 1 drop
Petitgrain – 1 drop

Vaporisation Blend 1

Basil – 1 drop
Cedarwood – 2 drops
Bergamot – 3 drops
Geranium –2 drops

or

Vaporisation Blend 2

Jasmine - 1 drop
Orange – 2 drops
Marjoram – 2 drops
Sandalwood – 3 drops

Inhalation Blend 1

Lavender – 1 drop
Orange – 1 drop
Neroli – 1 drop

or

Inhalation Blend 2

Bergamot –2 drops
Cedarwood – 2 drops

ARTHRITIS

Arthritis is an inflammation of one or more joints, characterised by swelling, warmth, and redness of the overlying skin; pain and restriction of motion is experienced.

Essential Oils: Basil, German Chamomile, Cypress, Eucalyptus, Frankincense, Juniper, Lavender, Lemon, Pine and Sage.

Application: Massage, Bathing.

Massage Blend 1

Basil – 10 drops
Juniper – 20 drops
Pine – 10 drops
Sage – 10 drops

or

Massage Blend 2

Chamomile (G) – 10 drops
Eucalyptus – 10 drops
Lavender – 20 drops
Lemon – 10 drops

or

Massage Blend 3

Eucalyptus – 10 drops
Frankincense – 10 drops
Juniper – 10 drops
Lavender – 20 drops

Bathing Blend 1

Cypress – 2 drops
Lemon – 1 drop
Sage – 2 drops

or

Bathing Blend 2

Frankincense – 2 drops
Pine – 1 drop
Sage – 2 drops

ASTHMA

Asthma inhibits the process of breathing and sufferers experience symptoms such as coughing, wheezing and emotional stress as the bronchial airways narrow. When the bronchial tube spasms, it makes it more difficult for air to make its way in or out of the lungs. Bacteria, allergens and a build up of mucus can govern the severity of the condition.

Essential Oils: Cedarwood, Eucalyptus, Frankincense, Geranium, Juniper, Lavender, Marjoram, Peppermint, Pine, Rosemary, Sage and Thyme.

Application: Massage, Vaporisation, Inhalation.

Massage Blend 1

(for children or acute adult conditions)

Eucalyptus – 10 drops	*Juniper – 10 drops*
Lavender – 20 drops	*Marjoram – 5 drops*
Cedarwood – 5 drops	

or

Massage Blend 2

Peppermint – 10 drops	*Pine – 10 drops*
Rosemary – 20 drops	*Sage – 10 drops*

Vaporisation Blend 1

Cedarwood – 2 drops	*Peppermint – 2 drops*
Eucalyptus– 2 drops	*Thyme – 2 drops*

or

Vaporisation Blend 2

Frankincense – 2 drops	*Geranium – 2 drops*
Lavender – 2 drops	*Marjoram – 2 drops*

Inhalation Blend 1

Eucalyptus – 1 drop
Peppermint – 1 drop
Thyme – 1 drop
Cedarwood – 1 drop

or

Inhalation Blend 2

Eucalyptus – 2 drops
Juniper – 1 drop
Pine – 1 drop

ATHLETE'S FOOT

Athlete's foot is a fungal infection of the skin between the toes encouraged by the presence of bacteria in warm, damp conditions.

Essential Oils: Bergamot, Cardamon, Cypress, Eucalyptus, Lavender, Palmarosa, Sage, Tea Tree.

Application: Massage, Footbath.

Massage Blend 1

Bergamot – 20 drops
Cardamon – 10 drops
Cypress – 10 drops
Eucalyptus – 10 drops

or

Massage Blend 2

Lavender – 20 drops
Palmarosa – 10 drops
Sage – 10 drops
Tea Tree – 10 drops

Footbath Blend 1

Eucalyptus – 2 drops
Sage – 2 drops
Tea Tree – 1 drop

or

Footbath Blend 2

Bergamot – 2 drops
Cardamon – 1 drop
Lavender – 2 drops

B

BACK PAIN

There are numerous reasons for the symptoms of back pain. It is important to determine the source or cause of the pain before receiving specific treatment. Its cause can be from kidney infection, injury, degenerative spine conditions or bad posture.

In this instance, the recipes address muscular skeletal influences.

Essential Oils: Black Pepper, Roman Chamomile, Clary Sage, Ginger, Lavender, Marjoram, Peppermint, Rosemary, Thyme and Vetiver.

Application: Massage, Bathing.

Massage Blend 1

Chamomile (R) – 15 drops
Ginger – 15 drops
Rosemary – 15 drops
Vetiver – 5 drops

or

Massage Blend 2

Black Pepper – 10 drops
Clary Sage – 20 drops
Peppermint – 15 drops
Thyme – 5 drops

or

Massage Blend 3

Chamomile (R) – 10 drops
Lavender – 10 drops
Marjoram – 20 drops
Vetiver – 10 drops

Bathing Blend 1

Clary Sage – 1 drop
Ginger – 1 drop
Rosemary – 3 drops

or

Bathing Blend 2

Chamomile (R) – 2 drops
Lavender – 2 drops
Marjoram – 1 drop

or

Bathing Blend 3

Peppermint – 2 drops
Rosemary – 2 drops
Thyme – 1 drop

BALDNESS/ALOPECIA

Baldness is an absence of hair from areas where it normally grows. It includes common baldness in men, which is familial, and in women where the hair loss (Alopecia) is associated with stress or the ageing process. It can be predetermined by our genetic make-up and influenced by the way we handle shock, trauma, illness or change.

Essential Oils: Cedarwood, Roman Chamomile, Clary Sage, Juniper, Lavender, Lemon, Lime, Neroli, Rosemary and Thyme.

Application: Massage, Hair Mask, Hair Rinse.

Massage Blend 1

Lemon – 10 drops | *Lime – 15 drops*
Rosemary – 20 drops | *Thyme – 5 drops*

or

Massage Blend 2

Chamomile (R) – 10 drops | *Clary Sage – 10 drops*
Lavender – 20 drops | *Neroli – 10 drops*

or

Massage Blend 3

Cedarwood – 20 drops | *Lavender – 10 drops*
Juniper – 10 drops | *Neroli – 10 drops*

Hair Mask Blend 1

Cedarwood – 1 drop
Juniper – 1 drop
Neroli – 1 drop
Lavender – 1 drop

or

Hair Mask Blend 2

Lemon – 1 drop
Rosemary – 1 drop
Thyme – 1 drop
Juniper – 1 drop

or

Hair Mask Blend 3

Chamomile (R) – 1 drop
Clary Sage – 1 drop
Lemon – 1 drop
Cedarwood – 1 drop

Hair Rinse Blend 1

Cedarwood – 1 drop
Juniper – 1 drop
Neroli – 1 drop
Rosemary – 1 drop

or

Hair Rinse Blend 2

Cedarwood – 1 drop
Chamomile (R) - 1 drop
Juniper – 1 drop
Lime – 1 drop

BITES AND STINGS

Bites from domestic and farm animals such as dogs or horses are generally harmless, but a tetanus injection may be necessary. The most common bites however are from the mosquito and ant. Both become inflamed and itchy however it is the ant bite which is ultimately more painful. Stings may arise from plant, insect or fish, the most common are from a bee or wasp.

Essential Oils: Eucalyptus, Lavender, Lemongrass, Marjoram, Patchouli, Peppermint and Tea Tree. Basil, Bergamot and Cedarwood are insect repellents.

Application: Swab, Spritz.

Swab – Blend 1

Lavender – 1 drop | *Patchouli – 1 drop*
Tea Tree – 1 drop

or

Swab – Blend 2

Eucalyptus – 1 drop | *Basil – 1 drop*
Marjoram – 1 drop

Spritz

Lavender – 1 drop | *Lemongrass – 1 drop*
Peppermint – 1 drop

Spritz (Repellent)

Basil – 1 drop | *Bergamot – 1 drop*
Cedarwood – 1 drop

BLISTERS

Blisters commonly occur on the feet due to pressure and/or a rubbing action from shoes. They are a swelling containing watery fluid and sometimes also blood or pus, within or just beneath the skin.

Essential Oils: Black Pepper, German Chamomile, Roman Chamomile, Cypress, Eucalyptus, Lavender, Marjoram, Palmarosa, Peppermint, Rosemary, Tea Tree and Vetiver.

Application: Compress, Footbath.

Compress Blend 1

Chamomile (G) – 1 drop
Chamomile (R) – 1 drop
Lavender – 1 drop
Tea Tree – 1 drop

or

Compress Blend 2

Cypress – 1 drop
Eucalyptus – 1 drop
Palmarosa – 1 drop
Tea Tree – 1 drop

Footbath Blend 1

Bergamot – 1 drop
Chamomile (G) – 1 drop
Lavender – 2 drops
Tea Tree – 1 drop

or

Footbath Blend 2

Chamomile (R) – 1 drop
Eucalyptus – 1 drop
Lavender – 2 drops
Palmarosa – 1 drop

or

Footbath Blend 3

Peppermint – 2 drops
Rosemary – 2 drops
Black Pepper – 1 drop

or

Footbath Blend 4

Marjoram – 1 drop
Vetiver – 2 drops
Lavender – 1 drop
Black Pepper – 1 drop

BLOOD PRESSURE

Blood pressure is the pressure of blood against the walls of the main arteries. Muscular exertion and emotional factors, such as fear, stress and excitement can all raise blood pressure.

The heartbeat is higher when the heart contracts, pumping blood out into the body and lower when the heart relaxes filling it with blood from the veins.

Essential Oils: For Hypotension: Basil, Lemon, Neroli, Peppermint and Rosemary.

Application: Massage, and Vaporisation.

Massage

Basil – 10 drops
Lemon – 10 drops
Neroli – 10 drops
Peppermint – 10 drops
Rosemary - 10 drops

Vaporisation

Basil – 1 drop
Lemon – 3 drops
Peppermint – 2 drops
Rosemary – 2 drops

Essential Oils for Hypertension: Clary Sage, Lavender, Marjoram, Neroli and Rose.

Application: Massage, and Vaporisation.

Massage

Clary Sage – 5 drops
Lavender – 15 drops
Marjoram – 10 drops
Neroli – 10 drops
Rose – 10 drops

Vaporisation

Lavender – 2 drops
Marjoram – 2 drops
Neroli – 3 drops
Rose – 1 drop

Precaution: Marjoram is contra-indicated for low blood pressure. It has sedating qualities. Do not use.

BOILS

A boil is a tender inflamed area of the skin containing pus. Bacteria entering through a hair follicle or a break in the skin usually cause the infection. Boils usually heal when the pus is released.

Essential Oils: Bergamot, German Chamomile, Roman Chamomile, Cedarwood, Lavender, Lemon, Myrrh, Patchouli, Petitgrain, Pine, Tea Tree, Thyme.

Application: Compress, Swabs, Direct.

Compress Blend 1

Chamomile (R) – 2 drops
Clary Sage – 1 drop
Lavender – 1 drop
Petitgrain – 1 drop

or

Compress Blend 2

Bergamot – 1 drop
Chamomile (G) – 2 drops
Myrrh – 1 drop
Tea Tree – 1 drop

or

Compress Blend 3

Thyme – 1 drop
Patchouli – 1 drop
Lemon – 2 drops

Swab Blend 1

Chamomile (G) – 2 drops
Lavender – 1 drop

or

Swab Blend 2

Cedarwood – 1 drop
Petitgrain – 1 drop
Pine – 1 drop

or

Swab Blend 3

Chamomile (G) – 1 drop
Chamomile (R) – 1 drop
Myrrh – 1 drop

Direct Blend 1

Lavender - 1 drop
Tea Tree – 2 drops

or

Direct Blend 2

Lavender – 1 drop
Myrrh – 1 drop
Tea Tree – 1 drop

BRONCHITIS

Bronchitis is an inflammation of the bronchial tubes resulting in a build-up of congestion. It is caused by bacterial infection which in turn increases mucous production. Acute bronchitis can be accompanied by a fever, persistent cough and a general lack of energy. Chronic bronchitis is without a fever and can last over several weeks or months and is usually accompanied by phlegm.

Essential Oils: Lavender, Cedarwood, Eucalyptus, Frankincense, Lemon, Marjoram, Myrrh, Peppermint, Pine, Rosemary, Sage, Sandalwood, Tea Tree and Thyme.

Application: Massage, Vaporisation, Inhalation.

Massage Blend 1

Peppermint – 10 drops
Sage – 10 drops
Tea Tree – 20 drops
Thyme – 10 drops

or

Massage Blend 2

Eucalyptus – 20 drops
Frankincense – 10 drops
Lemon – 10 drops
Pine – 10 drops

or

Massage Blend 3

Cedarwood – 10 drops
Lavender – 20 drops
Myrrh – 10 drops
Sandalwood – 10 drops

Vaporisation Blend 1

Eucalyptus – 2 drops
Lemon – 2 drops
Peppermint – 2 drops
Pine – 2 drops

or

Vaporisation Blend 2

Cedarwood – 2 drops
Pine – 2 drops
Tea Tree – 2 drops
Thyme – 2 drops

Inhalation Blend 1

Eucalyptus – 1 drop
Lemon – 1 drop
Sage – 1 drop
Marjoram – 1 drop

or

Inhalation Blend 2

Lemon – 1 drop
Peppermint – 1 drop
Tea Tree – 1 drop
Rosemary – 1 drop

BRUISES

An area of skin discoloration caused by the escape of blood from ruptured underlying vessels usually following injury. They can appear black, red or variations of the same and begin to change colour and yellow as they heal.

Essential Oils: Black Pepper, Roman Chamomile, Eucalyptus, Ginger, Juniper, Lavender, Lemongrass and Marjoram.

Application: Massage, Compress, Direct.

Massage Blend 1

Lavender – 20 drops | *Marjoram – 10 drops*
Chamomile (R) – 10 drops | *Juniper – 10 drops*

or

Massage Blend 2

Black Pepper – 5 drops | *Lavender – 25 drops*
Ginger – 5 drops | *Lemongrass – 15 drops*

Compress

Black Pepper – 2 drops | *Eucalyptus – 1 drop*
Ginger – 1 drop | *Lemongrass – 1 drop*

Direct

Juniper –1 drop | *Lavender – 2 drops*

BURNS

A burn is tissue damage caused by such agents as heat, chemicals, electricity or sunlight. Burns cause swelling and blistering and the pain associated with even minor burns can be extreme.

Recommended oil: Roman Chamomile, Lavender and Tea Tree.

Application: Massage, Bathing, Swab, Spritz.

Massage

Chamomile (R) - 10 drops *Lavender – 25 drops*
Tea Tree – 10 drops

Bathing

Chamomile (R) – 1 drop *Lavender – 3 drops*
Tea Tree – 1 drop

Lavender Swab

Lavender – 2 drops
Onto a cotton bud

Spritz

Lavender – 3 drops

C

CARPAL TUNNEL SYNDROME

Carpal Tunnel Syndrome is an uncomfortable disorder that occurs in the nerve pathway leading from the hands to the arms. Swelling can occur and a combination of pins and needles, numbness and pain affecting all of the hand except the little finger caused by a repetitive action such as typing.

Essential Oils: German Chamomile, Jasmine, Lavender, Myrrh, Peppermint, Petitgrain, and Rose.

Application: Massage, Direct.

Massage Blend 1

Chamomile (G) – 10 drops
Jasmine – 10 drops
Lavender – 20 drops
Petitgrain – 10 drops

Massage Blend 2

Jasmine – 10 drops
Lavender – 20 drops
Myrrh – 10 drops
Rose – 10 drops

Direct

Peppermint – 2 drops

CATARRH

Refers to the inflammation of a mucous membrane which subsequently produces excessive secretion of thick phlegm or mucus by the mucous membrane of the nose, nasal sinuses, naso-pharynx or air passages. It can also be associated with infection from a cold or flu or by irritants such as pollen or dust.

Essential Oils: Cardamon, Cedarwood, Eucalyptus, Juniper, Lavender, Lemon, Lime, Myrrh, Peppermint, Pine, Rosemary, Tea Tree and Thyme.

Application: Massage, Inhalation.

Massage Blend 1

Cedarwood – 20 drops *Eucalyptus – 10 drops*
Lemon – 10 drops *Myrrh – 10 drops*

or

Massage Blend 2

Lavender – 10 drops *Cedarwood – 20 drops*
Myrrh – 10 drops *Peppermint – 10 drops*

or

Massage Blend 3

Lemon – 10 drops *Cedarwood – 20 drops*
Lime – 10 drops *Peppermint – 10 drops*

or

Massage Blend 4

Lemon – 10 drops
Lime – 10 drops
Eucalyptus – 20 drops
Rosemary – 10 drops

Inhalation Blend 1

Eucalyptus – 2 drops
Pine – 1 drop
Peppermint – 1 drop

or

Inhalation Blend 2

Cardamon – 1 drop
Thyme – 1 drop
Eucalyptus – 1 drop
Pine – 1 drop

or

Inhalation Blend 3

Cedarwood – 1 drop
Juniper – 1 drop
Eucalyptus – 1 drop
Peppermint – 1 drop

or

Inhalation Blend 4

Cardamon – 1 drop
Peppermint – 1 drop
Eucalyptus – 1 drop
Tea Tree – 1 drop

CELLULITE

Cellulite is used to describe the "orange peel" affect many women, and some men, find on their thighs, hips, upper arms or buttocks. It is thought to be the result of water infiltrating body tissue and inter-dispersing with fat cells.

Essential Oils: Cedarwood, Cypress, Fennel, Lavender, Lemon and Lemongrass.

Application: Massage.

Massage Blend 1

Cedarwood – 10 drops *Cypress – 10 drops*
Lavender – 30 drops

or

Massage Blend 2

Cedarwood – 20 drops *Cypress – 10 drops*
Fennel – 10 drops *Lemongrass – 10 drops*

or

Massage Blend 3

Cypress – 10 drops *Fennel – 20 drops*
Lemon – 10 drops *Lemongrass – 10 drops*

CELLULITIS

Cellulitis is a medical condition resulting from an inflammation of the subcutaneous tissue due to a bacterial infection. It is most common on the lower legs and can feel uncomfortable or painful.

Essential Oils: Cypress, German Chamomile, Lavender, Tea Tree.

Application: Massage, Bathing.

Massage

Chamomile (G) – 10 drops *Cypress – 10 drops*
Lavender – 20 drops *Tea Tree –10 drops*

Bathing

Chamomile (G) – 2 drops *Cypress – 1 drop*
Lavender – 1 drop *Tea Tree – 1 drop*

CHILBLAINS

Are dusky red itchy swellings that develop on the extremities, either the hands or the feet, in cold weather. They can feel quite painful under pressure of shoes.

Essential Oils: Black Pepper, German Chamomile, Cypress, Eucalyptus, Juniper, Lavender, Lemon, Lemongrass, Mandarin, Neroli, Petitgrain, Rosemary and Tea Tree.

Application: Massage, Footbath, Direct.

Massage Blend 1

Chamomile (G) – 10 drops *Juniper – 10 drops*
Lavender – 20 drops *Mandarin – 10 drops*

or

Massage Blend 2

Chamomile (G) – 10 drops *Black Pepper – 10 drops*
Rosemary – 20 drops *Tea Tree – 10 drops*

or

Massage Blend 3

Lemongrass – 10 drops
Neroli – 10 drops
Petitgrain – 20 drops
Tea Tree – 10 drops

Footbath Blend 1

Chamomile (G) – 2 drops
Eucalyptus – 1 drop
Black Pepper – 1 drop
Juniper – 1 drop

or

Footbath Blend 2

Black Pepper – 1 drop
Rosemary – 2 drops
Eucalyptus – 1 drop
Tea Tree – 1 drop

or

Footbath Blend 3

Cypress – 1 drop
Mandarin – 1 drop
Lemon – 2 drops

Direct

Lavender – 2 drops

COLIC

Colic is associated with the digestive system and can be aggravated by over eating over ripe or under ripe fruit or fermented cheeses. It is usually associated with severe abdominal pain, usually of fluctuating severity, with waves of pain seconds or a few minutes apart.

Essential Oils: Roman Chamomile, Clary Sage, Fennel, Ginger, Lavender, Marjoram, Neroli and Peppermint.

Application: Massage, Bathing and Compress.

Massage Blend 1

Chamomile (R) – 20 drops *Lavender – 20 drops*
Neroli – 10 drops

or

Massage Blend 2

Clary Sage – 20 drops *Marjoram – 20 drops*
Chamomile (R) – 10 drops

Bathing Blend 1

Ginger – 1 drop *Lavender – 1 drop*
Chamomile (R) – 2 drops *Marjoram – 1 drop*

or

Bathing Blend 2

Fennel – 1 drop *Neroli – 1 drop*
Peppermint – 1 drop *Lavender – 2 drops*

Compress

Marjoram – 1 drop *Neroli – 2 drops*
Chamomile (R) – 1 drop

COLD SORES

Herpes Simlex I is the medical term for cold sores, those painful blisters that appear around the mouth and nose when you have a cold or flu, or simply when your immune system is low from too much work. Some people may also find they get cold sores in either extremely hot or cold weather. Stress is often an underlying cause, too.

Essential Oils: Eucalyptus, Geranium and Myrrh.

Application: Swab, Direct.

Swab

Eucalyptus – 1 drop *Geranium – 1 drop*
Myrrh – 1 drop

Direct

Myrrh – 1 drop

COMMON COLD

A widespread virus disease causing inflammation of the mucous membranes of the nose, throat and bronchial tubes. Coughing and sneezing can spread the infection and the symptoms vary but include, fever, aches and pains, fatigue, mucus, sore throat and sore eyes.

Essential Oils: Black Pepper, Eucalyptus, Ginger, Lavender, Lemon, Lime, Marjoram, Peppermint, Pine, Tea Tree and Thyme.

Application: Massage, Footbaths and Inhalation.

Massage Blend 1

Eucalyptus – 20 drops
Ginger – 10 drops
Peppermint – 10 drops
Pine – 10 drops

or

Massage Blend 2

Black Pepper – 10 drops
Lemon – 10 drops
Tea Tree – 20 drops
Thyme – 10 drops

or

Massage Blend 3

Eucalyptus – 20 drops
Lemon – 10 drops
Lime – 10 drops
Peppermint – 10 drops

Footbath Blend 1

Cardamon – 1 drop
Eucalyptus – 2 drops
Lemon – 1 drop
Pine – 1 drop

or

Footbath Blend 2

Black Pepper – 1 drop
Eucalyptus – 2 drops
Ginger – 1 drop
Lavender – 1 drop

or

Footbath Blend 3

Eucalyptus – 2 drops
Pine – 1 drop
Marjoram – 1 drop
Tea Tree – 1 drop

Inhalation

Eucalyptus – 1 drop
Lime – 1 drop
Peppermint – 1 drop
Tea Tree – 1 drop

CONSTIPATION

A condition in which bowel evacuations occur infrequently, or in which the faeces are hard and small, or where passage of faeces cause difficulty or pain.

Essential Oils: Black Pepper, Fennel, Ginger, Lemon, Marjoram, Mandarin, Rose and Sage.

Application: Massage.

Massage Blend 1

Black Pepper – 10 drops	*Fennel – 20 drops*
Ginger – 10 drops	*Lemon – 10 drops*

or

Massage Blend 2

Mandarin – 10 drops	*Sage – 10 drops*
Marjoram – 10 drops	*Rose – 20 drops*

or

Massage Blend 3

Sage – 10 drops	*Black Pepper – 10 drops*
Ginger – 10 drops	*Mandarin – 20 drops*

CRADLE CAP

Cradle Cap is a common condition in young babies in which crusty white or yellow scales form a "cap" on the scalp. It is due to an over activity of the sebaceous glands under the skin on the scalp.

Essential Oils: Cedarwood, Lavender and Patchouli.

Application: Massage, Bathing and Swab.

Massage

Cedarwood – 1 drop *Lavender – 1 drop*
Patchouli – 1 drop

Bathing

Cedarwood – 1 drop *Lavender – 1 drop*

Swab

Cedarwood – 1 drop *Lavender – 1 drop*

Precaution: Do not pick at the affected area, as it will leave the scalp raw and inflamed.

CRAMPS

A cramp is a prolonged involuntary action of a muscle or group of muscles. A painful contraction, it is sometimes caused by an imbalance of the salts in the body, but is more often the result of fatigue.

Essential Oils: Clary Sage, Ginger, Lavender, Mandarin, Marjoram, Peppermint, Petitgrain, Pine and Sage.

Application: Massage, Bathing

Massage Blend 1

Clary Sage – 10 drops *Ginger – 10 drops*
Pine – 10 drops *Sage – 20 drops*

or

Massage Blend 2

Lavender – 20 drops
Marjoram – 10 drops
Mandarin – 10 drops
Petitgrain – 10 drops

Bathing Blend 1

Peppermint – 2 drops
Pine – 2 drops
Petitgrain – 1 drop

or

Bathing Blend 2

Clary Sage – 1 drop
Mandarin – 1 drop
Lavender – 2 drops
Petitgrain – 1 drop

or

Bathing Blend 3

Marjoram – 2 drops
Mandarin – 2 drops
Petitgrain – 1 drop

CROUP

An acute inflammation and obstruction of the respiratory tract, involving the larynx and the main air passages in young children. It can be brought on by cold, wet conditions.

Essential Oils: Black Pepper, Eucalyptus, Juniper, Lavender and Marjoram.

Application: Massage, Aromatic Steam.

Massage

Black Pepper – 5 drops
Eucalyptus – 5 drops
Juniper – 10 drops
Lavender – 20 drops
Marjoram – 10 drops

Aromatic Steam

Eucalyptus – 5 drops
Juniper – 5 drops
Lavender – 2 drops
Marjoram – 3 drops

CUTS

Cuts can be minor or major according to the depth and length of the laceration. Cuts are usually the result of an injury to the skin from a sharp object. If a cut is quite deep, applying pressure on it to stop the bleeding is recommended and once the bleeding has been controlled, you are then able to disinfect the area.

Essential Oils: German Chamomile, Lavender, Patchouli, Sage.

Application: Swab, Direct.

Swab Blend 1

Chamomile (G) – 1 drop
Patchouli – 1 drop

or

Swab Blend 2

Lavender – 1 drop
Sage – 1 drop

Direct

Lavender – 1 drop

CYSTITIS

An inflammation of the urinary bladder, often caused by infection. It is usually accompanied by the desire to pass urine frequently, with a degree of burning experienced.

Essential Oils: Bergamot, Cedarwood, German Chamomile, Frankincense, Ginger, Juniper, Lavender, Palmarosa, Sandalwood and Tea Tree.

Application: Massage, Sitz Bath, Swab.

Massage Blend 1

Juniper – 10 drops | *Palmarosa – 10 drops*
Sandalwood – 20 drops | *Tea Tree – 10 drops*

or

Massage Blend 2

Bergamot – 10 drops | *Ginger – 10 drops*
Sandalwood – 20 drops | *Tea Tree – 10 drops*

Swab Blend 1

Chamomile (G) – 1 drop | *Lavender – 1* drop

or

Swab Blend 2

Frankincense – 1 drop | *Tea Tree – 1 drop*

Sitz Bath

Bergamot – 1 drop | *Lavender – 1 drop*
Cedarwood – 1 drop

D

DANDRUFF

Dandruff is the visible scaling from the surface of the scalp. It is the shedding of dead skin from the scalp and may also be caused by excessive sebum or a dry scalp.

Essential Oils: Cedarwood, Clary Sage, Patchouli, Rosemary, Sage, Tea Tree

Application: Hair Rinse, Warm Oil Mask.

Hair Rinse 1

Cedarwood – 1 drop *Rosemary – 1 drop*
Sage – 1 drop *Tea Tree – 1 drop*

or

Hair Rinse 2

Clary Sage – 1 drop *Patchouli – 1 drop*
Sage – 1 drop *Tea Tree – 1 drop*

Warm Oil Mask

Cedarwood – 1 drop *Rosemary – 1 drop*
Sage – 1 drop *Tea Tree – 1 drop*

DEPRESSION

Depression is a mental state characterised by excessive sadness. Activity can be agitated and restless or slow and retarded. Behaviour is governed by pessimistic or despairing beliefs, lack of sleep and poor concentration.

Essential Oils: Basil, Bergamot, Clary Sage, Frankincense, Neroli, Patchouli, Rose, Rosewood, Sandalwood, Vetiver and Ylang Ylang.

Application: Massage, Footbath, Vaporisation, Inhalation and Compress.

Massage Blend 1

Bergamot – 10 drops | *Clary Sage – 20 drops*
Frankincense – 10 drops | *Neroli – 10 drops*

or

Massage Blend 2

Frankincense – 20 drops | *Neroli – 10 drops*
Rose – 10 drops | *Ylang Ylang – 10 drops*

Footbath Blend 1

Frankincense – 2 drops | *Neroli – 1 drop*
Vetiver – 2 drops

or

Footbath Blend 2

Patchouli – 1 drop | *Rosewood – 2 drops*
Clary Sage – 2 drops

Vaporisation Blend 1

Bergamot – 3 drops
Frankincense – 2 drops
Clary Sage – 1 drop
Neroli – 2 drops

or

Vaporisation Blend 2

Frankincense – 2 drops
Rose – 2 drops
Neroli – 2 drops
Ylang Ylang – 2 drops

Inhalation

Neroli – 1 drop
Sandalwood – 1 drop
Rose – 2 drops

Compress Blend 1

Basil – 1 drop
Neroli – 1 drop
Clary Sage – 1 drop
Vetiver – 1 drop

or

Compress Blend 2

Bergamot – 1 drop
Neroli – 1 drop
Clary Sage – 1 drop
Ylang Ylang – 1 drop

DERMATITIS

Dermatitis is an inflammatory condition of the skin that can be caused by outside agents. Many forms of dermatitis are associated with allergic tendencies that are hereditary or may result from various animal, vegetable or chemical substances. Its appearance can be seen as red, irritated, blistered watery discharge and have fissures.

Essential Oils: Bergamot, Roman Chamomile, Cypress, Geranium, Lavender, Myrrh, Patchouli, Rose and Sandalwood.

Application: Massage, Bathing and Compress.

Massage Blend 1

Chamomile (R) – 5 drops
Bergamot – 15 drops
Lavender – 20 drops
Myrrh – 10 drops

or

Massage Blend 2

Bergamot – 15 drops
Cypress – 5 drops
Lavender – 20 drops
Rose – 10 drops

Bathing

Bergamot – 1 drop
Geranium – 1 drop
Rose – 2 drops
Sandalwood – 1 drop

Compress

Chamomile (R) – 1 drop
Geranium – 1 drop
Lavender – 1 drop
Patchouli – 1 drop

DIABETES

Diabetes is a disorder of the metabolism. It is characterised by excessive thirst and the production of large volumes of urine. Specific dietary requirements must be followed.

Essential Oils: Cypress, Eucalyptus, Geranium, Juniper, Lavender, Pine and Ylang Ylang.

Application: Massage and Bathing.

Massage Blend 1

Cypress – 10 drops	*Geranium – 15 drops*
Pine – 15 drops	*Ylang Ylang – 10 drops*

or

Massage Blend 2

Cypress – 10 drops	*Eucalyptus – 10 drops*
Juniper – 10 drops	*Lavender – 20 drops*

Bathing Blend 1

Geranium – 1 drop	*Juniper – 1 drop*
Pine – 1 drop	*Ylang Ylang – 2 drops*

or

Bathing Blend 2

Cypress – 1 drop	*Eucalyptus – 1 drop*
Lavender – 2 drops	*Pine – 1 drop*

DIARRHOEA

Diarrhoea is characterised by frequent bowel evacuation or the passage of abnormally soft or liquid faeces. It causes the muscle of the intestinal wall to work overtime, pushing food through the stomach faster e.g. bacteria, shock, fear and anxiety can cause this condition.

Essential Oils: Cypress, Roman Chamomile, Geranium, Ginger, Lavender, Myrrh, Neroli, Orange, Patchouli, Rose and Sandalwood.

Application: Massage.

Massage Blend 1

Ginger – 10 drops	*Lavender – 20 drops*
Rose – 10 drops	*Sandalwood – 10 drops*

or

Massage Blend 2

Myrrh – 10 drops	*Neroli – 20 drops*
Orange – 10 drops	*Patchouli – 10 drops*

or

Massage Blend 3

Chamomile (R) – 10 drops	*Ginger – 10 drops*
Myrrh – 10 drops	*Neroli – 20 drops*

or

Massage Blend 4

Cypress – 10 drops	*Geranium – 10 drops*
Patchouli – 10 drops	*Lavender – 20 drops*

DIGESTION/INDIGESTION

Digestion is the process in which ingested food is broken down in the alimentary canal into a form that can be absorbed and assimilated by the tissues of the body.

Indigestion occurs when the digestive system finds it difficult to break down food and utilise nutrients. Symptoms can include abdominal pain, constipation, diarrhoea or flatulence.

Essential Oils: Basil, Fennel, Ginger, Juniper, Lavender, Mandarin, Peppermint

Application: Massage.

Massage Blend 1

Basil – 10 drops
Fennel – 10 drops
Peppermint – 20 drops
Ginger – 10 drops

or

Massage Blend 2

Ginger – 20 drops
Juniper – 10 drops
Lavender – 10 drops
Mandarin – 10 drops

or

Massage Blend 3

Fennel – 10 drops
Ginger – 20 drops
Juniper – 10 drops
Peppermint – 10 drops

E

EARACHE

Earache is characterised by severe pain in either or both ears and head behind the ears. They can accompany a head cold and may even be due to disease of the jaw joints, neck, throat or teeth. Earache can be experienced acutely when flying in an aircraft.

Essential Oils: Eucalyptus, Lavender, Peppermint and Tea Tree.

Application: Massage, Aromatic Cotton Ball.

Massage

Eucalyptus – 10 drops	*Lavender – 20 drops*
Peppermint – 10 drops	*Tea Tree – 10 drops*

Aromatic Cotton Ball

Lavender – 1 drop	*Peppermint – 1 drop*

ECZEMA

Eczema may be due to an allergy or could be the result of skin irritation. There are various underlying causes. It can be characterised by reddening and vesicle formation, scaling, itchy, weeping and crusting of the skin. The distress of dealing with this condition can prolong its symptoms.

Essential Oils: Bergamot, Chamomile (Roman), Juniper, Lavender, Myrrh, Palmarosa and Patchouli.

Application: Massage, Bathing, Compress.

Massage Blend 1

Bergamot – 15 drops	*Chamomile (R) – 5 drops*
Juniper – 10 drops	*Lavender – 20 drops*

or

Massage Blend 2

Bergamot – 10 drops	*Lavender – 20 drops*
Myrrh – 10 drops	*Palmarosa – 10 drops*

Bath Blend 1

Chamomile (R) – 1 drop	*Lavender – 2 drops*
Palmarosa – 1 drop	*Patchouli – 1 drop*

or

Bath Blend 2

Bergamot – 1 drop	*Chamomile (R) – 1 drop*
Lavender – 2 drops	*Myrrh – 1 drop*

Compress Blend 1

Bergamot – 1 drop	*Chamomile (R) – 1 drop*
Lavender – 1 drop	*Myrrh – 1 drop*

or

Compress Blend 2

Bergamot – 1 drop	*Juniper – 1 drop*
Lavender – 1 drop	*Patchouli – 1 drop*

ELBOW TENDINITIS

Elbow Tendinitis is the inflammation of the muscles and tendons around the elbow due to the repetitive use of the forearm muscles over an extended period of time.

Essential Oils: German Chamomile, Eucalyptus, Lavender, Lemon, Thyme.

Application: Massage and Compress.

Massage

Chamomile (G) – 10 drops *Eucalyptus – 20 drops*
Lavender – 10 drops Lemon – 10 drops

Compress

Chamomile (G) – 1 drop *Eucalyptus – 1 drop*
Lavender – 1 drop *Thyme – 1 drop*

ENDOMETRIOSIS

Endometriosis refers to the condition where the lining of the uterus (endometrium) develops in other parts of the body, i.e., stray fragments from the endometrium escape and colonise in the pelvic cavity.

Essential Oils: Roman Chamomile, Clary Sage, Cypress, Rose and Geranium.

Application: Massage, Bathing and Compress.

Massage Blend 1

Chamomile (R) – 10 drops
Clary Sage – 20 drops
Geranium – 10 drops
Rose – 10 drops

or

Massage Blend 2

Chamomile (R) – 10 drops
Clary Sage – 10 drops
Geranium – 10 drops
Rose – 20 drops

Bathing

Chamomile (R) – 2 drops
Geranium – 1 drop
Rose – 2 drops

Compress

Chamomile (R) – 1 drop
Clary Sage – 2 drops
Cypress – 1 drop

F

FAINTING *(Light headedness)*

Fainting occurs when there isn't enough blood to the brain. This can happen after a severe emotional shock or fright when the blood is directed to the abdominal area, which in turn lowers the blood supply to the brain.

Essential Oils: Black Pepper, Peppermint and Rosemary.

Application: Massage, Aromatic Sniff.

Massage

Black Pepper – 15 drops *Peppermint – 15 drops*
Rosemary – 20 drops

Aromatic Sniff

Peppermint – 2 drops *Rosemary – 1 drop*

FATIGUE

Fatigue can occur either mentally or physically. It is the associated tiredness that follows prolonged or intense activity, which can be either acute or chronic.

Essential Oils: Basil, Black Pepper, Cardamon, Ginger, Lavender, Peppermint, Petitgrain, Rosemary and Vetiver.

Application: Massage, Bathing and Vaporisation.

Massage Blend 1

Basil – 10 drops *Cardamon – 20 drops*
Rosemary – 10 drops *Vetiver – 10 drops*

or

Massage Blend 2

Cardamon – 10 drops *Ginger – 10 drops*
Lavender – 20 drops *Petitgrain – 10 drops*

Bathing Blend 1

Ginger – 1 drop
Rosemary – 1 drop
Petitgrain – 2 drops
Peppermint – 1 drop

or

Bathing Blend 2

Cardamon – 1 drop
Petitgrain – 2 drops
Lavender – 2 drops

Vaporisation

Black Pepper – 2 drops
Ginger – 2 drops
Cardamon – 2 drops
Petitgrain – 2 drops

FEET *(tired, aching)*

There is such a large number of bones and muscles in the feet that subsequently a variety of complaints can affect them. Injury, sprains, poor posture, pressure and over activity can cause the feet to ache or feel sore.

Essential Oils: Ginger, Peppermint, Petitgrain, Rosemary and Sage.

Application: Massage and Footbath.

Massage

Ginger – 10 drops
Rosemary – 20 drops
Peppermint – 10 drops
Sage – 10 drops

Footbath Blend 1

Ginger – 1 drop
Petitgrain – 2 drops
Peppermint – 1 drop
Rosemary – 1 drop

or

Footbath Blend 2

Ginger – 1 drop

Rosemary – 2 drops

Sage – 2 drops

FEVER

A fever is simply a rise in the body's temperature above normal and can result if the body is fighting an infection. It can accompany bacterial or viral infections and can be symptomatic of shivering, headache, nausea, constipation or diarrhoea and a rise in temperature above 40.5c. may cause delirium in young children.

Essential Oils: Basil, Eucalyptus, Ginger, Lemon, Lemongrass, Lime, Peppermint, Sage

Application: Bathing (Tepid) and Compress.

Bathing Blend 1

Eucalyptus – 2 drops

Lemon – 1 drop

Lime – 1 drop

Peppermint – 1 drop

or

Bathing Blend 2

Basil – 1 drop

Ginger – 2 drops

Lemongrass – 1 drop

Sage – 1 drop

Compress (Cold)

Eucalyptus – 4 drops

FLATULENCE

Flatulence is a condition we suffer when excessive gas in the intestinal tract is produced. This results in the expulsion of gas or air from the stomach through the mouth as in belching or a sensation of abdominal distention in which the gas is expelled through the anus.

Essential Oils: Basil, Black Pepper, Fennel, Lavender, Lemon, Lemongrass, Lime, Marjoram and Peppermint.

Application: Massage.

Massage Blend 1

Basil – 10 drops
Lime – 10 drops
Lemongrass – 10 drops
Fennel – 20 drops

or

Massage Blend 2

Black Pepper – 10 drops
Fennel – 10 drops
Lemon – 20 drops
Peppermint – 10 drops

or

Massage Blend 3

Basil– 10 drops
Lavender –10 drops
Fennel – 10 drops
Marjoram – 20 drops

FLU

Influenza is a highly contagious viral infection that affects the respiratory system. Symptoms commence after an incubation period of 1-4 days and can include fever, loss of appetite, weakness and general aches and pains.

Essential Oils: Bergamot, Black Pepper, Eucalyptus, Fennel, Ginger, Lavender, Lemon, Marjoram, Pine, Rosemary, Rosewood, Sage, Tea Tree and Thyme.

Application: Massage, Bathing, Vaporisation, Inhalation and Compress.

Massage Blend 1

Black Pepper – 10 drops
Fennel – 10 drops
Pine – 10 drops
Tea Tree – 20 drops

or

Massage Blend 2

Ginger – 10 drops
Lemon – 20 drops
Rosemary – 10 drops
Thyme – 10 drops

or

Massage Blend 3

Eucalyptus – 10 drops
Lavender – 10 drops
Marjoram – 10 drops
Sage – 10 drops
Rosewood – 10 drops

Bathing Blend 1

Eucalyptus – 2 drops
Fennel – 1 drop
Lemon – 1 drop
Pine – 1 drop

Vaporisation Blend 1

Eucalyptus – 2 drops
Fennel – 2 drops
Pine – 2 drops
Tea Tree – 2 drops

or

Vaporisation Blend 2

Eucalyptus – 2 drops
Lemon – 3 drops
Pine – 2 drops
Thyme – 1 drop

Inhalation Blend 1

Eucalyptus – 1 drop
Tea Tree – 1 drop
Thyme – 1 drop

or

Inhalation Blend 2

Bergamot – 1 drop
Lavender –1 drop
Tea Tree – 1 drop
Rosewood – 1 drop

Compress (fever)

Eucalyptus – 4 drops

FLUID RETENTION

As the name implies, fluid retention occurs when the body retains excess fluid. This causes swelling around the ankles, hands, eyes and other parts of the body.

Essential Oils: Cypress, Fennel, Frankincense, Grapefruit, Juniper and Patchouli.

Application: Massage, Bathing and Footbath.

Massage

Frankincense – 10 drops *Juniper – 20 drops*
Patchouli – 20 drops

Bathing

Cypress – 1 drop *Frankincense – 2 drops*
Grapefruit – 2 drops

Footbath

Fennel – 1 drop *Frankincense – 2 drops*
Juniper - 2 drops

FOLLICULITIS

Folliculitis is a condition of the skin where hair follicles become infected and inflamed. The infection penetrates the deeper layers of the skin, spreading rapidly leaving the skin feeling tender as it emits a discharge.

Essential Oils: Lavender, Tea Tree.

Application: Massage and Compress.

Massage

Lavender – 10 drops *Tea Tree – 40 drops*

Compress

Lavender – 1 drop *Tea Tree – 3 drops*

FOOT ODOUR

Foot odour may simply result from wearing the same shoes and socks on a daily basis or shoes and socks that don't allow the feet to breath. Natural fibres should always be chosen. Hygiene is imperative, as too are dietary habits as a number of fungal disorders can occur in the presence of bacteria.

Essential Oils: Sage and Tea Tree

Application: Footbath, Spritz.

Footbath

Sage – 3 drops *Tea Tree – 2 drops*

Spritz

Sage – 2 drops *Tea Tree – 1 drop*

FRACTURES

A fracture of a bone is a breakage, which is either complete or incomplete. A simple fracture involves a clean break with little damage to the surrounding tissue and no break to the surface skin. If the bone pierces through the skin the fracture becomes a compound or open fracture. These recipes are for simple fractures.

Essential Oils: Bergamot, Lavender, Rosemary, Sandalwood and Thyme.

Application: Massage

Massage Blend 1

Bergamot – 10 drops
Lavender – 10 drops
Sandalwood – 10 drops
Rosemary – 20 drops

or

Massage Blend 2

Bergamot – 10 drops
Lavender – 20 drops
Rosemary – 10 drops
Thyme – 10 drops

FRIGIDITY

Frigidity usually relates to the lack of sexual desire in either men or women. It can also relate to the inability to achieve orgasm during sexual intercourse. Lack of confidence, low self esteem, fear or stress are feelings that can accompany this condition.

Essential Oils: Black Pepper, Cardamon, Roman Chamomile, Clary Sage, Jasmine, Lavender, Orange, Patchouli, Rose, Rosewood, Sandalwood, Vetiver and Ylang Ylang.

Application: Massage, Bathing and Vaporisation.

Massage Blend 1

Cardamon – 10 drops
Clary Sage – 20 drops
Orange – 10 drops
Vetiver – 10 drops

or

Massage Blend 2

Jasmine – 10 drops
Lavender – 10 drops
Rose – 10 drops
Sandalwood – 20 drops

or

Massage Blend 3

Chamomile (R) – 10 drops
Cardamon – 10 drops
Rosewood – 20 drops
Ylang Ylang – 10 drops

Bathing Blend 1

Cardamon – 2 drops
Jasmine –1 drop
Orange –1 drop
Rose – 1 drop

or

Bathing Blend 2

Black Pepper – 1 drop
Clary Sage – 1 drop
Patchouli – 2 drops
Rosewood – 1 drop

Vaporisation Blend 1

Orange – 3 drops
Patchouli – 1 drop
Sandalwood – 2 drops
Ylang Ylang – 2 drops

or

Vaporisation Blend 2

Chamomile (R) – 2 drops
Jasmine – 2 drops
Rose – 3 drops
Vetiver – 1 drop

G

GALLSTONES

Gallstones occur in the gall bladder. They form when there is too much cholesterol or pigments in the bile. They are hard masses composed of bile pigments, cholesterol and calcium salts in varying proportions and can begin as the size of a sand granule and grow to the size of an egg.

Essential Oils: Fennel, Lemon, Peppermint, Rose and Rosemary.

Application: Massage, Bathing.

Massage Blend 1

Lemon – 10 drops
Peppermint – 20 drops
Rosemary – 10 drops
Rose – 10 drops

or

Massage Blend 2

Fennel – 10 drops
Rose – 20 drops
Rosemary 20 drops

or

Massage Blend 3

Peppermint – 20 drops
Rose – 10 drops
Rosemary – 20 drops

Bathing Blend 1

Fennel – 1 drop *Lemon – 2 drops*

Rosemary – 2 drops

or

Bathing Blend 2

Fennel – 2 drops *Rose – 2 drops*

Rosemary – 1 drop

GINGIVITIS

Gingivitis is the inflammation of the gums. It can be due to bacterial infection or lack of stimulation to the tissue from the toothbrush. Symptoms can be unpleasant, pain, bleeding gums, receding gums and bad breath.

Essential Oils: Fennel, Lavender, Myrrh, Peppermint, Rose, Tea Tree.

Application: Mouth Wash – dispense 1-2 drops of your chosen essential oil into half a glass of tepid water. Agitate the water with a stainless steel spoon. You may choose to add half a teaspoon of honey to the mixture. This is an ideal way to produce an antiseptic gargle for gum infection or as a mouthwash and gargle for sore throats.

Mouth Wash Blend 1

Myrrh – 1 drop *Tea Tree – 1 drop*

or

Mouth Wash Blend 2

Lavender – 1 drop *Rose – 1 drop*

or

Mouth Wash Blend 3

Fennel – 1 drop *Peppermint – 1 drop*

GOUT

Gout is a disease in which a defect in uric acid metabolism causes an excess of the acid and its salts to accumulate in the bloodstream and the joints respectively. Severe pain often accompanies gout with the joint often becoming red and inflamed.

Essential Oils: Basil, Fennel, Juniper, Pine and Rosemary.

Application: Massage, Bathing, Footbath.

Massage Blend 1

Fennel – 10 drops *Juniper – 10 drops*
Pine – 10 drops *Rosemary – 20 drops*

or

Massage Blend 2

Basil – 10 drops *Fennel – 10 drops*
Juniper – 20 drops *Pine – 10 drops*

Bathing Blend 1

Basil – 1 drop *Juniper – 2 drops*
Rosemary – 2 drops

or

Bathing Blend 2

Fennel – 1 drop *Pine – 2 drops*
Rosemary – 2 drops

Footbath

Fennel – 1 drop *Juniper – 2 drops*
Pine 2 drops

GRIEF

Grief usually occurs in the presence of a sense of loss. Loss is a part of everyone's life and requires acknowledgement, participation and the passage of time to heal the change. Loss of relationship, business, object or opportunity either by death or destruction can cause grief.

Essential Oils: Bergamot, Cedarwood, Roman Chamomile, Clary Sage, Frankincense, Jasmine, Lavender, Marjoram, Neroli, Rose, Rosewood and Sandalwood.

Application: Massage, Bathing and Vaporisation.

Massage Blend 1

Lavender – 15 drops
Marjoram – 10 drops
Rosewood – 10 drops
Jasmine – 5 drops
Rose – 10 drops

Massage Blend 2

Chamomile (R) – 20 drops
Frankincense – 10 drops
Clary Sage – 10 drops
Neroli – 10 drops

Bathing Blend 1

Bergamot – 1 drop
Jasmine – 1 drop
Rosewood – 1 drop
Cedarwood – 1 drop
Sandalwood – 1 drop

or

Bathing Blend 2

Chamomile (R) –1 drop
Rose – 1 drop
Rosewood – 1 drop
Lavender – 1 drop
Sandalwood – 1 drop

Vaporisation Blend 1

Bergamot – 3 drops
Chamomile (R) – 2 drops
Clary Sage – 1 drop
Marjoram – 2 drops

or

Vaporisation Blend 2

Cedarwood – 2 drops
Rose – 2 drops
Jasmine – 2 drops
Sandalwood – 2 drops

H

HAEMORRHOIDS

Haemorrhoids are an enlargement of the normal spongy blood filled cushions in the walls of the anus, which is usually a consequence of prolonged constipation or, occasional diarrhoea. The main symptom is bleeding at the end of defecation.

Essential Oils: Bergamot, Cedarwood, Cypress, Eucalyptus, Neroli, Patchouli and Sandalwood.

Application: Massage, Sitz Bath.

Massage Blend 1

Cedarwood – 10 drops
Cypress – 10 drops
Neroli – 20 drops
Sandalwood – 10 drops

or

Massage Blend 2

Bergamot – 10 drops
Cypress – 10 drops
Eucalyptus – 20 drops
Patchouli – 10 drops

Sitz Bath Blend 1

Bergamot – 1 drop
Cedarwood – 1 drop
Cypress – 1 drop

or

Sitz Bath Blend 2

Bergamot – 1 drop
Patchouli – 1 drop
Sandalwood – 1 drop

HAY FEVER

Hay fever is an allergic reaction affecting the lining of the nose. It is usually due to the pollen of grasses, trees and other plants, characterised by the inflammation of the membrane lining of the nose and sometimes of the eyes.

Essential Oils: Cypress, Eucalyptus, Lavender, Marjoram, Neroli and Sandalwood.

Application: Massage and inhalation.

Massage Blend 1

Lavender – 20 drops
Marjoram – 10 drops
Neroli – 10 drops
Sandalwood – 10 drops

or

Massage Blend 2

Lavender – 30 drops
Neroli – 10 drops
Sandalwood – 10 drops

or

Massage Blend 3

Eucalyptus –10 drops
Lavender – 30 drops
Marjoram – 10 drops

Inhalation Blend 1

Cypress – 2 drops *Lavender – 2 drops*

or

Inhalation Blend 2

Cypress – 2 drops *Lavender – 1 drop*
Sandalwood – 1 drop

HEADACHES

Headaches vary in intensity and the pain is felt deep within the skull. Most headaches are caused by emotional stress or fatigue, but some are symptoms of intra cranial disease.

Essential Oils: Basil, German Chamomile, Eucalyptus, Lavender, Lemongrass, Marjoram, Orange, Peppermint, Rosemary, Rosewood and Tea Tree

Application: Massage, Inhalation, Direct.

Massage Blend 1

Chamomile (G) – 10 drops *Basil – 10 drops*
Lavender – 15 drops *Orange – 15 drops*

or

Massage Blend 2

Eucalyptus – 20 drops *Lemongrass – 10 drops*
Peppermint – 10 drops *Tea Tree – 10 drops*

or

Massage Blend 3

Basil – 10 drops
Lavender – 10 drops
Marjoram – 10 drops
Orange – 10 drops
Rosewood – 10 drops

Inhalation Blend 1

Basil – 1 drop
Eucalyptus – 1 drop
Peppermint – 1 drop
Rosemary – 1 drop

or

Inhalation Blend 2

Basil – 1 drop
Chamomile (G) – 1 drop
Marjoram – 1 drop
Orange – 1 drop

Direct

Basil – 1 drop
Lavender – 1 drop

HEAD LICE

Head lice is commonly associated with childhood. The tiny lice attach themselves to the hair shafts and become resilient to chemicals that are used to control them. Itching is the main symptom and the lice must be treated in an initial treatment and then subsequently a week later to ensure eradication.

Essential Oils: Eucalyptus, Lemon, Lime, Tea Tree and Thyme.

Application: Warm Oil Mask (Hair).

Warm Oil Mask (Double Strength)

Eucalyptus – 2 drops
Lime – 2 drops
Thyme – 2 drops
Lemon – 1 drop
Tea Tree – 1 drop

HEARTBURN

Heartburn is a discomfort or pain, usually burning in character, that is felt behind the breastbone and often appears to rise from the abdomen towards or into the throat. It may be accompanied by the appearance of acid or bitter fluid in the mouth.

Essential Oils: Basil, Bergamot, Fennel, Ginger, Lemon, Marjoram and Peppermint.

Application: Massage, Direct.

Massage Blend 1

Basil – 10 drops
Ginger – 10 drops
Bergamot – 10 drops
Peppermint – 20 drops

or

Massage Blend 2

Fennel – 20 drops
Lemon – 10 drops
Ginger – 10 drops
Peppermint – 10 drops

or

Massage Blend 3

Basil – 10 drops
Ginger – 10 drops
Bergamot – 10 drops
Marjoram – 20 drops

Direct

Fennel – 1 drop
Peppermint – 1 drop

HERPES

Herpes Simplex II refers to the same condition as a cold sore. In this case, appearing on the genitals. It is not known whether it is two viruses or simply the same one manifesting differently.

Essential Oils: Bergamot, Eucalyptus, Geranium, Lavender, Myrrh, Rose, Tea Tree.

Application: Massage, Bathing and Swab.

Massage Blend 1

Bergamot – 10 drops
Lavender – 20 drops
Myrrh – 10 drops
Tea Tree – 10 drops

or

Massage Blend 2

Eucalyptus – 10 drops
Geranium – 10 drops
Lavender – 20 drops
Rose – 10 drops

Bath Blend 1

Bergamot – 1 drop
Lavender – 1 drop
Myrrh – 1 drop
Rose – 2 drops

or

Bath Blend 2

Bergamot – 1 drop
Eucalyptus – 2 drops
Geranium – 1 drop
Tea Tree – 1 drop

Swab 1

Bergamot – 1 drop *Myrrh – 1 drop*

or

Swab 2

Lavender – 1 drop *Tea Tree – 1 drop*

Precaution: It is important to refrain from sexual activity when the sores become apparent.

I

IMMUNE DEFICIENCY

The immune system is responsible for the body's protection against invading bacteria, viruses or fungi by the presence of specific antibodies which act against the organisms concerned. Antibodies are manufactured specifically to deal with antigens associated with different diseases as they are encountered.

Essential Oils: Cedarwood, Cypress, Ginger, Lemongrass, Mandarin, Neroli, Petitgrain, Pine, Rose, Rosewood, Sandalwood and Tea Tree.

Application: Massage, Bathing and Inhalation.

Massage Blend 1

Cedarwood – 10 drops
Petitgrain – 10 drops
Rose – 10 drops
Sandalwood – 20 drops

or

Massage Blend 2

Ginger - 10 drops
Lemongrass – 10 drops
Mandarin – 10 drops
Neroli – 20 drops

Bath Blend 1

Cypress – 1 drop
Mandarin – 1 drop
Pine – 1 drop
Tea Tree – 2 drops

or

Bath Blend 2

Neroli – 2 drops
Rose – 1 drop
Rosewood – 1 drop
Sandalwood – 1 drop

Inhalation Blend 1

Ginger – 1 drop
Mandarin – 1 drop
Neroli – 1 drop
Rosewood – 1 drop

or

Inhalation Blend 2

Lemongrass – 1 drop
Neroli – 1 drop
Petitgrain – 1 drop
Tea Tree – 1 drop

IMPOTENCE

Impotence is the inability in a man to have sexual intercourse. There are different forms of impotence and apart from medical support, the following Essential Oils are offered as a means to address the condition both physically and emotionally.

Essential Oils: Black Pepper, Ginger, Jasmine, Patchouli, Rose, Rosewood, Sandalwood and Ylang Ylang.

Application: Massage, Bathing and Vaporisation.

Massage Blend (Men)

Jasmine – 10 drops
Patchouli – 5 drops
Rose – 10 drops
Sandalwood – 15 drops
Ylang Ylang – 10 drops

or

Massage Blend (Women)

Black Pepper – 5 drops
Ginger – 5 drops
Jasmine – 10 drops
Sandalwood – 10 drops
Ylang Ylang –10 drops
Rosewood – 10 drops

Bath Blend 1

Jasmine – 1 drop
Rose – 1 drop
Sandalwood - 1 drop
Ylang Ylang – 2 drops

or

Bath Blend 2

Black Pepper - 1 drop
Patchouli – 1 drop
Ginger – 1 drop
Ylang Ylang – 2 drops

Vaporisation

Rose – 2 drops
Sandalwood – 2 drops
Ylang Ylang – 2 drops
Rosewood – 2 drops

Vaporisation

Jasmine – 2 drops
Sandalwood – 2 drops
Ylang Ylang – 2 drops
Rosewood – 2 drops

INSOMNIA

Insomnia is the inability to fall asleep or to remain asleep for an adequate length of time, so that tiredness becomes a prolonged experience. Insomnia may be associated with a disease, particularly if there are painful symptoms, but is more often caused by worry.

Essential Oils: German Chamomile, Roman Chamomile, Jasmine, Orange, Lavender, Mandarin, Marjoram, Petitgrain, Rose, Sandalwood, Vetiver and Ylang Ylang.

Application: Massage, Bathing and Vaporisation.

Massage Blend 1

Chamomile (R) – 10 drops
Marjoram – 10 drops
Lavender – 20 drops
Vetiver – 10 drops

or

Massage Blend 2

Orange – 10 drops
Petitgrain – 10 drops
Rose – 10 drops
Sandalwood – 20 drops

or

Massage Blend 3

Chamomile (G) – 5 drops
Jasmine – 10 drops
Mandarin – 15 drops
Ylang Ylang – 20 drops

Bathing Blend 1

Lavender – 2 drops
Marjoram – 1 drop
Rose – 2 drops

or

Bathing Blend 2

Jasmine – 1 drop
Mandarin – 3 drops
Orange – 1 drop

or

Bathing Blend 3

Marjoram – 1 drop
Orange – 2 drops
Petitgrain – 1 drop
Vetiver – 1 drop

Vaporisation Blend 1

Jasmine – 2 drops
Petitgrain – 1 drop
Rose – 2 drops
Sandalwood – 3 drops

or

Vaporisation Blend 2

Marjoram – 2 drops
Petitgrain – 2 drops
Orange – 3 drops
Vetiver – 1 drop

or

Vaporisation Blend 3

Jasmine – 2 drops
Orange – 3 drops
Lavender – 2 drops
Ylang Ylang – 1 drop

J

JET LAG

Jet lag occurs when we change the natural pattern of our bodies. Flying long distances (10 or more hours) disrupts the stability of our circadian rhythms and eating, sleeping and working patterns become disrupted. When our bodies time clock is disrupted, it takes times to readjust to the new rhythm.

Essential Oils: Cardamon, Cypress, Ginger, Lavender, Lemon, Lime, Peppermint, Rosemary, Rosewood, Vetiver and Ylang Ylang.

Application: Massage, Compress and Bathing.

Massage Blend 1

Lavender – 30 drops
Rosewood – 10 drops
Ylang Ylang – 10 drops

or

Massage Blend 2

Cardamon – 10 drops
Lavender – 20 drops
Cypress – 10 drops
Ylang Ylang – 10 drops

or

Massage Blend 3

Cypress – 10 drops
Lime –10 drops
Peppermint – 5 drops
Lemon – 20 drops
Ginger – 5 drops

Bathing Blend 1

Lemon – 2 drops
Peppermint – 1 drop
Lime – 1 drop
Rosemary – 1 drop

or

Bathing Blend 2

Ginger – 1 drop
Rosemary – 2 drops
Lime – 1 drop
Vetiver – 1 drop

or

Bathing Blend 3

Cardamon – 1 drop
Ylang Ylang – 2 drops
Lavender – 1 drop
Rosewood – 1 drop

or

Bathing Blend 4

Lavender – 2 drops
Vetiver – 1 drop
Ylang Ylang – 1 drop
Cardamon – 1 drop

Compress Blend 1

Lavender – 2 drops
Ylang Ylang - 2 drops

or

Compress Blend 2

Cardamon – 2 drops
Lemon – 1 drop
Lime – 1 drop

or

Compress Blend 3

Ginger – 1 drop
Ylang Ylang – 2 drops
Rosewood – 1 drop

L

LARYNGITIS

Laryngitis is an inflammation of the larynx and vocal folds, due to infection by bacteria or viruses. The folds lose their vibrance and the voice becomes husky or is lost completely.

Essential Oils: Clary Sage, Cypress, Frankincense, Pine, Sandalwood, Tea Tree.

Application: Massage or Direct

Massage Blend 1

Cypress – 10 drops
Pine – 10 drops
Sandalwood – 20 drops
Tea Tree – 10 drops

or

Massage Blend 2

Clary Sage – 10 drops
Frankincense – 10 drops
Pine – 10 drops
Sandalwood – 20 drops

Direct Blend 1

Clary Sage – 1 drop
Sandalwood – 1 drop

or

Direct Blend 2

Frankincense – 1 drop
Sandalwood – 1 drop

LOSS OF APPETITE

Loss of appetite usually accompanies illness or emotional stress.

Essential Oils: Roman Chamomile, Fennel, Ginger, Juniper, Lime and Palmarosa.

Application: Massage, Bathing and Vaporisation.

Massage Blend 1

Fennel – 15 drops
Ginger – 10 drops
Juniper – 25 drops

or

Massage Blend 2

Chamomile (R) – 15 drops	*Ginger – 15 drops*
Lime – 10 drops	*Palmarosa – 10 drops*

Bathing Blend 1

Fennel – 1 drop	*Ginger – 1 drop*
Juniper – 1 drop	*Palmarosa – 2 drops*

or

Bathing Blend 2

Chamomile (R) – 3 drops	*Ginger – 2 drops*

Vaporisation

Chamomile (R) – 2 drops	*Fennel – 2 drops*
Ginger – 1 drop	*Lime – 3 drops*

LOSS OF LIBIDO

Most sexual problems are of a psychological nature, contributing to a lack of sexual drive and a desire not to make love. Most people experience loss of libido at least a couple of times in their lives. If loss of libido is more of a concern either personally or within a relationship, talking to a skilled support person is highly recommended.

Essential Oils: Clary Sage, Jasmine, Neroli, Orange, Patchouli, Sandalwood, Vetiver and Ylang Ylang.

Application: Massage, Bathing and Vaporisation.

Massage Blend 1

Clary Sage – 10 drops
Jasmine – 10 drops
Neroli – 20 drops
Ylang Ylang – 10 drops

or

Massage Blend 2

Jasmine – 5 drops
Orange – 15 drops
Sandalwood – 20 drops
Vetiver – 10 drops

Bath Blend 1

Patchouli – 1 drop
Sandalwood – 2 drops
Vetiver – 1 drop
Ylang Ylang – 1 drop

or

Bath Blend 2

Clary Sage – 1 drop
Orange – 2 drops
Patchouli – 1 drop
Vetiver – 1 drop

Vaporisation

Clary Sage – 3 drops
Jasmine – 2 drops
Neroli – 2 drops
Ylang Ylang – 1 drop

M

MEASLES

Measles is a highly infectious virus disease that tends to appear in epidemics every 2-3 years and mainly affects children. After an incubation period of 8-15 days, symptoms resembling those of a cold develop accompanied by a high fever. Small red spots with white centres may appear on the inside of the cheeks.

Essential Oils: Roman Chamomile, German Chamomile, Eucalyptus, Lavender, Tea Tree

Application: Bathing, Compress.

Bathing Blend 1

Chamomile (R) – 2 drops
Chamomile (G) –1 drop
Eucalyptus – 1 drop
Lavender – 1 drop

or

Bathing Blend 2

Chamomile (R) – 1 drop
Chamomile (G) –1 drop
Eucalyptus – 1 drop
Lavender – 1 drop
Tea Tree – 1 drop

Compress Blend 1

Chamomile (R) – 2 drops *Lavender – 2 drops*

or

Compress Blend 2

Chamomile (G) – 2 drops *Lavender – 2 drops*

MENOPAUSE

Menopause is that time in a woman's life when ovulation stops and menstruation ceases. There is a change in the balance of sex hormones in the body, which sometimes leads to hot flushes, heart palpitations, depression, headaches, irritability, night sweats, water retention, palpitations and dizziness.

Essential Oils: Bergamot, Clary Sage, German Chamomile, Roman Chamomile, Fennel, Geranium, Neroli, Patchouli, Rose and Sage.

Application: Massage, Bathing, Vaporisation, Inhalation and Compress.

Massage Blend 1

Neroli – 20 drops *Rose – 10 drops*

Patchouli – 10 drops *Sage – 10 drops*

or

Massage Blend 2

Bergamot – 10 drops
Clary Sage – 20 drops
Geranium – 10 drops
Rose – 10 drops

Bathing Blend 1

Chamomile (R) – 2 drops
Chamomile (G) – 1 drop
Neroli – 1 drop
Rose – 1 drop

or

Bathing Blend 2

Fennel – 1 drop
Geranium – 1 drop
Neroli – 2 drops
Sage – 1 drop

Vaporisation Blend 1

Fennel – 2 drops
Geranium – 2 drops
Neroli – 2 drops
Sage 2 drops

or

Vaporisation Blend 2

Clary Sage – 2 drops
Geranium – 2 drops
Rose – 2 drops
Neroli – 2 drops

Inhalation

Chamomile (R) – 1 drop
Geranium – 2 drops
Neroli – 1 drop

Compress Blend 1

Neroli – 1 drop
Geranium – 1 drop
Clary Sage – 2 drops

or

Compress Blend 2

Chamomile (R) - 1 drop *Geranium – 1 drop*
Patchouli – 1 drop

MENSTRUATION

Menstruation is the discharge of blood and of fragments of endometrium from the vagina at intervals of about one month in women of child-bearing age. Menstruation is that stage of the menstrual cycle during which the endometrium, thickened in readiness to receive a fertilised egg cell , is shed because fertilisation has not occurred.

Essential Oils: Basil, Bergamot, Roman Chamomile, Clary Sage, Fennel, Ginger, Jasmine, Lavender, Lemongrass, Mandarin, Marjoram, Myrrh, Peppermint, Rose and Rosemary

Application: Massage, Bathing and Compress.

Massage Blend 1

Bergamot – 20 drops *Clary Sage – 10 drops*
Jasmine – 10 drops *Lavender – 10 drops*

or

Massage Blend 2

Chamomile (G) – 10 drops *Bergamot – 10 drops*
Fennel – 10 drops *Lavender – 20 drops*

or

Massage Blend 3

Clary Sage – 10 drops
Marjoram – 10 drops
Lemongrass – 20 drops
Rosemary – 10 drops

or

Massage Blend 4

Basil – 20 drops
Mandarin – 10 drops
Ginger - 10 drops
Rose – 10 drops

Bathing Blend 1

Clary Sage – 2 drops
Myrrh – 2 drops
Marjoram – 2 drops
Rose – 2 drops

or

Bathing Blend 2

Chamomile (R) – 1 drop
Fennel – 1 drop
Clary Sage – 1 drop
Marjoram – 2 drops

or

Bathing Blend 3

Clary Sage – 1 drop
Peppermint – 1 drop
Fennel –1 drop
Jasmine – 2 drops

or

Bathing Blend 4

Sage – 1 drop
Geranium – 1 drop
Rose – 2 drops
Clary Sage – 1 drop

Compress Blend 1

Marjoram – 1 drop
Jasmine – 1 drop
Chamomile (R) – 1 drop
Myrrh – 1 drop

or

Compress Blend 2

Chamomile (R) – 1 drop
Lavender – 1 drop
Clary Sage – 1 drop
Mandarin – 1 drop

MIGRAINE

Migraine is a condition resulting from a spasm and subsequent over dilation of certain arteries in the brain which causes a recurrent throbbing headache that characteristically affects one side of the head. Symptoms include visual disturbance, numbness and/or weakness of the limbs.

Essential Oils: Basil, German Chamomile, Clary Sage, Jasmine, Lavender, Lemongrass, Marjoram, Peppermint, Rose and Rosemary.

Application: Massage, Bathing, Direct.

Massage Blend 1

Jasmine – 10 drops
Marjoram – 10 drops
Lavender – 10 drops
Rose – 20 drops

or

Massage Blend 2

Chamomile (G) – 10 drops *Basil – 10 drops*
Lemongrass – 10 drops *Rosemary – 20 drops*

or

Massage Blend 3

Clary Sage – 10 drops *Lavender – 20 drops*
Marjoram – 10 drops *Rose – 10 drops*

Bathing Blend 1

Basil – 3 drops *Lemongrass – 1 drop*
Rosemary – 1 drop

or

Bathing Blend 2

Chamomile (G) – 2 drops *Clary Sage – 1 drop*
Jasmine – 1 drop *Rose – 1 drop*

Direct Blend

Basil – 1 drop *Peppermint – 1 drop*

MOUTH ULCERS

Mouth Ulcers are painful round or oval spots inside the mouth. They are often a sign of being run down or under stress, but can also be caused by infection or injury to the tongue and mouth.

Essential Oils: German Chamomile, Roman Chamomile, Marjoram, Myrrh, Rose, Sage and Tea Tree.

Application: Direct, Mouth Wash.

Direct Blend 1

Myrrh – 1 drop
Tea Tree – 1 drop

or

Direct Blend 2

Chamomile (G) – 1 drop
Tea Tree – 1 drop

Mouth Wash Blend 1

Marjoram – 1 drop
Myrrh – 1 drop
Tea Tree – 1 drop

or

Mouth Wash Blend 2

Chamomile (R) – 1 drop
Chamomile (G) – 1 drop
Rose – 1 drop

or

Mouth Wash Blend 3

Marjoram – 1 drop
Sage – 1 drop
Tea Tree – 1 drop

or

Mouth Wash Blend 4

Chamomile (R) – 1 drop
Myrrh – 1 drop
Rose – 1 drop

MUMPS

Mumps is a common virus infection mainly affecting school-age children. Symptoms appear 2-3 weeks after exposure: fever, headache, and vomiting may precede a typical swelling of the parotid salivary glands.

Essential Oils: German Chamomile, Roman Chamomile, Eucalyptus, Lavender, Sage and Thyme.

Application: Massage, Bathing and Compress.

Massage Blend 1

Chamomile (G) – 10 drops *Eucalyptus – 20 drops*
Chamomile (R) – 10 drops *Sage – 10 drops*

or

Massage Blend 2

Chamomile (G) – 10 drops *Lavender – 20 drops*
Chamomile (R) – 10 drops *Sage – 10 drops*

Bathing Blend 1

Chamomile (G) – 1 drop *Chamomile (R) – 1 drop*
Lavender – 2 drops *Thyme – 1 drop*

or

Bathing Blend 2

Chamomile (G) – 1 drop *Eucalyptus – 1 drop*
Lavender – 1 drop *Sage – 2 drops*

Compress

Eucalyptus – 3 drops *Lavender – 1 drop*

MUSCLE SORENESS

The major function of muscles is to produce movement of the body and to maintain its position. Muscle soreness can occur in the presence of injury e.g. when tiny tears appear in your muscles after demanding exercise. Over activity can produce a build up of lactic acid, which causes soreness and stiffness until it clears.

Essential Oils: Basil, Black Pepper, Eucalyptus, Ginger, Lemongrass, Marjoram, Peppermint, Rosemary and Sage.

Application: Massage and Bathing.

Massage Blend 1

Eucalyptus – 20 drops *Lemongrass – 10 drops*
Rosemary – 10 drops *Sage - 10 drops*

or

Massage Blend 2

Basil – 10 drops *Black Pepper – 10 drops*
Ginger – 10 drops *Peppermint - 20 drops*

Bathing Blend 1

Basil – 1 drop *Marjoram – 2 drops*
Peppermint – 1 drop *Sage – 1 drop*

or

Bathing Blend 2

Black Pepper – 2 drops
Peppermint – 1 drop
Eucalyptus – 1 drop
Rosemary – 1 drop

N

NAPPY RASH

Nappy rash is a red skin rash within the napkin area, usually caused by chemical irritation or infection. Wet, soiled nappies act as an irritant to the skin.

Essential Oils: Bergamot, German Chamomile, Roman Chamomile, Lavender and Patchouli.

Application: Massage.

Massage Blend 1

Chamomile (G) – 10 drops
Lavender – 20 drops
Bergamot – 10 drops
Patchouli – 10 drops

or

Massage Blend 2

Chamomile (R) – 10 drops
Lavender – 10 drops
Bergamot – 20 drops
Patchouli – 10 drops

NAUSEA, VOMITING

Nausea is the feeling that one is about to vomit as experienced in sea sickness and in morning sickness during early pregnancy. Actual vomiting occurs subsequently.

Essential Oils: Fennel, Ginger and Peppermint.

Application: Massage, Inhalation and Compress.

Massage

Fennel – 20 drops *Ginger – 10 drops*
Peppermint – 20 drops

Compress

Fennel – 2 drops *Ginger – 1 drop*
Peppermint – 1 drop

Inhalation

Fennel – 1 drop *Ginger – 2 drops*
Peppermint – 1 drop

NIGHTMARES

Nightmares are the condition in which a child (usually aged 2-4 years), soon after falling asleep, starts screaming and appears terrified. The child cannot be comforted because they remain mentally inaccessible; the attack ceases when the child wakes up fully and the nightmare is never remembered. Attacks sometimes follow a stressful experience.

Essential Oils: Bergamot, Roman Chamomile, Frankincense, Marjoram, Neroli and Rose.

Application: Massage, Bathing and Vaporisation.

Massage Blend 1

Frankincense – 10 drops *Marjoram – 20 drops*
Neroli - 10 drops *Rose – 10 drops*

or

Massage Blend 2

Chamomile (R) – 10 drops *Bergamot – 10 drops*
Frankincense – 20 drops *Neroli – 10 drops*

Bathing

Bergamot – 1 drop *Chamomile (R) – 1 drop*
Neroli – 1 drop *Rose – 2 drops*

Vaporisation

Chamomile (R) – 2 drops *Frankincense – 2 drops*
Neroli – 2 drops *Rose – 2 drops*

NOSEBLEEDS

Bleeding from the nose is associated with either minor injuries, fever, high blood pressure, or blood disorders. The blood often comes from a vessel just inside the nostril in which case applying pressure on the side of the nose may stop the flow.

Essential Oils: Cypress, Geranium and Lavender

Application: Inhalation.

Inhalation Blend 1

Cypress – 2 drops

Lavender – 2 drops

or

Inhalation Blend 2

Cypress – 2 drops

Lavender – 1 drop

Geranium – 1 drop

O

OBESITY

Obesity is a condition in which excess fat has accumulated in the body, mostly in the subcutaneous tissues. Obesity is usually considered to be present when a person is 20% above the recommended weight for his/her height and build.

Recommended oil: Cedarwood, Eucalyptus, Fennel, Geranium, Grapefruit, Juniper, Lemon, Sage, Lime, Mandarin, Peppermint and Rosemary.

Application: Massage.

Massage Blend 1

Cedarwood – 20 drops
Juniper – 10 drops
Fennel – 10 drops
Peppermint – 10 drops

or

Massage Blend 2

Eucalyptus – 20 drops
Lime – 10 drops
Grapefruit – 10 drops
Sage – 10 drops

or

Massage Blend 3

Lemon – 10 drops
Mandarin – 10 drops
Geranium – 10 drops
Rosemary – 20 drops

or

Massage Blend 4

Eucalyptus – 10 drops
Mandarin – 10 drops
Fennel – 20 drops
Peppermint – 10 drops

OEDEMA

Oedema is an excessive accumulation of fluid in the body tissues, popularly known as dropsy. The resultant swelling may be local, as with an injury or inflammation, or more general, as in heart or kidney failure.

Essential Oils: Cedarwood, German Chamomile, Frankincense, Grapefruit, Juniper, Lavender and Lemon.

Application: Massage, Bathing, and Footbath.

Massage Blend 1

Chamomile (G) – 10 drops
Frankincense – 20 drops
Juniper – 10 drops
Lavender – 10 drops

or

Massage Blend 2

Cedarwood – 10 drops
Juniper – 20 drops
Grapefruit – 10 drops
Lemon – 10 drops

Bathing Blend 1

Cedarwood – 1 drop
Grapefruit – 1 drop
Frankincense – 2 drops
Juniper – 1 drop

or

Bathing Blend 2

Chamomile (G) – 2 drops
Juniper – 1 drop
Grapefruit – 1 drop
Lemon – 1 drop

Footbath

Frankincense – 1 drop
Lemon – 1 drop
Juniper – 2 drops
Chamomile (G) – 1 drop

P

PALPITATIONS

Palpitations are experienced as an awareness of the heartbeat. This is normal with fear, emotion or exhaustion. It may also be a symptom of neurosis over activity or heart disease.

Essential Oils: Cardamon, Frankincense, Lavender, Mandarin, Neroli, Petitgrain, Rose and Ylang Ylang.

Application: Massage, Bathing and Vaporisation.

Massage Blend 1

Lavender – 20 drops
Mandarin – 10 drops
Neroli – 10 drops
Ylang Ylang – 10 drops

or

Massage Blend 2

Cardamon – 10 drops
Frankincense – 10 drops
Neroli – 20 drops
Rose – 10 drops

or

Massage Blend 3

Lavender – 20 drops
Mandarin – 10 drops
Rose – 10 drops
Ylang Ylang – 10 drops

Bathing Blend 1

Lavender – 1 drop
Mandarin – 1 drop
Petitgrain – 1 drop
Rose – 2 drops

or

Bathing Blend 2

Frankincense – 1 drop
Mandarin – 1 drop
Rose – 2 drops
Ylang Ylang – 1 drop

Vaporisation Blend 1

Lavender – 2 drops
Mandarin – 2 drops
Petitgrain – 2 drops
Rose – 2 drops

or

Vaporisation Blend 2

Cardamon – 2 drops
Frankincense – 2 drops
Neroli – 2 drops
Rose – 2 drops

PRE-MENSTRUAL TENSION

Premenstrual tension (PMT) is a condition of nervousness, irritability, emotional disturbance, headache, and/or depression affecting some women for up to about ten days before menstruation. The condition is associated with the accumulation of salt and water in the tissues and usually disappears soon after menstruation begins.

Essential Oils: Roman Chamomile, Clary Sage, Frankincense, Geranium, Jasmine, Lavender, Mandarin, Neroli and Rose.

Application: Massage, Bathing and Vaporisation.

Massage Blend 1

Chamomile (R) – 10 drops
Clary Sage – 20 drops
Frankincense – 10 drops
Geranium – 10 drops

or

Massage Blend 2

Geranium – 10 drops
Lavender – 20 drops
Neroli – 10 drops
Rose – 10 drops

Bathing Blend 1

Jasmine – 1 drop
Lavender – 1 drop
Mandarin – 1 drop
Neroli – 2 drops

or

Bathing Blend 2

Clary Sage – 1 drop
Frankincense – 2 drops
Geranium – 1 drop
Rose – 1 drop

Vaporisation Blend 1

Jasmine – 2 drops
Lavender – 2 drops
Mandarin – 2 drops
Neroli – 1 drop
Rose – 1 drop

or

Vaporisation Blend 2

Chamomile (R) – 2 drops
Frankincense – 2 drops
Jasmine – 2 drops
Lavender – 2 drops

R

RASHES

A rash is a temporary eruption on the skin, usually typified by reddening – either discrete red spots or generalised reddening – which may be accompanied by itching. A rash may be local or occur in the presence of infection or disease such as chicken pox or measles.

Essential Oils: German Chamomile, Roman Chamomile, Lavender, Myrrh, Patchouli, Rose and Sandalwood.

Application: Massage, Compress and Spritz.

Massage Blend 1

Lavender – 20 drops
Myrrh – 10 drops
Patchouli – 10 drops
Sandalwood – 10 drops

or

Massage Blend 2

Chamomile (R) – 10 drops
Lavender – 20 drops
Patchouli – 10 drops
Rose – 10 drops

Compress Blend 1

Chamomile (R) – 2 drops
Lavender – 2 drops

or

Compress Blend 2

Chamomile (G) – 1 drop *Lavender – 1 drop*
Patchouli – 2 drops

Spritz

Chamomile (G) – 1 drop *Lavender – 1 drop*
Patchouli – 1 drop

REPETITIVE STRAIN INJURY (RSI)

Repetitive Strain Injury (RSI) is the pain associated with loss of function in a limb resulting from its repeated movement or sustained static loading.

Essential Oils: Black Pepper, Frankincense, Ginger, Juniper, Lavender, Marjoram and Petitgrain.

Application: Massage and Compress.

Massage Blend 1

Black Pepper – 10 drops *Ginger – 10 drops*
Juniper – 20 drops *Petitgrain – 10 drops*

or

Massage Blend 2

Frankincense – 10 drops *Juniper – 10 drops*
Lavender – 20 drops *Petitgrain – 10 drops*

Compress Blend 1

Ginger – 1 drop *Juniper – 1 drop*
Lavender – 1 drop *Petitgrain – 1 drop*

or

Compress Blend 2

Frankincense – 1 drop	*Ginger – 1 drop*
Lavender – 1 drop	*Marjoram – 1 drop*

S

SCABIES

Scabies is a skin infection and is typified by severe itching, red spots and often secondary infection. A female mite tunnels in the skin to lay her eggs and the newly hatched mites pass from person to person by close contact. The itching represents a true allergic reaction.

Essential Oils: Bergamot, Lavender, Peppermint, Rosemary, Tea Tree and Thyme.

Application: Massage, and Bathing.

Alternate blends daily for four weeks.

Massage Blend 1

Bergamot – 10 drops	*Lavender – 20 drops*
Tea Tree – 10 drops	*Thyme – 10 drops*

or

Massage Blend 2

Peppermint – 10 drops
Rosemary – 10 drops
Tea Tree – 20 drops
Thyme – 10 drops

Bathing Blend 1

Bergamot – 2 drops
Lavender – 1 drop
Tea Tree – 2 drops

or

Bathing Blend 2

Peppermint – 1 drop
Rosemary – 2 drops
Tea Tree – 1 drop
Thyme – 1 drop

SCARS

Minor and major injury to the skin can leave a visual repair site. Scar tissue is produced as a result of the healing process. Essential Oils can help the skin's repairing process and as such the following topical applications are recommended on either new or old repair sites.

Essential Oils: Lavender, Mandarin, Neroli, Palmarosa, Patchouli and Petitgrain.

Application: Massage, Direct.

Massage Blend 1

Lavender – 20 drops
Palmarosa – 10 drops
Patchouli – 10 drops
Petitgrain – 10 drops

or

Massage Blend 2

Lavender – 10 drops	*Mandarin – 10 drops*
Neroli – 20 drops	*Patchouli – 10 drops*

Direct Blend 1

Lavender – 1 drop	*Patchouli – 1 drop*

or

Direct Blend 2

Lavender – 1 drop	*Neroli – 1 drop*

SHINGLES (HERPES ZOSTER)

Shingles is caused by the varicella-zoster virus, which also causes chickenpox. This occurs when the immune system is weakened and the dormant virus is activated. Symptoms include acute skin sensitivity and a classic rash running around one half of the midriff.

Essential Oils: Basil, Bergamot, Eucalyptus, Geranium, Lavender, Peppermint, Rose, Sage and Tea Tree.

Application: Massage, Bath.

Massage Blend 1

Geranium – 10 drops	*Lavender – 20 drops*
Rose – 10 drops	*Sage – 10 drops*

or

Massage Blend 2

Bergamot – 20 drops	*Eucalyptus – 10 drops*
Peppermint - 10 drops	*Tea Tree – 10 drops*

or

Massage Blend 3

Eucalyptus – 10 drops	*Peppermint – 10 drops*
Sage – 20 drops	*Tea Tree – 10 drops*

Bathing Blend 1

Bergamot –2 drops	*Geranium – 1 drop*
Rose –1 drop	*Tea Tree – 1 drop*

or

Bathing Blend 2

Basil – 1 drop	*Geranium – 1 drop*
Lavender – 1 drop	*Rose – 2 drops*

SHOCK

Shock is the condition associated with circulatory collapse, when the arterial blood pressure is too low to maintain an adequate supply of blood to the tissues. Symptoms usually include cold, sweaty skin, a weak rapid pulse, irregular breathing, dry mouth, dilated pupils and a reduced flow of urine.

Essential Oils: Roman Chamomile, Lavender, Neroli, Peppermint and Petitgrain.

Application: Massage, Bathing and Inhalation.

Massage Blend 1

Lavender – 10 drops
Neroli – 10 drops
Peppermint – 20 drops
Petitgrain – 10 drops

or

Massage Blend 2

Chamomile (R) – 10 drops
Lavender – 20 drops
Neroli – 10 drops
Petitgrain – 10 drops

Bathing Blend 1

Lavender – 1 drop
Neroli – 1 drop
Peppermint – 1 drop
Petitgrain – 2 drops

or

Bathing Blend 2

Chamomile (R) – 1 drop
Lavender – 1 drop
Neroli – 2 drops
Petitgrain – 1 drop

Inhalation Blend 1

Chamomile (R) –2 drops
Lavender – 1 drop
Neroli – 1 drop

or

Inhalation Blend 2

Lavender – 2 drops
Neroli – 1 drop
Petitgrain – 1 drop

SINUSITIS

Sinusitis is an inflammation of one or more of the mucous-membrane-lined air spaces in the facial bones that communicate with the nose. It is often associated with inflammation of the nasal lining and may be acute or chronic.

Essential Oils: Cedarwood, Eucalyptus, Lavender, Palmarosa, Peppermint, Sage, Tea Tree and Thyme.

Application: Massage, Inhalation.

Massage Blend 1

Cedarwood – 20 drops
Eucalyptus – 10 drops
Palmarosa – 10 drops
Tea Tree – 10 drops

or

Massage Blend 2

Eucalyptus – 20 drops
Sage – 10 drops
Tea Tree – 10 drops
Thyme – 10 drops

or

Inhalation Blend 1

Marjoram – 1 drop
Peppermint – 1 drop
Sage – 1 drop
Thyme – 1 drop

or

Inhalation Blend 2

Cedarwood – 1 drop
Eucalyptus – 1 drop
Lavender – 1 drop
Palmarosa – 1 drop

SPRAINS

A sprain is an injury to a ligament caused by sudden over stretching. As the ligament is not severed, it gradually heals, but this may take several months.

Essential Oils: Black Pepper, German Chamomile, Eucalyptus, Grapefruit, Jasmine, Lavender, Marjoram, Rose and Rosemary.

Application: Massage (gentle) and Cold Compress.

Massage Blend 1

Chamomile (G) – 10 drops *Black Pepper – 10 drops*
Eucalyptus – 20 drops *Grapefruit – 10 drops*

or

Massage Blend 2

Black Pepper – 10 drops *Eucalyptus – 20 drops*
Grapefruit – 10 drops *Rosemary – 10 drops*

or

Massage Blend 3

Chamomile (G) – 20 drops *Jasmine – 10 drops*
Marjoram – 10 drops *Rose - 10 drops*

Compress Blend 1

Black Pepper – 1 drop *Eucalyptus – 2 drops*
Rosemary – 1 drop

or

Compress Blend 2

Lavender – 2 drops
Marjoram – 1 drop
Rose – 1 drop

STRESS/NERVOUS TENSION

Stress relates to any factor or influence that threatens the health of the body or has an adverse affect on its functioning, such as injury, disease or worry.

Essential Oils: Basil, Bergamot, Cedarwood, Clary Sage, Geranium, Lavender, Marjoram, Neroli, Patchouli, Petitgrain, Rose and Sandalwood.

Application: Massage, Bathing and Vaporisation.

Massage Blend 1

Neroli – 10 drops
Petitgrain – 10 drops
Rose – 10 drops
Sandalwood – 20 drops

or

Massage Blend 2

Cedarwood – 10 drops
Basil – 10 drops
Bergamot – 10 drops
Lavender – 20 drops

or

Massage Blend 3

Geranium – 10 drops
Lavender – 20 drops
Marjoram – 10 drops
Patchouli – 10 drops

or

Massage Blend 4

Bergamot – 10 drops
Clary Sage – 10 drops
Neroli – 10 drops
Sandalwood – 20 drops

Bath Blend 1

Bergamot – 2 drops
Neroli – 1 drop
Petitgrain – 1 drop
Sandalwood – 1 drop

or

Bath Blend 2

Cedarwood – 2 drops
Lavender – 1 drop
Marjoram – 1 drop
Neroli – 1 drop

or

Bath Blend 3

Basil – 2 drops
Bergamot – 1 drop
Petitgrain – 1 drop
Rose – 1 drop

Vaporisation Blend 1

Basil – 2 drops
Lavender – 2 drops
Neroli – 2 drops
Rose – 2 drops

or

Vaporisation Blend 2

Bergamot – 2 drops
Cedarwood – 2 drops
Petitgrain – 2 drops
Sandalwood – 2 drops

STRETCH MARKS

Stretch marks are characterised by red lines appearing on the skin. They become white over time, and are due to a rapid increase in the expansion of the skin e.g. pregnancy, or weight gain. They usually appear around the buttocks, thighs and stomach.

Essential Oils: Jasmine, Lavender, Mandarin, Neroli, Petitgrain, Rose and Sandalwood.

Application: Massage.

Massage Blend 1

Mandarin – 10 drops
Petitgrain – 10 drops
Rose – 10 drops
Sandalwood – 20 drops

or

Massage Blend 2

Jasmine – 10 drops
Neroli – 10 drops
Petitgrain – 20 drops
Rose – 10 drops

or

Massage Blend 3

Lavender – 10 drops
Mandarin – 5 drops
Petitgrain – 10 drops
Rose – 5 drops
Sandalwood – 20 drops

SUNBURN

Sunburn causes damage to the skin by excessive exposure to the sun's rays. Sunburn may vary from reddening of the skin to the development of large painful fluid filled blisters which may cause shock if they cover a large area.

Essential Oils: German Chamomile, Roman Chamomile, Lavender and Tea Tree.

Application: Massage, Bathing, Spritz.

Massage

Chamomile (R) – 10 drops *Lavender – 20 drops*
Chamomile (G) – 10 drops *Tea Tree – 10 drops*

Bathing

Chamomile (G) – 2 drops *Chamomile (R) – 1 drop*
Lavender – 1 drop *Tea Tree – 1 drop*

Spritz

Chamomile (G) – 1 drop *Chamomile (R) – 1 drop*
Lavender – 1 drop *Tea Tree – 1 drop*

T

THRUSH

Thrush is a fungal infection affecting the mucous membrane of the vagina. The fungus responsible is Candida albicans, and the symptoms include inflammation, itchiness and a thick vaginal discharge.

Essential Oils: Bergamot, Eucalyptus, Lavender, Myrrh, Palmarosa and Tea Tree.

Application: Massage, Douche, Sitz Bath.

Massage Blend 1

Eucalyptus – 10 drops *Lavender – 20 drops*
Myrrh – 10 drops *Tea Tree – 10 drops*

or

Massage Blend 2

Bergamot – 20 drops *Lavender – 20 drops*
Tea Tree – 10 drops

Douche

Lavender – 1 drop *Tea Tree – 2 drops*

Sitz Bath Blend 1

Bergamot – 1 drop *Lavender – 1 drop*
Tea Tree – 2 drops

or

Sitz Bath Blend 2

Lavender – 1 drop	*Myrrh – 2 drops*
Tea Tree – 1 drop	

TONSILLITIS

Tonsillitis is the inflammation of the tonsils due to bacterial or viral infection, causing a sore throat, fever, and difficulty in swallowing.

Essential Oils: Bergamot, Black Pepper,, German Chamomile, Geranium, Ginger, Peppermint, Tea Tree and Thyme.

Application: Massage, Mouth Wash and Direct.

Massage Blend 1

Ginger – 10 drops	*Peppermint – 10 drops*
Tea Tree – 20 drops	*Thyme – 10 drops*

or

Massage Blend 2

Bergamot – 20 drops	*Black Pepper – 10 drops*
Chamomile (G) – 10 drops	*Geranium – 10 drops*

Direct

Peppermint – 1 drop	*Tea Tree – 2 drops*

Mouth Wash Blend

Tea Tree – 2 drops	*Bergamot – 1 drop*

TOOTHACHE

Teeth are one of the hard structures in the mouth used for cutting and chewing food. Toothache is often caused by an invading bacteria which causes decay. Dental attention is necessary and the essential oil offered here is for temporary relief only.

Essential Oils: Peppermint.

Application: Direct.

Direct
Peppermint – 1 drop

U

URINARY TRACT INFECTION

The Urinary Tract relates to the entire system of ducts and channels that conduct urine from the kidneys to the exterior. Infection can be caused by bacteria which develops in the rectal area, colonises with the vagina, enters the urethra and ascends into the bladder.

Essential Oils: Bergamot, Black Pepper, Eucalyptus, Juniper, Marjoram, Myrrh, Sandalwood, Tea Tree, and Vetiver.

Application: Massage, Sitz Bath daily, and Swab.

Massage Blend 1

Bergamot – 10 drops

Eucalyptus 10 drops

Juniper – 20 drops

Marjoram – 10 drops

or

Massage Blend 2

Black Pepper – 10 drops

Myrrh – 10 drops

Sandalwood – 20 drops

Tea Tree – 10 drops

Sitz Bath Blend 1

Bergamot – 1 drop

Sandalwood – 1 drop

Tea Tree – 2 drops

or

Sitz Bath Blend 2

Marjoram – 1 drop

Tea Tree – 2 drops

Vetiver – 1 drop

Swab Blend 1

Myrrh – 1 drop

Tea Tree – 1 drop

Vetiver – 1 drop

or

Swab Blend 2

Juniper – 1 drop

Myrrh – 1 drop

Sandalwood – 1 drop

V

VARICOSE VEINS

Varicose veins are veins that are distended, lengthened and tortuous. The superficial veins of the legs are most commonly affected. Other sites include the oesophagus and testes.

These recipes address the veins of the legs.

Essential Oils: Bergamot, Roman Chamomile, Clary Sage, Cypress, Grapefruit, Lemon, Neroli, Petitgrain, Rosemary, Sandalwood and Vetiver

Application: Massage (extremely lightly). Compress.

Massage Blend 1

Cypress – 20 drops
Grapefruit – 10 drops
Neroli – 10 drops
Sandalwood – 10 drops

or

Massage Blend 2

Chamomile (R) – 20 drops
Bergamot – 10 drops
Cypress – 10 drops
Lemon – 10 drops

or

Massage Blend 3

Clary Sage – 10 drops
Lemon – 10 drops
Rosemary – 10 drops
Vetiver – 20 drops

Compress Blend 1

Cypress – 1 drop
Lemon – 1 drop
Neroli – 1 drop
Petitgrain – 1 drop

or

Compress Blend 2

Bergamot – 1 drop
Chamomile (R) – 1 drop
Grapefruit – 1 drop
Vetiver – 1 drop

or

Compress Blend 3

Clary Sage – 1 drop
Neroli – 1 drop
Rosemary – 1 drop
Sandalwood – 1 drop

W

WARTS

Warts are a benign growth on the skin caused by infection. Common warts are firm horny papules found mainly on the backs of the hands.

Essential Oils: Lemon, Lime and Thyme.

Application: Swab.

Swab

Lemon – 1 drop
Lime – 1 drop
Thyme – 1 drop

WHOOPING COUGH

Whooping cough is an acute infectious disease, primarily in infants, caused by the bacterium Bordetella pertussis, which affects the respiratory tract. A cough develops which becomes increasingly severe accompanied by a whoop.

Essential Oils: Basil, Eucalyptus, Lavender, Lemon Peppermint, Tea Tree and Thyme.

Application: Massage, Vaporisation, Inhalation.

Massage Blend 1

Basil – 10 drops
Lavender – 20 drops
Tea Tree – 10 drops
Thyme – 10 drops

or

Massage Blend 2

Basil – 10 drops
Lemon – 10 drops
Tea Tree – 20 drops
Thyme – 10 drops

Vaporisation Blend 1

Lemon – 2 drops
Peppermint – 2 drops
Tea Tree – 2 drops
Thyme – 2 drops

or

Vaporisation Blend 2

Basil – 2 drops
Lemon – 2 drops
Peppermint – 2 drops
Tea Tree – 2 drops

Inhalation Blend 1

Eucalyptus – 2 drops
Lemon – 1 drop
Peppermint – 1 drop

or

Inhalation Blend 2

Basil – 1 drop
Lemon – 1 drop
Tea Tree – 1 drop
Peppermint – 1 drop

WOUNDS

A wound is a break in the structure of an organ or tissue caused by an external agent. Bruises, grazes, tears, cuts, punctures, and burns are all examples of wounds.

Essential Oils: Lavender, Patchouli and Tea Tree.

Application: Swab, Spritz.

Swab

Lavender – 1 drop
Patchouli –1drop
Tea Tree – 1 drop

Spritz

Lavender – 1 drop
Patchouli – 1 drop
Tea Tree – 1 drop

CHAPTER FIVE

Tips for Women

BY NOURISHING AND PROTECTING YOUR SKIN regularly with pure essential oils you will develop a healthy glow, while maintaining a constant state of wellbeing.

There are so many ways to nourish and moisturise your skin and make it look and feel great. Many essential oils give great delight when used for pampering the body, and you can rest assured that their naturalness will be doing nothing but good all-round.

Skin: The Body's Largest Organ

Our skin is a living breathing organ and requires attention, protection and nourishment. For this reason, it is important to understand how your skin works and how best it can be nourished. Few people realise that the skin is the largest organ of the body. In a person weighing around 75kg (165lb), the skin will constitute approximately 3kg, whereas the liver is a mere 1.5kg. The skin is only about 1-2mm deep on most areas of your body, although on the palms of the hands and soles of the feet it is greater – about 4mm.

The skin is composed of three distinct layers. The epidermis, the surface layer which continually renews itself as new cells are formed and old ones are shed. The dermis, a deeper layer which contains the connective tissue that attribute the skin with its remarkable strength and suppleness. And the deepest layer, the sub-cutaneous tissue, which is responsible for nourishment and insulation.

The skin is endowed with a very good supply of blood which is brought to the surface by tiny capillaries, and is also teeming with nerve endings which are responsible for our perception of touch and pain.

One of the skin's main functions is the elimination of wastes, sweat, and excess sebum, the lubricating oil produced by the sebaceous glands (which are most active during puberty, playing a part in the development of greasy skin and spots). These are excreted through tiny pores, which cover the entire surface of the skin. Oxygen and carbon dioxide also pass in and out of the skin, in a kind of respiration akin to that which takes place in the lungs.

Some modern medicines, such as those for sea sickness and travel sickness, come as patches which you stick onto the skin, usually on the neck or upper body. The medication is absorbed through the skin and into the blood. Likewise, essential oils have the ability to pass through the epidermis, to seep into the capillaries of the dermis which then carry them in a "time released" action to the various organs, glands and tissues of the body. Once an essential oil has been absorbed the epidermis acts as a reservoir for a time before it enters into the bloodstream. The oils are also taken up by the lymph fluid which bathes every cell. Most essential oil ingredients are metabolised by enzymes before being excreted. They are excreted by the urine, faeces, skin and breath.

Skin Care

Many people these days choose to care for their skin using only pure plant extracts. Why? Because they are natural, digestible and effective. I personally blend natural skin care products (relevant to the Resource Guide in the back pages) and essential oils to maximise the results and achieve hydration, repair, replenishment and ease. For those of you who wish to use only aromatherapy I offer the following considerations.

You can begin by adding a few drops of essential oils to preparations such as hand creams, face cleansers and moisturisers to use up your existing products. In fact, doing this regularly motivated me to develop my own skin care range and share it with others.

And with essential oils it doesn't take a lot of time or money to change your complexion. It is important to cleanse and nourish the skin daily and continue a healthy diet that works for you. The skin's repair processes are ever-changing. The cell renewal process happens very fast in young children and slows down as we get older hence the skin requires more moisture as it ages.

Helping remove dead skin cells by exfoliating and soaking with natural products and aromatic compressing will also create a healthier looking skin.

The Blends for Life Skin Care Programme

YOUR FACE

From our adolescent years we are taught to cleanse, tone and moisturise to protect our skin. These fundamental principles continue to be important. Yet the more we do above and beyond this can enhance the results we desire. Additional eye, throat and neck treatments are useful.

For many years I have fed my skin when I fed my body: during the day. I now realise that my skin actually communicates its needs to me. Usually all I have to do is pay attention to the signals during the day and night. If moisture is required, then I shall provide it. Programmes are great as long as they produce the results that you are seeking. It is always important to monitor your skin and be willing to change.

A good rule of thumb is think natural, think digestible and celebrate the choice you make.

This particular programme is designed to assist the skin in its natural elimination and rebuilding processes. Allow time to see the results of your efforts. Patience helps the skin settle into a new pattern. This particular programme is designed to keep your skin well hydrated and it is best supported by drinking 2 litres of water a day.

MORNING AROMATIC PROGRAMME

Step 1: Compress

Utensils: water, basin, face cloth/gauze or cloth.

Essential Oils: Lavender, to soften and rebuild. Bergamot to cleanse and tonify. Mandarin to refeshen and Sandalwood to moisturise.

Fill a medium-sized bowl or half bathroom basin with very warm water (for more sensitive skin use luke-warm only). Add 3-6 drops in total of your chosen essential oils and agitate the water-surface (one essential oil will do). Immerse your cloth into the aromatic water and squeeze out the excess. While it's still very warm, place the cloth over the entire face and press it firmly all over, as if pressing the water into the skin. Repeat this at least four times. Compressing the skin helps to soak and soften the skin. It also promotes the removal of dead cells.

Compress Blend 1 (Inflamed)

Chamomile (G) – 1 drop
Eucalyptus – 1 drop
Juniper – 1 drop
Lavender – 1 drop

Compress Blend 2

Bergamot – 1 drop
Rose – 1 drop
Lavender – 1 drop
Sandalwood – 1 drop

Compress Blend 3

Cedarwood – 1 drop
Patchouli – 1 drop
Rose – 1 drop
Ylang Ylang – 1 drop

Spritz Blend 1

Lavender –1 drop
Mandarin – 1 drop
Palmarosa – 1 drop
Rose – 1 drop

Spritz Blend 2

Cedarwood – 1 drop
Orange – 1 drop
Neroli – 1 drop
Sandalwood – 1 drop

Step 2: *Toning*

Essential Oils: Lime, to tonify and invigorate. Orange, to soften and refresh. Ylang Ylang, to regulate. Lemon, as an astringent, Lavender to settle and calm.

Fill a glass bottle with 200mls of warm water, add 3-6 drops in total of your chosen essential oils and shake the bottle vigorously to disperse the oil. Using a cotton wool pad or spritz attachment, wipe or spray your skin with the aromatic water avoiding the eyes. You can of course, add other ingredients such as a teaspoon of witch hazel.

Step 3: *Moisturise*

Essential Oils: Lemon, to strengthen broken capillaries. Lavender, to assist regeneration of cells. Sandalwood, to nourish and moisturise. Bergamot, Cedarwood or Mandarin for oily skin. Clary Sage, Sandalwood, German Chamomile or Lavender for sensitive skin. Rosewood, Lavender, Sandalwood for skin that looks older than its years.

I recommend to blend your massage oils together, Jojoba comprising of at least 80%. Take a few drops of Jojoba and add 1 drop of your chosen oil. Smooth over the face to complete. Your makeup can easily be applied over this.

Apply a protective eye cream (remember no essential oils around the eyes).

In the Shower

It is easy to prepare an aromatic wash (swab) to take into the shower with you. You can prepare it by dispensing 2-3 drops of your chosen essential oils into an empty bottle. Add about 200mls of warm water to the bottle and shake well. Sprinkle the aromatic water over your body, then brush your entire body using a natural body brush or loofah. When you finish your skin will feel smooth and your mind will be clear to begin the day. Wet or dry skin brushing is fantastic. This can be done once or twice a week.

EVENING AROMATIC PROGRAMME

***Step 1:** Compressing*

Follow Step 1 from morning compress procedure, selecting the oils of your choice.

***Step 2:** Cleanse*

Use a natural facial cleanser to remove makeup (refer to Resource Guide). Remove with cotton wool, not tissues. Remove eye makeup with cotton wool too.

***Step 3:** Compress Again*

***Step 4:** Toning*

Follow Step 2 from morning procedure.

***Step 5:** Moisturise again*

Add additional moisturising agents as and when your skin requires.

Warm Facial Mask

Once a week you can treat your skin to a warm oil mask. Apply your eye cream for further protection and choose an essential oil combination for your facial mask from the recipe section.

This mask applied weekly will assist the moisture content of the skin. To apply this mask, use a pastry brush.

Utensils: An apparatus to warm your massage base oil, essential oils, a pastry brush, cold pressed massage base oil.

Once the 10mls of massage base oil is warmed add your 2-4 drops of essential oil. Apply the warm oil in a thin layer over the throat and facial area, over the nose and through to the hairline in a long sweeping stroke.

Avoid the eye sockets. Have a small bowl for the eyes with an infusion of Chamomile tea prepared. Soak cotton wool pads in it and when you are lying down with your mask on, refresh the eye tissue with the cotton wool pads.

Leave the mask on the face and throat area for anything from five to 10 minutes, taking advantage of this time to lie with your feet elevated. Listen to some relaxing music and breathe those healing vapours deep into the lungs. When complete, remove with a warm wet flannel or towel.

Your skin will glow from the invisible sheen that remains. Aromatic water in a spray pack can be utilised to refresh and further rehydrate the skin after any treatment or simply spritz throughout the day.

For particularly oily or blemished skin, you can steam (see Inhalation) prior to the facial mask.

FACIAL MASSAGE

For all facial massages, use 3-5 drops of essential oil into 10ml of Peach kernel oil as a base or add Avocado for a richer blend.

Normal Skin

Bergamot – 2 drops
Lavender – 1 drop
Sandalwood – 1 drop
Rosewood – 1 drop

Oily Skin

Basil – 1 drop
Cypress – 3 drops
Lemon – 1 drop

For Acne or Blemished Skin

Cedarwood – 1 drop
Cypress – 1 drop
Tea Tree – 3 drops

For Prematurely Ageing Skin

Ylang Ylang – 1 drop
Vetiver – 1 drop
Rosewood – 3 drops

For Dry or Mature Skin

Lavender – 3 drops
Sandalwood – 2 drops
Palmarosa – 1 drop
Geranium – 1 drop
Frankincense – 1 drop
Rose – 2 drops

Massage Blend 1. (Hydrate)

Lavender – 20 drops
Mandarin – 10 drops
Palmarosa – 10 drops
Rose – 10 drops

Massage Blend 2. (Moisturising)

Cedarwood – 20 drops *Lavender – 10 drops*
Neroli – 10 drops *Rosewood – 10 drops*

Massage Blend 3. (Healing)

Chamomile (G) – 10 drops *Eucalyptus – 10 drops*
Juniper – 10 drops *Lavender – 15 drops*
Rosewood – 5 drops

Massage Blend 4. (Tonifying)

Cypress – 10 drops *Grapefruit – 20 drops*
Lemon – 10 drops *Lime – 10 drops*

Massage Blend 5. (Sensitive)

Chamomile (G) – 5 drops *Juniper – 15 drops*
Chamomile (R) – 20 drops *Lavender – 10 drops*

Massage Blend 6. (Oily Skin)

Cedarwood – 20 drops *Clary Sage – 10 drops*
Chamomile (R) – 10 drops *Lemon – 10 drops*

Massage Blend 7. (Combination Skin)

Cedarwood – 10 drops *Geranium – 25 drops*
Ylang Ylang – 10 drops *Lemon – 5 drops*

Massage Blend 8. (Congested)

Juniper – 15 drops *Lemongrass – 15 drops*
Sage – 15 drops *Thyme – 5 drops*

To use the above blends as a moisturiser, reduce the number of drops and mls of base oils.

FACIAL STEAM/INHALATION

Before you begin, please protect any broken capillaries with protective eye cream. This method of application may not suit people who have highly sensitive skin.

Facial Steam (Normal Skin)

Bergamot – 1 drop
Geranium – 1 drop
Eucalyptus – 1 drop

Facial Steam (Oily Skin)

Lemon – 1 drop
Frankincense – 1 drop
Juniper – 1 drop

Facial Steam (Dry and Mature Skin)

Jasmine – 1 drop
Lavender – 1 drop
Patchouli – 1 drop

Facial Steam (Acne or Infected Skin)

Tea Tree – 1 drop
Cedarwood – 1 drop
Sage – 1 drop

FACIAL MASKS

2 dessert spoons of Clay and 2 drops of essential oil

Facial masks are an excellent follow up to the steaming procedure. A natural clay mask is ideal. Blend the clay with distilled or filtered water until it forms a paste.

Essential oils are then added. Blend the mask well.

Apply the mask with a pastry brush. The clay has a drawing action on the skin and is especially good for oily or infected skin conditions. You can do this weekly.

The essential oils to add for the facial mask are as follows:

Clay Facial Mask (Dry and Mature Skin)

Lavender – 1 drop *Rosewood – 1 drop*
Chamomile (R) – 1 drop

Clay Facial Mask (Oily Skin)

Cypress – 1 drop *Lemongrass – 1 drop*
Juniper – 1 drop

Clay Facial Mask (Normal Skin)

Geranium – 1 drop *Lavender – 1 drop*
Palmarosa – 1 drop

Note: The facial mask for normal skin should not be used on extremely sensitive skin as it is quite stimulating and drawing. Avoid areas prone to broken capillaries. Dry skin types can leave their mask on for five to 10 minutes, oily skin up to 15 minutes. A further addition to these masks can be a teaspoon of honey, which is very nourishing to the skin.

Here are further suggestions for a good start to the day:

Step 1.

Light your oil vaporiser. Select a combination of oils to wake up your senses, perhaps something energising or invigorating.

Step 2.

Breathing exercises enhance lung capacity and nourish every cell. Most of the air movement is accounted for by the action of the diaphragm, which is a voluntary muscle controlled at will. It enables the vital oxygen of our blood and elimination of carbon dioxide. Breathing deeply is an essential health aid, and daily practice works wonders. Begin by resting your hands on your rib cage at your sides just above the waist, breathe out completely. Inhaling through the nose to a count of four, first fill your abdomen (you'll see your fingers open to a space between them) and then fill your chest without raising the shoulders. Hold your breath for a count of eight then let it out through your mouth as you count slowly to four, noticing how your rib cage shrinks beneath your hands and pulling in with your abdomen until you have released as much air as possible and tightly contract your abdominal muscles. Repeat four to eight times.

Step 3.

Regular physical activity helps overcome or reduce depression and fatigue. Do some stretching (perhaps yoga) before commencing your chosen activity. Regular aerobic exercise pumps up vitality, improves muscle tone and circulation and detoxifies your body. I personally enjoy a brisk early morning walk.

Step 4.

After exercise, it's time to cleanse with a brisk body brush in the shower. With the skin dampened, brush from side-to-side with a natural bristle body brush. This really wakes you up.

or

A wake up bath feels great at the start of the day. Add your energising oils to the surface, agitate the water and climb in.

Step 5.

Now, take time to moisturise your skin with natural skin care products and your favourite essential oils.

HAIR CARE

Applications and Recipes

For hundreds of years herbal preparations and oils have been used to improve the health and condition of the hair; to add lustre and shine; to increase circulation or to stimulate growth. Essential oils create an aromatic halo around the head – a true delight to behold.

Essential oils do not alter your natural hair colour, but they can help to enhance it. Bleached hair can also be helped by essential oil rinses. Essential oils are natural mediums which help rebalance the skin after chemical colouring of the hair.

One of the pathways essential oils use to enter the body is via the hair follicles. Therefore, hair treatments and rinses using the essential oils are of great benefit to overall health.

While hair itself is dead, the vitality and condition of the scalp can be treated effectively with chosen preparations, and the hair can be made to shine by using rinses. For example, Lemon essential oil will help rid the hair of residual alkaline after shampooing. This will make the hair shine with a natural lustre.

Sage used as a final rinse has been known to disguise the greying of hair. Massaging the scalp with Rosemary and Juniper will stimulate and encourage new hair growth and improve circulation.

Damaged Hair

Hair can be damaged by many different things: the weather, perming, colouring, crimping, bleaching, or even by frequent washing with a strong shampoo. If your hair is damaged, lacking lustre or feeling dry, the once-a-week warm oil treatment will replace vital nutrients, making the hair feel and look better, while at the same time feeding the scalp.

Once you start to use the essential oil treatments on your hair, you will see marked improvements in your hair texture and appearance.

HAIR RINSES

Sandalwood, Rosemary and Sage can give dark hair lustre and shine. Lemon and Chamomile can lighten and brighten fair hair. While Orange, Mandarin and Bergamot enhances red or ginger hair. Add one drop of each essential oil to 1 litre of water in a glass bottle well sealed, shake vigorously and allow at least 24 hours for the oils to be taken up by the water. Use as a final rinse to impart shine and lustre to the hair and aromatise the head area while providing a nourishing treatment to the scalp.

You will notice a marked difference in the way you feel after an aromatherapy hair treatment. Many people experience greater clarity, more energy and a care-free feeling as body heat continues to emit oils into the air.

Hair Rinse Blend 1 (Dandruff)

Sage – 1 drop *Cedarwood – 2 drops*
Tea Tree – 1 drop

Hair Rinse Blend 2 (Dark Hair)

Rosemary – 2 drops
Sandalwood – 1 drop
Bergamot – 1 drop

Hair Rinse Blend 3 (Fair Hair)

Lemon – 3 drops
Chamomile – 1 drop

Add these essential oil combinations to one litre of water and shake vigorously in the bottle before use. Pour through the hair and leave in.

WARM OIL MASKS

Warm Oil Mask (Sensitive)

Lavender – 2 drops
Bergamot – 1 drop
Sandalwood – 1 drop

Warm Oil Mask (Oily Hair)

Bergamot – 2 drops
Sage – 1 drop
Cypress – 1 drop

Warm Oil Mask (Anti-Dandruff)

Tea Tree – 2 drops
Rosemary – 1 drop
Cedarwood – 1 drop

Warm Oil Mask (Damaged)

Geranium – 1 drop
Lavender – 1 drop
Sandalwood – 2 drops

Warm Oil Mask (Stimulate)

Rosemary – 2 drops
Lemon – 1 drop
Cardamon – 1 drop

Warm Oil Mask (Calming)

Lavender – 2 drops *Neroli – 1 drop*
Palmarosa – 1 drop

Warm Oil Mask (Clarity)

Lemon – 2 drops *Rosemary – 1 drop*
Black Pepper – 1 drop

Massage Blend 1 (Greasy Hair)

Bergamot – 20 drops *Sage – 20 drops*
Cypress – 10 drops

Massage Blend 2 (Dandruff)

Eucalyptus – 20 drops *Tea Tree – 20 drops*
Cedarwood – 10 drops

Massage Blend 3 (Damaged Hair)

Geranium – 10 drops *Sandalwood – 20 drops*
Lavender – 20 drops

Massage Blend 4 (Hair Loss)

Juniper – 10 drops *Cedarwood – 20 drops*
Rosemary – 20 drops

Blend these combinations into a base of 100mls of cold pressed vegetable oil. Jojoba is particularly good as a base. Apply to dry hair, massaging well into the scalp and leave in for about 20 minutes. In order to maximise oil penetration wrap the hair inside a hot towel.

Note: When removing the treatment, shampoo must be added and worked through before wetting hair. Wash thoroughly and shampoo again.

HAND CARE

Our hands are often neglected and it is important to care for these hard workers that are continually exposed to the elements. To begin, soak the hands in a bowl of warm water with two drops of Lavender oil. Soak the hands to soften the skin and warm them to promote circulation for greater oil penetration. Gently dry the hands.

For this next step, which is your oil treatment, the oil can be warmed, (follow the instructions from the warm oil mask) before applying to the hands.

Once the oil is slightly warmed, take the oil into the palm of the hand and massage over the back and front of the hand and fingers, stroking the fingers from the hand to the tips, pulling and stretching each one.

Twist down each finger, drawing gently downward, applying firm pressure. Press and release, sliding down the sides of each finger and as you reach the tip apply firm pressure to the nail and release. Massage between each bone up the hand toward the wrist again stroking with firm pressure.

Massage through the palm of the hand and onto the pad of the thumb, stretching out the hand gently but firmly. Now begin the massage treatment of the second hand.

You can leave the oil on overnight by simply wearing a pair of cotton gloves to bed to protect your linen and infuse the oil into the skin.

In 10mls of massage base oil add the following:

Warm Oil Mask Blend 1.

Lavender – 2 drops
Sandalwood – 1 drop
Geranium – 1 drop

or

Warm Oil Mask Blend 2

Patchouli – 1drop
Rosewood – 2 drops
Frankincense – 1 drop

NAILS

For brittle nails use 10mls of massage base oil and add 4 drops of Lemon oil. Massage into the cuticle area which serves to nourish the nail bed, strengthening the nails.

NB: With any citrus oil do not use in the presence of ultra-violet light.

FEET

Treat your feet with a foot bath. Add 5 drops of your essential oils, agitating the water before placing the feet in. Soak for 10 minutes then massage the feet while submerged in the warm water.

Footbath Blend 1 (aching or tired feet)

Juniper – 2 drops
Lavender – 1 drop
Rosemary – 2 drops

Footbath Blend 2 (for perspiring feet)

Cypress – 2 drops
Sage – 2 drops
Bergamot – 1 drop

Footbath Blend 3 (for swollen ankles)

Grapefruit – 1 drop
Juniper – 2 drops
Cypress – 1 drop
Frankincense – 1 drop

Note: The same oil treatment applied to the hands can be applied to the feet. Place a pair of socks on after oil application.

CHAPTER SIX

Women's Concerns

YOU AND YOUR BABY

SCIENCE HAS GONE TO GREAT LENGTHS TO DISCOVER the cycles of our solar system and of our weather, yet the biological cycles of a woman remain something of a mystery even for modern medicine.

It has been estimated that 50 per cent of women in the reproductive age group suffer from premenstrual syndrome (PMS) and up to 10 per cent of these women suffer devastating symptoms which often make their life a misery.

Menopausal problems, dysmenorrhoea (period pains) and post natal depression are some symptoms which can be experienced by women and can make life tough and hard to cope with.

Aromatherapy can assist women to relieve traumatic problems associated with PMS, post natal depression, menopausal problems and other uniquely female conditions.

Possessing potent medical qualities, essential oils will act to balance the natural physiological functions of your body just as they do in plants.

The oils, apart from having a very sound therapeutic role to play can lift our spirits and work wonders on our emotions. Hormones are the most powerful chemicals in our bodies. They have the power to be physically and emotionally debilitating, or allow us to feel wonderfully alive.

Once you start using the oils on a regular basis, your body rapidly responds and your senses become more acute.

Premenstrual Syndrome

Premenstrual Syndrome is a common ailment faced by many women today and although a lot more is known about the condition now, many people " doctors and lay persons alike " continue to inquire and question, when the subject is raised.

Working with the essential oils, in conjunction with good lifestyle practices such as a healthy diet, regular exercise and taking care not to let stress get the better of you, will help you overcome the debilitating effects of premenstrual syndrome.

When the natural flow of female hormones from the ovaries is insufficient or ends too soon, the metabolism of many tissues and organs of the female body are disrupted.

Aromatherapy can help the body find a balance proactively supporting the natural functions of the body in an wholistic practice of prevention, rather than waiting for symptoms to occur, then acting to eradicate them. You can begin one week prior to your menstrual cycle, begin massaging your body with a focus on the pelvic girdle.

The following oils are most useful to address PMS:

Geranium, Clary Sage, Fennel, Lavender, Mandarin, Frankincense, Roman Chamomile, Jasmine, Rose and Neroli.

A combination of up to three oils can be selected and blended into your massage base oil and worn regularly. One drop of each can also be dispensed onto a tissue and inhaled throughout the day. Every woman will experience her menstrual cycle differently. Some can have dramatic mood swings that affect not only the way they feel emotionally, but how they feel physically. Some symptoms may be fatigue, abdominal discomfort, bloating, nausea and migraines.

DYSMENORRHOEA *(Period Pains)*

Women are designed to bleed every month for a large part of their lives, a reminder of our fertility and life giving qualities. However, any accompanying pain or discomfort can be greatly relieved with essential oils in conjunction with care for our bodies.

Clary Sage is an essential oil which has the ability to ease dysmenorrhoea.

What Causes Period Pains?

At the end of each menstrual cycle, the fall in oestrogen and progesterone secretion by the ovaries precipitates the shedding of the layer of cells lining the uterine cavity (endometrium) in the form of blood. This shedding is accompanied by the release of prostaglandins into the uterus and menstrual blood. In some women there is an excess of prostaglandins in the menstrual blood and this can cause painful contractions of the uterine muscles.

Here are some massage blends to help alleviate the discomfort of period pains:

Massage Blend 1 (Painful Period)

Clary Sage – 20 drops | *Peppermint – 10 drops*
Basil – 10 drops | *Eucalyptus – 10 drops*

or

Massage Blend 2 (Painful Period)

Clary Sage – 25 drops | *Basil – 10 drops*
Ginger – 5 drops | *Fennel – 10 drops*

or

Massage Blend 3 (Irregular Period)

Basil – 20 drops | *Geranium – 15 drops*
Chamomile (R) – 5 drops | *Rose – 10 drops*

or

Massage Blend 4 (Irregular Period)

Basil – 10 drops | *Clary Sage – 25 drops*
Chamomile (R) – 10 drops | *Fennel – 5 drops*

FLUID RETENTION

Our general health plays a crucial role in determining whether we sufficiently eliminate waste liquids from our body. Fluid retention is a major concern for many women. Quite often, our weight can go up and down within days because our body isn't functioning well enough to eliminate fluids effectively.

The body is a smart biological system. Water retention is often a life-saving mechanism, especially during pregnancy. If you are dehydrated your body will automatically store fluid until the drought is over, so continue to drink one to two litres of water a day.

Water retention can often be addressed using specific essential oils. Juniper oil is a known natural and safe diuretic. Useful essential oils for the treatment of water retention are:

Cypress, Juniper, Frankincense, Rosemary, Sage, Grapefruit.

Massage Blend 1 (Drainage)

Juniper – 25 drops *Sage – 15 drops*
Rosemary – 10 drops

or

Massage Blend 2 (Drainage)

Grapefruit – 20 drops *Juniper – 15 drops*
Frankincense – 15 drops

Bathing Blend

Juniper – 4 drops *Rosemary – 2 drops*
Frankincense – 2 drops

You can massage your body regularly with your blend to assist in the release of excess fluids for a three week period only. Soaking in the bath can be a perfect time to ease your body, the feeling of weightlessness in water is of benefit itself. Elevate your legs to assist the flow of fluids in the body. Using even pressure massage each leg from the feet towards the groin area with both hands wrapped around the ankle and move with a light but firm stoke as you go. Another alternative is to treat the feet and ankles with a foot bath. (*See Chapter 7*).

MENOPAUSE

It is said that both ovaries have a limited active life span on average 35-45 years. The word – menopause – simply means the stopping of cyclical menstrual bleeding. This occurs on average, at 50 years of age, the normal range is between 45 and 55 years. There is a slow-down in ovarian activity with resultant hormonal imbalance for as long as five years before menstrual bleeding finally stops.

Unfortunately, during these years of hormonal change, a large percentage of women can feel generally unwell, physically and emotionally. All the signals let you know that more time is needed for yourself, opposed to giving so much to others.

Once again, aromatherapy is the perfect complement to this time of change. Through regular use of the essential oils, we are able to bring about a marked balancing effect in the body. Many women who have taken on aromatic support to nurture themselves during menopause have avoided some of the unpleasant symptoms and continued to live a vital life both physically and emotionally.

Useful essential oils for the menopause phase are:

Bergamot, Clary Sage, German Chamomile, Roman Chamomile, Fennel, Geranium, Jasmine, Neroli, Patchouli, Rose and Sage.

Application: Massage, Bathing, Vaporisation, Inhalation and Compress.

Massage Blend 1

Neroli – 20 drops | *Rose – 10 drops*
Patchouli – 10 drops | *Sage – 10 drops*

Massage Blend 2

Bergamot – 10 drops | *Clary Sage – 20 drops*
Geranium – 10 drops | *Rose – 10 drops*

Bathing Blend 1

Chamomile (G) – 1 drop | *Chamomile (R) – 2 drops*
Neroli – 1 drop | *Rose – 1 drop*

Bathing Blend 2

Fennel – 1 drop | *Geranium – 1 drop*
Neroli – 2 drops | *Sage – 1 drop*

Vaporisation Blend 1

Fennel – 2 drops | *Geranium – 2 drops*
Neroli – 2 drops | *Sage – 2 drops*

Vaporisation Blend 2

Clary Sage – 2 drops | *Geranium – 2 drops*
Rose – 2 drops | *Neroli – 2 drops*

Inhalation

Chamomile (R) – 1 drop | *Geranium – 2 drops*
Neroli – 1 drop

Compress Blend 1

Neroli – 1 drop | *Geranium – 1 drop*
Clary Sage – 2 drops

Compress Blend 2

Chamomile (R) - 1 drop | *Geranium – 1 drop*
Patchouli – 1 drop

THRUSH

Thrush is a common yeast infection which afflicts the vagina and can be most uncomfortable. Candida Albicans is the organism responsible for thrush. Symptoms are a white vaginal discharge, redness and itching of the vulva.

Tea Tree oil is gaining recognition around the world for its effectiveness in treating thrush and other bacterial infections and can be used highly diluted in a douche. Bergamot, Eucalyptus, Lavender, Myrrh, Palmarosa and Tea Tree are also very effective essential oils for the treatment of this condition.

Sitz Bath

Lavender – 1 drop
Tea Tree – 1 drop
Myrrh – 1 drop

Douche

Lavender – 2 drops
Tea Tree – 1 drop

Other useful blends to address Varicose Veins and Cellulite:

Varicose Veins Massage Blend

Cypress – 20 drops
Geranium – 20 drops
Lemongrass – 10 drops

Cellulite Massage Blend

Cypress – 20 drops
Fennel – 20 drops
Rosemary – 10 drops

or

Cypress – 20 drops
Grapefruit – 20 drops
Juniper – 10 drops

AROMATHERAPY AND YOUR BABY

Until recently, newborns were assumed to be helpless, unsensing and unresponsive creatures, who had little awareness of what was going on around them. Parents were often told that their infants were essentially blind at birth and could not taste, smell or feel pain.

Research has now shown that babies enter the world

with all sensory systems functioning and are well-prepared to learn about their new environment. That is why it is so important that their first sensations be positive ones. The first fragrances to hit our nostrils will give us distinct impressions about this new world we have entered.

Because our sense of smell resides in the same part of the brain as our memories, certain smells and combinations of smells can trigger specific memories. Therefore, those very first smells that meet us at birth have a profound impact.

Those parents who are keen to bring their child into the world to the sounds of gentle music, dimmed lighting and nurturing words can also add calming fragrances to make the experience even more pleasant and full of positive memories.

The art of aromatherapy can aromatically link us with our children, increasing our sensory connection to each other and the world in which we live.

PREGNANCY

Pregnancy Precautions: No topic application of essential oils during first 16 weeks, thereafter one aromatherapy body massage per week.

Essential oils to avoid during pregnancy:

Basil, Clary Sage, Cypress, Fennel, Ginger, Lemongrass, Marjoram, Peppermint, Thyme, Rose, Rosemary and Sage.

THE LAST FEW WEEKS

Your baby is almost ready to be born. The final stages of growth are occurring for your little one in preparation for his/her entry into the world. In this final burst of growth your little one is gaining layers of fat to assist in temperature regulation for when it comes into the world.

During this time there are many sensations and feeling which are heightened and it is normal for the mother to feel challenged. For many this final phase can feel like an emotional roller coaster ride, with the added pressure of family and friends ringing with their love and concern to see how well you're doing. While some mothers feel anxious with the anticipation, others may seem calm and revel in these weeks of preparation time. The best tip I can give you in these preceding weeks is to give time to yourself; relax in a short aromatic bath; compress your face during anxious moments in the day; sit quietly with your feet soaking in an aromatic foot bath and have your vaporiser alight in order to constantly create environments and aromatic moods that support you. Make the most of this time before your baby arrives. Remember to halve the recommended dosage of essential oils for bathing and massage.

CHILDBIRTH

Giving birth these days is very different from when our mothers were going through the same process.
Going into an unfamiliar environment for this wonderful event in itself can be an ordeal, there are a few if any familiar faces, seldom is there recognisable equipment in place, and rarely are there comforting smells. If this is the case for your labour then you must plan ahead so that you create your perfect surroundings. Every woman will go through this like any other experience in their own unique way so I have put together a selection of oils to assist you.

EQUIPMENT TO TAKE WITH YOU

Oil Vaporiser – to create and maintain your environment which will support you.

Essential Oils for Vaporising – Frankincense, Clary Sage, Geranium, Marjoram, Rose, Rosewood.

Essential Oils for Massage – Bergamot, Roman Chamomile, Lavender, Mandarin, Neroli, Petitgrain.

A Massage Base Oil – to blend your massage oil.

A Blending Bowl – to make up your blend.

A Face Cloth – to compress the face

Music – if appropriate.

N.B. If a vaporiser is not allowed then I suggest to use a tissue and inhale your essential oils neat.

Marjoram will assist in creating a relaxing atmosphere. As it is known as the most sedating of all the oils, this may be just the oil if you're feeling extremely anxious or tense.

Frankincense is wonderful during this time for its ability to allay fears.

Lavender for its calming and nurturing quality. Its physical properties will be wonderful in assisting in uterine pain. With its soothing properties, it will assist to dispel the intensity of emotions that are certainly present during birth. If feelings of panic are present Lavender, Geranium and Neroli are the team to use.

Rose oil being one of the most precious essential oils brings strength and security with its presence. An incredibly powerful oil to use in matters of the heart; this is a special time for bonding with the heart of your new born. At this time during labour, there is the amazing paradox – the pain of the birth and the pleasure of your new arrival are just minutes apart.

Geranium is the balancer and takes care of emotional distress. It will provide comfort and balance in the environment.

Neroli will leave you feeling steady and calm and relieve any tendency of hysteria.

COMING INTO THE WORLD

At the moment of birth the child loses its embryonic coverings; exposed to a new environment it embraces the force of gravity. This is why a child is usually born head first, because it's the heaviest part of your baby's body.

The real moment of birth is when the child's head passes through the mother's pelvis. There are enormous differences in a child before it is born and after birth. The enormity of the changes, adjustments and adaptations that the new born has to make to the immediate surroundings demand that one approach the little child with the utmost gentleness and tenderness. This is the time to consider carefully everything that will assail your baby's senses.

Your baby is incredibly vulnerable and open to the initial experiences that it encounters. You know only too well how your own first impressions of situations impact upon your life. Your baby at birth hasn't developed the ability to filter our information or understand their first encounters.

They are a sensory sponge, absorbing the essence of life into their cells which will be stored as references for the future. As they grow they will learn step by step how to develop their physical expression. This process is monitored primarily by the mother, who listens instinctively to her baby's delicate breathing. But she also listens sensuously to the essence of its soul.

Within the first three years of you child's life especially, we as parents and care givers, are responsible for the sensory contribution that we make to our children. By being kind to their senses, that which they touch, smell, see, taste and hear will provide them with the sensory tools to make their lives a masterpiece.

We constantly remind each other that our children are not ours, that we have them on loan and that they belong to themselves. We are sure that they assist us to grow and develop and that a lot of the time we feel that we are the students and they are the teachers. One thing for sure is that developing gratitude, the simple art of being grateful for all the experiences that you encounter as a parent with your child, helps to see you through the sunshine and darkness of the unpredictable, hurried journey of parenthood.

COMING HOME

I mentioned the notion earlier that our new born babe is like a sensory sponge, imagine absolutely everything being discovered for the first time! Although your baby's conscious process is not fully awake its sensory antennae is alert and active. As guardians we provide for their sensory conditions even at this early stage.

In the very early months your little one will have no real relationship between night and day. They can be just as active at 2 o'clock in the morning as they can in the middle of the day. They have not yet adopted the pattern of sleeping at night and waking during the day that many adults live by. They have their own rhythms and to begin with, yours will be totally disrupted.

To balance your self during these early days which are often demanding, it's time to implement some aromatic strategies. Consider:

Bathing: to relax, re-balance and nurture

Compressing: to wake yourself up or to put yourself back to sleep.

Vaporisation: to create a calm, serene environment.

WHAT OILS TO USE

Remember that newborn babies are particularly sensitive, it's important to always keep dosages low when you are working with children. Babies should not receive essential oils each day and when you do use them, only one drop for any topical application is required.

Here are some essential oils to introduce to your baby: Mandarin, Orange, Roman Chamomile and Rose, Lavender, Sandalwood and Cedarwood.

One of the gentlest, most effective ways to treat various common baby ailments is to use a vaporiser, allowing the essential oils to evaporate and circulate through the baby's room. Place your vaporiser well away from the baby, then add the oils, 3-4 drops will do to produce a delicate fragrance.

Keep all essential oils well away from your baby's face and hands so that they don't rub them into their eyes. Never use essential oils directly on your baby's skin.

Most babies delight in bath-time, and coupling it with a delightful aroma will help to reinforce positive memories and address any ailments your infant might have, e.g. coughs, colds, eczema or cradle cap.

For a small child's bath add one drop of essential oil mixed in honey. Organic bran added to the bath oil and mixed into the bath water has been known to soothe children with sensitive skin.

Make sure the water is at body temperature and that baby has plenty of room to kick and splash. Use soft, fluffy towels washed in pure soap to pat the baby dry afterwards, and rub some massage base oil into the baby's skin, and wipe any excess oil out of creases from the baby's skin.

MASSAGE

Massage is also an excellent way to introduce babies and small children to the healing effects of aromatherapy. Medical scientists have confirmed that loving touch is essential for the healthy psychological health of both infant and mother.

Babies need to be touched in a loving way to establish closeness, trust and security with their parents. This reassures infants that they are accepted and helps them to grow up with a feeling of their own self-worth.

In early childhood we reach out instinctively towards pleasure – for love, comfort and affection. Regular massages not only help babies emotionally, they also help to strengthen and tone the muscles and prevent colic.

Use cold pressed massage base oil and avoid mineral oil on a baby as it tends to dry the skin and cannot be absorbed. Sweet Almond oil or Jojoba oil is an ideal base for the following blend.

MASSAGE BLEND

Cold pressed Olive Oil is also nourishing to the skin. Prepare a space for the massage where you and baby will not be interrupted and make sure the room is free from drafts and is warm.

Directly after a bath is a good time to massage. Mother or Dad can massage baby; the nurturing body contact will further develop the bond between parents and child.

Warm the oil to body temperature by first rubbing it between your fingers, then use gentle, confident strokes along baby's body. Always stroke towards the heart.

Your baby will indicate its pleasure or discomfort with your massaging technique and you will come to know what it enjoys most.

Regularly oiling the scalp will assist in keeping the head free of cradle cap. Make sure you gently wipe away excess oil after massage – particularly in creases – to avoid rashes.

A nurturing massage is a gentle way to entice baby to sleep, so it is best done at the end of the day, after bath time.

Here are some New Born tips to consider:

Avoid using soap and water on your new born baby. Your baby when born is covered in a greasy protective substance called vermix caseosa one of whose functions is that of nourishment. Soap and water will remove this protective coating and deprive your baby of vital nourishment during the first days of its life. To clean your baby initially, gently wipe over a smear of cold pressed massage base oil. Take care to wipe the surface of the skin carefully so that you leave the natural protective coating in tact as it is reabsorbed by the body itself and disappears in a few days.

When you wipe your baby's bottom clean, complete by gently rubbing some cold pressed Olive Oil into their skin. This will help protect your baby against the chemical reaction that can take place on the skin from faeces and urine, especially if it is left in contact with the skin for a prolonged period.

Make your baby's resting place a haven for your newborn baby's body and soul. The room that your little one dwells in should always be kept warm. This will provide relaxation, safety and stability, especially during the first days and weeks.

Use an essential oil vaporiser in your baby's resting place. You can choose essential oils that will help your baby to rest quietly and peacefully. Lavender and Roman Chamomile are two favourites for new born babes.

Wool is a perfect insulator. You may have knitted or been given a soft wool vest, this is perfect worn over their chest and back. A woolen bonnet will help your baby to keep warm. A wool underlay to line the cradle is also ideal. Woolen pilchers can be purchased as an alternative to plastic pants to cover those nappies and further contribute to their warmth.

Baby Blends

1 drop of essential oil into 10mls of massage base oil.

Colic and Digestive Problems

Lavender – 1 drop

Inflammed Skin

Chamomile (G) – 1 drop

Cradle Cap

Cedarwood – 1 drop

Colds and Sniffles

Eucalyptus – 1 drop

This can also be used in a vaporiser.

Nappy Rash

Lavender – 1 drop

Winter Protection

Sandalwood – 1 drop

Restful Sleep

Lavender – 1 drop

TEETHING

Babies usually cut their teeth around six months of age. It is painful for them and causes irritability, dribbling, chewing and sometimes a flushed cheek or fever.

Essential oils: Eucalyptus, German Chamomile, Roman Chamomile and Lavender. Tepid water.

Application: Bathing, Compress

Bath Blend 1 (Fever)

Chamomile (R) – 1 drop *Eucalyptus – 1 drop*

or

Bath Blend 2 (Irritated Skin)

Chamomile (G) – 1 drop *Lavender – 1 drop*

Dispense 2 drops into full baby bath, agitate the water and bathe baby to soothe and comfort. Add 1 drop of Eucalyptus if a fever is present.

Compress

Eucalyptus – 1 drop

GROWING PAINS

Children are constantly getting into scrapes of one sort or another. Essential oils can help fight infection and promote healing. By employing your remedies for problems such as cuts and scrapes, stings and burns, colds and sniffles, you are showing your child they can take care of themselves, without the need to run off to the doctor each time something happens. This encourages the child to take control of his/her own healing in later years. Of course, always seek medical advice if you are uncertain, or if the problem persists.

Older children love lemon, orange and oils with a floral scent, and you can adjust the drops of essential oil for each application, e.g. 5yrs-10yrs – increase from 1 drop to 2 or 3 drops into 10mls of massage base oil and 2 drops into a full bath.

AROMATHERAPY ENVIRONMENT

By vaporising the sedating and more soothing essential oils in the evening, you can create an harmonious and peaceful environment. These essential oils include: Lavender, Chamomile and Orange

PREPARING FOR BED

Complete the child's daily activities with a ten-minute soak in an aromatic bath using the following blend:

Sleepy time blend

Cedarwood – 1 drop *Lavender – 1 drop*

After finishing the bath, lightly pat the skin dry and prepare an aromatic massage blend using Lavender, Chamomile and Geranium into a base of Sweet Almond Oil or Jojoba Oil. Using long, flowing strokes massage your blend over the whole body for the most beneficial treatment.

If the child is still lively, vaporise six drops of Lavender, two each of Marjoram and Orange in your child's bedroom 1 hour before retiring. Shut the door to ensure that the room contains the sleep-inducing vapor. Your child is sure to have a deep and restful sleep!

CALMING THE HYPERACTIVE CHILD

Some preservatives and additives and food allergies can overstimulate children fairly rapidly. It's important to note what a child has eaten just before a temper tantrum or hyperactive state. Keeping preservatives and additives out of the diet can help to calm a hyperactive child, and aromatherapy can help calm the child or even change its mood.

There are many changes in a child's life, from the physical changes they experience (losing teeth, growing taller, voice deepening etc), to the emotional changes that occur with each year, and then there are the changes that can occur in the family, at school and in the neighborhood. Aromatherapy can be used to assist children through both minor and major transitions, even when they may not be aware such transitions are occurring.

Trauma in the home can dramatically impact a child's life, and yet it is sometimes inevitable with divorce, loss of a loved one, a new child in the family, having to move to another area etc. Sometimes the only constant will be the child's personal belongings and the familiar aromas. Vaporising aromatic blends to make the house feel warm and inviting can provide a stabilising effect for children even during the most traumatic or changeable times.

It is possible to influence creativity, alter attitudes and sharpen our children's senses by exposing them to specific fragrances. While working with a group of students at the University of Wisconsin in America, Professor Arch Minchin discovered that by exposing students to different naturally occurring aromas, he could substantially influence their moods and energy levels. Professor Minchin has established that smells can influence where you stand or sit in a room, how long you will stay and how much you will enjoy yourself and enjoy the company of others in the room with you.

This can be extremely valuable for those parents and teachers who seek the best performance from their children.

DO'S AND DON'TS

- Don't place essential oils directly on children's skin.
- Don't use aromatherapy every day on babies.
- Use only highly diluted blends for babies.
- Avoid mineral oils as massage oils.
- Don't place vaporisers, candles or steamers where little hands can reach them.

- Do consult a doctor if problem persists.
- Do keep essential oils stored up high and away from your child's access.

MY EXPERIENCE OF PARENTING

Several years before I decided to have children I was already a student of Anthroposophy, the work of Rudolf Steiner, who gave a philosophical view of the nature of human beingness. He believed that human beings consisted of a threefold nature of body, mind and spirit.

He was said to be an investigator of the spirit world, skillfully interpreting his findings into a philosophy and science that could be examined and practised. His investigations led him to develop a philosophy about man kind. Agriculture (known as bio-dynamic agriculture), medicine (known as anthroposophical medicine), education (Rudolf Steiner Schools) and art which embraced such things as water colour paintings and eurhythmy (sound expressed though movement).

I still refer to these teachings today both as an individual and as a mother. My two boys experienced Rudolf Steiner education and I shared the direct benefits I saw expressed through Jacob and Joshua's developing years.

During my pregnancy I had a wonderful time preparing for my son's arrival. When natural light shines through silk, it filters the light and produces a beautiful clear hue. So instead of a net over Jacob and Joshua's crib I had my own individually dyed silk draping.

Selecting the pure silk canopies in rose pink for their cradles were special experiences which I skill have and treasure today.

There are many wonderful principles that Rudolf Steiner offered to parents, parents to be, and of course, children. I strongly recommend reading some of his work and incorporating some of the creative and nurturing principles into your child's life.

Every young person needs someone to talk to because human beings don't receive "The Manual" on how to be the perfect parent or child we assume there isn't one. There is no manual, no perfect parent nor perfect child. We do say, however, that within every baby born, there is the rich potential of opportunity and possibility yet to be realised.

Therefore, the best we can do in any given moment is to bring to the relationship all the resources that we currently have available to us and trust that we are making the right decisions based on the current references and information that we have. Combine this with love, honour and respect and trust your self that you will provide the best guidance and care for your child. Endeavour to be open to practices or principles that nourish the body and soul.

As parents it is our responsibility to develop the art of listening – with our ears as well as our instincts. Most of the time our children are communicating their needs, we need to develop our flexibility in the way that we listen continually so that we get the heart of their message, not our interpretation alone. Asking questions, open questions that begin with what, when, where, why, how and who allow for greater conversation beyond the boundaries of yes and no answers.

Some young people need more support than their families can give; someone who cares enough to lend a listening ear can make a big difference to them especially when they are undergoing changes. Significant changes occur in a young person's life cycles, especially around 7, 14 and 21. As a parent I've always endeavoured to do what's right for myself and my children. Many times my children have disagreed with me, and that's their right.

A good tip that was once shared with me, and I come to value is honour the confidence of others who share with you. It supports trust in each other. It takes courage to share, and respect to honour it. When your child chooses to share in confidence with someone else and the person tells you about it to keep you informed, protect the messenger – who brings the message. It may be valuable advice to help your child through a time of need. It is a case of being generous enough to allow your child to enjoy and share the gift of close loving relationships with others and respecting the close loving relationships that you have with others. These gifts can be mutually beneficial.

As life has it, there may not always be someone to talk to right when you need them. As adults we have more resources available to us, after all, we usually have both the funds and know how to change environments, whether it be as simple as taking a drive or booking in for a massage to ease the stresses of the moment. As adults we are now educated about stress release strategies to make changes in our lives. The problem for young people is, for the most part, adults consider them "lucky" and stress free. They are often trying to become the people they think we want them to be.

Children and the Art of Play

Creating the Environment for Creativity

I have taken great pleasure as a mother preparing my children's "play" or "work" environment too. I had a wonderful time gathering their toys, for the most part before they were born. Even though many years have now passed, it seems like yesterday and I look forward to the possibility of doing the same for my grandchildren one day.

Sea shells are fantastic, especially the larger curled ones. When you put them to your ear you can hear the sound of the ocean inside them. Use mother of pearl and cockle shells, they bring variety in colour and texture. For children under 3, make sure that the shells are firm enough not to easily crumble or break.

Rocks and stones are also another natural toy. They provide a wide-range of interest with their different shapes, sizes and textures. Again, don't give children under 3 small stones, because a baby will put them straight into his or her mouth. A basket of different sized river stones are ideal.

Drift wood is great. It is clean, smooth and light and comes in lots of interesting shapes. For children over three, you can also collect some short little stumpy pieces of wood and old small branches with dried leaves still strongly attached, especially when the bark remains in tact. Other pieces may need smoothing with sand paper. You can also collect autumn leaves and pine cones when they are accessible. They make all sorts of things from natural resources. They created rivers and houses and fairy gardens, and they were so beautiful I didn't want to pack them up.

Feathers, all different colours, shapes and sizes are greatly appreciated. Once again for those children around three or little ones who aren't going to put them into their mouths to suck on.

Other play tools to purchase can be crystals. Either raw or polished, these always make interesting treasures. Natural wooden boxes are also a great idea (help them to paint them if they want colour). Pieces of plain or coloured silk, large and small sizes make wonderful cubby houses or rivers.

The big hit with children is to have lots and lots of wooden blocks. Building up big towers and constructions and knocking them down to begin again is essential to a child's growth and development.

There are some specialty toy stores where you can purchase wooden shaped animals. There are no details of eyes or fur, they are neither coloured nor engraved, enabling your child to use their imagination to create the personality and character of the animal for themselves. You may be lucky enough to have a grandparent, friend or relative who is good with wood work, they may shape some animals for you.

Once you have collected all your natural toys, you simply place each type, e.g. stones etc into different baskets and perhaps place them in a circular fashion in their play room. You will be amazed at how creative your young person will be, creating houses, rivers, forests and cities etc. As their imagination becomes stimulated, their creativity runs wild.

The pack up is easy and I recommend that you encourage your young people to put all their play toys back into the appropriate baskets when they have completed their play.

Little ones 6 months – 1 year of age do well to have a small selection placed onto the floor so that they can reach for them or roll to them at will. Make sure that the objects that you provide for them are safe enough in size to go into their mouths.

CHAPTER SEVEN

Massage & Intimacy

Massage

EVERYONE NEEDS TO RELAX, TO ESCAPE THE stresses of daily living. We can listen to music, lie and watch the movement of clouds or the glowing of stars, sit on the beach and watch the waves or stroll along the shoreline searching for shells, watch the children playing in a park–these are all ways we inadvertently use to still the mind, to regain a sense of our own wholeness in the innocence of the moment.

As children, we climb trees and run around barefoot. We are at home with ourselves and our basic nature, but as we grow older we spend more and more time living in our heads.

For thousands or years, some form of massage or laying on of hands has been used to heal and soothe the sick. To the ancient Greek and Roman physicians, massage was one of the principal means of healing and relieving pain. Once again, I look to the Father of Medicine, Hippocrates, who wrote: "The physician must be experienced in many things, but assuredly in rubbing, for rubbing can bind a joint that is too loose, and loosen a joint that is too rigid".

Massage is one of the oldest and simplest of all therapies. For pure pleasure and/or to bring about a relaxation response in the body there is probably nothing better than the caring touch of a loved one or friend.

Massage means contact and it is of vital importance to all human beings. It gives reassurance, warmth, pleasure, comfort and renewed vitality. It has us feel connected.

Touch is a language we all use to show our feelings to demonstrate to others that they are loved, wanted or appreciated.

Massage can be stimulating or soothing, depending upon the speed and depth of your strokes. This is why it can make a person feel alive and ready for a sporting endeavour, or conversely, relaxed and sleepy. It can also help relieve tension, soothe away headaches, relax taut and aching muscles and banish insomnia.

MASSAGE WITH TRUST

This is a special massage which establishes and maintains trust between couples. It rekindles sensory energy. Once you commit yourself to the principles of The Touch of Honour Massage, you will learn to feel more secure with your partner.

We recommend that this massage is offered and received free of any sexual activity. It is good to make an appointment with your partner so that you can prepare for the event in advance. It also builds a sense of excitement and anticipation – an energy that both of you will enjoy being part of.

Of course, this massage – like any other – is best given and received with love and care. If you are not in a committed relationship, perhaps you have a friend who would love to share your massage. It is, however, difficult to give yourself this particular massage, so try and find a buddy – you may be surprised how much richer your friendship becomes.

PARTNER BACK MASSAGE

This is a "mini massage" – a rubdown of your partner's back – which can really add value to each other's health and wellbeing.

I have discovered that when a weekly mini massage is given to each other, connection and intimacy is created, thus dependencies and needs in the relationship diminish.

I suggest making a suitable time each week – a time commitment you keep even if it happens to fall in the middle of a disagreement. You may find that your little massage makes you realise that the tiff is really unimportant after all.

Prepare a mini treatment blend. You will only require 5mls per back massage. The recipes for all personal treatments can be chosen on intuition, likes and feelings.

I suggest that this particular massage be done with a sloping back, neck and shoulder region – perhaps by having your partner kneel on all fours with the neck hanging downwards (this is great for a 10-minute treatment each). This position makes for easy massage of the tissue in those vital areas.

Otherwise, support the chest and abdominal area with four pillows – this allows the neck to fall forward relaxed and allows massage movements to be executed without any discomfort to your partner. Take turns.

Another option is to have the receiver straddle a chair so their back is exposed.

The neck and shoulder area is where most people store tension. The neck muscles are always working, relaxing and contracting, even when we sleep.

Our Back-to-Back Massage is an ideal mini-treatment for each other. Of course, the obligatory blend of essential oils is needed to make it all worthwhile. The oils will help your body cleanse itself of toxins and the manipulation keeps the muscles healthy, flexible and toned.

CARRYING OUT THE MASSAGE

An essential oil blend, care and sensitivity, a little time and energy, and a good pair of hands – that is all you need to begin practising massage. There are a few points you should consider, however, when implementing your massages.

It is always best to set the scene in advance, so that you are well prepared for the massage session BEFORE you begin.

The room should be of even and warm temperature. You will break the entire flow of the massage if you have to stop to go in search of some more oil, a heater, an extra blanket, or whatever. And you will defeat the whole purpose of the exercise if your partner cannot relax because he or she is chilly or too hot or uncomfortable in some other way. Always use the entire flat surface of your hands.

Think about your own comfort, as the giver, as well. To give a good massage you will need to be able to move freely, so comfortable clothes are a must. Make sure you continually check your posture, it is important that your back is flat so keep the abdominal muscles pulled in tightly as you move about.

Crucial to the success of any massage is your state of mind and the state of mind of your partner. Before giving a treatment, prepare yourself mentally and talk to your partner to find out if there are any special problem areas which should be attended to or concerns they may have.

Focus your energy when giving the massage. Remember that massage is a two-way flow of touch and response, a mutual exchange of energy.

THE BASIC STROKES

You will soon build your own language of touch once you start to massage on a regular basis, but it helps to have some idea of the basic strokes which experienced masseurs/masseuses use.

GLIDING STROKES

Like waves rippling over rocks, these gentle rhythmic strokes glide over the skin, they are used on all areas of the body. The Long Stroke is the basic gliding stroke. Move your hands together along your partner's body. When you come to the limit of your natural reach, separate your hands and pull along the sides of the body. Circle around to bring them back together and repeat the stroke. Feathering is a brief, delicate stroke which brushes over the surface of the skin. It is mainly used to break contact gently, the strokes fading away like echoes of what has gone before. Broad circling is another gliding stroke. Move your hands in fairly wide circles, as if doing the breast stroke in miniature. This stroke can also serve to spread the oil more evenly over the body.

MEDIUM-DEPTH STROKES

Following on from the gliding stokes, you can now start to work more deeply on the large muscle masses, using a kneading action. In this action stroke each hand to echo the other's movement in a continuously alternating rhythm, relaxing the muscles, draining away waste products, and aiding circulation.

DEEP TISSUE STROKES

Deep and focussed, these friction movements make use of thumbs, fingertips or heels of hands to reach right down into the tissue to where more hidden tensions may lie. Having soothed and relaxed your partner with the broader, lighter gliding and medium-depth strokes, you penetrate below the superficial muscle layers or work around the joints with deep tissue strokes.

PERCUSSION STROKES

These movements are stimulating, rather than relaxing. These strokes are performed repeatedly with alternate hands. Hacking, cupping and pummelling with you fists or hands are all fairly noisy to apply, but have a marvellous regenerating effect. The main value of percussion strokes is to stimulate the soft-tissue areas, such as thighs and buttock, toning the skin and improving the circulation.

Caution: Do not massage over varicose veins and ensure the heavier strokes of massage are towards the heart.

THE BASIC MASSAGE SEQUENCE

There is no hard and fast rule as to what areas of the body should be massaged first or last, but many experienced massage workers follow a basic sequence. This sequence is:

1. *Back*
2. *Shoulders and neck*
3. *Back of legs*
4. *Arms and hands*
5. *Front of legs*
6. *Front of torso*
7. *Face and scalp*

Of course, you may prefer to carry out your massage in a different sequence. The important thing is to make mental notes as to how your receivers respond and to act according to their needs and wishes.

It is vital to get the right blend of essential oils for your massage, depending upon the type of massage you are going to give and, again, the needs and wishes of the receiver. The choices are endless: to be relaxed, enlivened and refreshed.

CONDITIONS TO AVOID

There are certain conditions that make massage inadvisable. These include skin eruptions, such as boils or infectious rashes, inflamed joints, tumours or any undiagnosed lumps, and cardiovascular problems, such as thrombosis, phlebitis and varicose veins. Also, deep abdominal work during pregnancy should be avoided.

Relaxation Blend

Bergamot – 3 drops
Lavender – 3 drops
Rosewood – 4 drops

Magic Moment Blend

Orange – 2 drops
Sandalwood – 4 drops
Jasmine – 4 drops

Serenity Blend

Lavender – 3 drops
Mandarin – 4 drops
Patchouli – 3 drops

Stress Blend

Neroli – 3 drops
Cedarwood – 3 drops
Pettigrain – 4 drops

Post Training Blend

Juniper – 3 drops
Rosemary – 4 drops
Lemongrass – 3 drops

Rejuvenation Blend

Frankincense – 4 drops
Black Pepper – 2 drops
Neroli – 4 drops

All of these blends should be placed into 20mls of massage base oil.

Intimacy

Aromatic oils can be used very effectively to create a mood for intimacy and lovemaking. Nothing is more stimulating to the senses than to return home after an intimate dinner for two and be greeted with the sensually-stimulating aroma of Ylang Ylang or Rose filling the air.

With just a few drops of essential oil and a little imagination, you can give your love life a wonderful new dimension. Many women have said using essential oils have helped them recharge the batteries in their sex lives. Certainly, the oils have been used very effectively to stimulate flagging sex drives in both males and females. Passion is at the heart of truly loving someone and aromatherapy stirs and arouses passion.

The alluring oils will help you to respond positively to your partner. If you are both contributing to a deep-seated love and respect for one another, the essential oils can truly work wonders.

For centuries aromatic preparations have been part of the love making ritual.

Certain essential oils have “heady”, euphoric characteristics, so why not take your favourite and imbue your bedroom. Create an aromatic setting that will sweep you and your partner into a mood of awareness and sexual excitement. Remember, creating the environment is an important part of seduction.

Jasmine, Rose, Patchouli, Orange, Cardamon and Ylang Ylang are ideal for bedrooms and seduction. Rose is arguably the favourite perfume of all time and is an integral ingredient in many modern-day perfumes. A drop of oil on a pillow or between the sheets can work wonders.

APHRODISIACS

Certain essential oils have long been praised for their aphrodisiac qualities. One of the reasons why they work so fast and effectively is that they act directly on the limbic portion of the brain, which is also responsible for sexual behaviour and response.

In a less direct way, other essences possess the ability to spark fatigued reproductive glands into action, and so work to revive a waning interest in sex.

LOVE MAKING

Touching and caressing must play a major role in lovemaking. Prolonged fondling and caressing stimulates the body's sexual hormones and heightens arousal so that the energetic charge and sensory fulfillment is far higher. Add to this the power of aromatic essences and the stimulation of the senses that they bring and you can learn to reach new heights of ecstasy.

Touch alone can be a satisfying experience, and being sensually aroused does not necessarily have to lead to intercourse. An intimate and prolonged sensual experience can be very valuable for both partners, because either one may not always want to go all the way. There is real magic to be found in your relationship if you spend time exploring each other's body. Making time and commitment for this as separate from actually making love is a very important technique for enhancing your relationship.

Particularly if you're tired or stressed or feel you've given all you can in any one day, non-conditional caressing can play a nurturing role in these instances. Often gentle stroking and caressing with no expectation or agenda at hand can, in a caring and honouring way motivate and inspire lovemaking.

Many people find the experience of being caressed for an extended period even more intimate than lovemaking, and may need to accustom themselves gradually to these new dimensions of pleasure. To reach new heights of ecstasy, let your body surrender to the loving touch of your partner.

To enhance the mood and raise the spirits of both partners, consider the following blends which are ideal in a massage base oil of 20mls. You could also add them to your vaporiser (8 drops):

Massage Blend 1
Clary Sage - 3 drops
Sandalwood - 3 drops
Ylang Ylang - 4 drops

Massage Blend 2
Ylang Ylang - 3 drops
Patchouli - 2 drops
Orange - 5 drops

Massage Blend 3
Neroli - 4 drops
Sandalwood - 3 drops
Rose - 3 drops

HONOURING RHYTHMS

No matter how much we love our partner, sometimes we have more enthusiasm for intimacy than at other times. Levels of intimacy can rise and fall dramatically without it being any reflection on the quality of the relationship.

We each have personal rhythms on a mental, physical and emotional level that scientists have been able to track and even to predict into the future. Each rhythm has a high, low and critical point each month, and depending on the position of these rhythms, we may feel tired/energetic, emotionally strong/weak, mentally dull or acute.

You can make use of essential oils to help balance the myriad of emotions you may experience. By using carefully chosen blended oils, couples can also maintain a more balanced interaction rather than being on an emotional and physical roller coaster. The following is a great blend to balance even the most charged moment.

Massage Blend 4

Geranium - 3 drops
Cedarwood - 2 drops
Orange - 5 drops

EROTIC MASSAGE

While using sensual massage is ideal for building up trust and a strong sense of intimacy between partners, erotic massage is designed to lift the sexual relationship to even loftier heights. Also, many partners find it impossible to experience such high levels of ecstasy without taking it to some kind of sexual completion. Massage is the ultimate in foreplay!

Scent works mainly on the instinctive centres, stimulating our basic primal urge- sexual excitement. When preparing for an erotic massage, we recommend that you choose oils that align with the smell of human sexual hormones and pheromones such as the base notes that have a strong connection to our physical being. Oils such as Sandalwood, Vetiver, Cedarwood and Rose are very arousing.

During massage, both the giver and the receiver can benefit from the aromatic energy created by the essential oils and the natural body odours they have stimulated during the massage. Your touch can be a little firmer during erotic massage, although starting out with light, titillating strokes will bring your partner to a higher level of ecstasy. You must always rely on feedback from your partner when giving a massage, respecting their wishes to stop at any time.

Below I've listed two blends which will assist in bringing your partner to levels of heightened sexual awareness. Just a quick note to remind you that I firmly advocate safe sex.

Massage Blend 5

Rose - 2 drops
Neroli - 2 drops
Patchouli - 1 drop
Ylang Ylang - 3 drops

or

Rose – 2 drops
Ylang Ylang – 2 drops
Sandalwood – 2 drops
Jasmine – 2 drops

ABSTINENCE

Men and women can be sensuous and sexual even if they're not in a sexual relationship with a partner. At different times in our lives we may either choose to abstain from sex for a while, or find ourselves without a partner. That doesn't mean we have to relinquish our sexuality for the duration. In this day and age, some of the most sensuous people choose to be celibate from time to time. These can be healing times when we hold our sexual energy within and use it to enhance our creativity.

Celibacy is not about denial, and it certainly doesn't mean we can't enjoy the healing energy of orgasms. In fact, many people, especially women, discover more about their body and their sexual desire when they are without a partner and left to gratify their inner yearnings.

If you choose to be celibate, it can give you the space you really need in a sexual relationship. You will also find the strength to know what you want in a sexual relationship when you decide that your celibacy experience is complete.

TIPS FOR LOVE MAKING

- Set aside a special space for your aromatherapy blending.
- Make sure you're not interrupted when mixing or applying essential oils.
- Never use essential oils on the skin without diluting them first.
- Avoid using citrus oils on the skin in the presence of ultra violet light.

– Never use essential oils around the eyes.
– Geranium and Ylang Ylang are not to be used on red and inflamed skin.
– Rosemary should not be used on people who have epilepsy.
– Thyme oil should be used with caution around the mouth and genital area and near mucous membranes.
– Basil and Marjoram should not be worn topically during the first three months of pregnancy.
– Use only those oils that are safe for the skin for massage.
– Store blends in dark bottles out of direct sunlight.

AROMATIC TOOLS IN RELATIONSHIPS

There are some wonderful aromatic techniques that can be adopted in relationships. I suggest these to add real value and love to a relationship.

THE AROMATIC FOOTBATH

Thousands of men and women now enjoy the benefits of an aromatic footbath.

Prepare a special environment before you begin.

I suggest the bowl be three-quarters filled with fairly warm water. Add five drops of your chosen essential oils.

Footbath Blend

Rosemary – 2 drops *Tea Tree – 1 drop*
Sage – 2 drops

This is a great combination for reviving tired or sore feet. When your partner comes home you can have the bowl prepared and invite them to indulge in a footbath. The giver of the footbath gets to experience a wonderful aromatherapy inhalation and the receiver gets to experience bliss. The whole energy dynamics of one partner massaging and bringing pleasure to the other, provides a wonderful opportunity to connect.

The entire performance can last as little as five minutes or as long as 20 minutes – either way the results are amazing. This experience engages vapours at a deep level and engenders humility and respect and, most of all, caring.

It is important when working with the feet to make initial contact with the right foot first. Allow the feet to be weightless in the water and massage under the water level. Move with firm, slow pressure in circular motions. Don't break contact with the foot until you complete the massage, then move to the other.

As the masseur, make sure your own back is supported during the process, keep it straight and have a towel on hand to dry the feet. Do all the lifting and moving for your loved one. Make the experience tender and caring

– make it like the footbath you'd love to receive.

After drying the feet, a warm oil blend can be massaged in, or simply slip on a pair of woolly socks. By working on the feet it polarises the two extremes of the body taking the focus away from the head where we spend most of our time thinking.

THE AROMATIC BATH

The aromatic bath is best taken with your partner, treating your loved one to special pampering makes bath time fun. Of course, if you are single, you can enjoy the delights of an aromatic bath to nurture and care for yourself.

Create the perfect ambience. Choose a blend of romantic essential oils, or a combination to relax and revitalise. You can enhance the mood with candles as your only source of lighting. Light your vaporiser to further enhance the aromatic water.

Make sure you have a flannel and a small rolled-up towel to support your neck if you intend staying in the bath for a while. Lean back and enjoy!

A good technique is to start with six candles for lighting. Wring out your flannel and place it over your face. Take in some nice deep breaths to heighten relaxation. Keep pressing the warm flannel to your face about five times. As you relax blow out a candle – the change in light further enhances relaxation. Blow out all the candles over the duration of your bath, except one which should remain the only source of light.

Bathing Blend 1

Ylang Ylang – 1 drop *Patchouli – 2 drops*
Orange – 2 drops

Bathing Blend 2

Sandalwood – 2 drops *Jasmine – 2 drops*
Ylang Ylang – 1 drop

Alternatively, you can make up a masculine combination:

Bathing Blend 3

Cardamon – 1 drop *Sandalwood – 2 drops*
Bergamot – 2 drops

Or a distinctly feminine combination:

Bathing Blend 4

Orange – 2 drops *Jasmine – 2 drops*
Ylang Ylang – 1 drop

RELAXING BATHS

The best way to use essential oils for an aromatic bath is to add them drop by drop once the bath is fully drawn. Make sure you are ready to climb in and that the doors and windows are closed so that you can take in the full healing benefits. Here are two of my favourite relaxation bath combinations for you to try. Of course, once you begin using the essential oils on a regular basis, you will soon develop your own blends, based on a little advice I have given along with your creativity.

Bathing Blend 5

Chamomile (R) – 2 drops
Geranium – 2 drops
Rosewood – 2 drops

Bathing Blend 6

Bergamot – 2 drops
Pettigrain – 2 drops
Cedarwood – 1 drop

Massage Blend 1

Rose – 20 drops
Mandarin – 10 drops
Ylang Ylang – 20 drops

Massage Blend 2

Ylang Ylang – 10 drops
Cardamon – 20 drops
Sandalwood – 20 drops

Massage Blend 3

Ylang Ylang – 10 drops
Jasmine – 10 drops
Orange – 20 drops
Clary Sage – 10 drops

CHAPTER EIGHT

Tips for Men

Aromatherapy for Hair Care & Balding

WHILE AMERICAN ACTOR STEVE MARTIN MAKES light of balding, for many men it's no laughing matter. Male self-image and self-confidence can be greatly reduced by baldness. Indeed, men seem to worry about their hair (or lack thereof) about as much as women worry about their weight. It's a sensitive issue, but one which can be addressed with aromatherapy.

Basically, our genetic makeup determines how much hair we lose as we age. Fortunately, the essential oils have proven quite helpful in reducing hair loss by improving the health of the scalp and the person in general. Remember, too, that the way we handle stress, shock, trauma, illness or change can influence the degree of hair loss we experience.

Several new drugs and potions have helped stimulate hair growth, and cosmetic surgery has helped many men, but these are drastic measures.

I believe the first step for all men concerned about hair loss should be to work with essential oils as part of a new hair care program. Several of the essential oils can very effectively stimulate atrophied hair follicles into producing hair growth

Don't expect the essential oils to work miracles. They can't restore a full head of hair overnight, but they can help a great deal. It's important to realise that you'll be doing your hair a great service if you work on the whole body with the essential oils – not just your head. The circulatory and lymphatic systems should also be worked on, particularly through massage.

Essential Oils to Stimulate Hair Growth

Juniper, Rosemary, Neroli, Lavender, Geranium, Basil, Cypress, Sandalwood and Cedarwood.

Massage Blend 1 (Hair Growth)

Rosemary – 10 drops
Juniper – 10 drops
Cedarwood – 20 drops
Cypress – 10 drops

Massage Blend 2 (Hair Loss)

Juniper – 10 drops
Rosemary – 20 drops
Cedarwood – 20 drops

Add to 100mls Jojoba oil and massage into the scalp night and morning. To remove oil from the hair, apply shampoo before adding water to emulsify the oil, then rinse.

You can place two drops of each of the same oils into 100mls of distilled water as a final aromatic hair rinse each time you wash your hair.

Pre-Shave Soak

Utensils: 1 clean flannel or face cloth, Lavender oil.

Fill the bathroom basin with warm to hot water.

Add a few drops of Lavender essential oil. Agitate the water to disperse the oil molecules.

Soak the flannel in the aromatic water and squeeze the excess water out. Leave the cloth damp.

Soften the skin by using a pressing and releasing action with the face cloth. You simply press the flannel into the skin then move to another part of the face. Move over the entire face and neck area. Do this three or four times before shaving. This cleanses the skin, opens the pores and prepares it for shaving.

Aromatic Aftershave

You will need any combination of three of the following oils: *Lavender, Bergamot, Tea Tree (as an antiseptic), Cedarwood, Sandalwood, Geranium, Cardamon, Black Pepper, Palmarosa.*

100ml glass bottle.

Add 2 drops each of Lavender, Bergamot and Tea Tree for example, to a blending bottle filled with 100mls of pure water. Shake the bottle vigorously with the lid intact to disperse the oil through the water.

Splash a small amount of this blend on the face to tone and soothe the skin after shaving and prior to moisturising. Create your own favourite combinations.

Skin Regeneration/Moisturiser

Shaving daily can be quite drying to the skin. This moisturising blend will quickly help to soften and regenerate, leaving you feeling revitalised.

Blend 1 drop of Lavender with 1ml of Jojoba oil and smooth it onto the skin. (Soothes and settles the skin after shaving and softens regrowth.)

For a more "earthy" blend, use 1 drop of Cedarwood with 1ml Jojoba oil. *(Regenerates the skin after shaving.)*

THE EVENING CLEANSE

It's important to cleanse and tone as per the pre-shave soak every evening before retiring (see Pre-Shave Soak method in this chapter). The soaking procedure prepares you for sleep, removing the dirt and grime of the day and softening the skin to prepare it for overnight regeneration. This soaking can be done with many essential oils. We recommend the following selections:

Grapefruit – 2 drops
Geranium – 2 drops
Sandalwood – 2 drops

Lavender – 2 drops
Black Pepper – 2 drops

Cardamon – 2 drops
Palmarosa – 2 drops
Frankincense – 2 drops

Lavender – 2 drops
Bergamot – 2 drops
Cedarwood – 2 drops

ACNE SCARRING

Mornings and Evenings

Apply Lavender oil neat to the skin with a cotton bud to small areas only. If treating larger areas, the essential oil must be blended into a base massage oil.

COMPRESSES

Mornings and Evenings

Chamomile – 2 drops
Patchouli – 2 drops

Lavender – 2 drops

Add the oils to a basin of warm to hot water and agitate to disperse the oils. Drop in a clean face cloth and squeeze excess water out. Press cloth to the skin. Repeat this six times.

SHAVING

The ancient Egyptians literally hacked away the whiskers with pumice stone, and some African tribes singed off their facial hair with hot irons! Thankfully, the safety razor was invented in 1762.

If you have coarse, fast-growing facial hair or sensitive skin, you'd probably love some tips to make this everyday task an enjoyable one. And no wonder! Shaving every day is akin to scraping sandpaper over your face, and it can sometimes injure the protective layers of the skin and cause a great deal of discomfort.

But that's just the beginning. In the hope of achieving some soothing relief and a refreshing fragrance, many men use synthetic aftershave products which are often full of harsh chemicals. On some skins, these products can cause a blotchy red rash or even small pimple-like bumps.

If you have ever experienced skin irritation after using commercial skin care and aftershave products, you should seriously consider switching completely to natural products such as essential oils. The correct oils will not only soothe the skin after shaving and give it a wonderful, fresh feeling, they'll also make you smell great, will promote a feeling of wellbeing and, when used properly, won't irritate the skin. In fact, they will even have a therapeutic effect!

Antiseptic After-Shave Splash

Cardamon – 2 drops
Ylang Ylang – 2 drops
Mandarin – 2 drops

Mix into a 100ml bottle filled with water. Agitate.

Pour a small amount into your hands and splash it on the face.

Passion After-Shave Splash

Palmarosa – 2 drops
Jasmine – 2 drops
Black Pepper – 2 drops

Mix into a 100ml bottle filled with water.

Take a small amount into your hands and splash it on the face.

Skin Repair (Sensitivity) Blend

Lavender – 25 drops
Bergamot – 10 drops
Sandalwood – 15 drops

Mix into 100mls of Jojoba oil.

Massage a small amount into the skin in the mornings.

Tonifying Blend (For open pores)

Lemon – 10 drops *Grapefruit – 5 drops*
Sage – 20 drops *Cypress – 15 drops*
Mix into 100mls of Jojoba oil.

Dab onto the skin with a cotton ball.

CARE FOR THE GENITAL AREA

Essential oils can greatly assist male hygiene and sexual health. Try the following wash and massage blends. *(Avoid direct contact with gland area)*

Antibacterial Wash Blend

Bergamot – 2 drops *Lavender – 2 drops*
Tea Tree – 2 drops

Massage Blend 1 (Anti-inflammatory)

Bergamot – 10 drops *Lavender – 25 drops*
Chamomile (G) – 15 drops
Add to 100mls of Jojoba oil.

Massage Blend 2 (Rejuvenating)

Juniper – 10 drops *Lavender – 25 drops*
Sandalwood – 15 drops
Add to 100mls of Jojoba oil.

Stress Management

We are all aware of stress to some extent. We might witness stress, of the type exercise enthusiasts voluntarily undergo, or stress from bickering with a loved one or running a business that is highly demanding.

Distress, however, is another thing altogether. This is when our stress becomes chronic, perhaps as a result of a series of ongoing events, with the result being that we lose energy, and we become frustrated and feel like victims.

Everyone handles stress differently. Stress takes place within ourselves and must be addressed individually. It is a force that can strain and deform, or motivate and empower. The essential oils can help us calm our emotions, clear our minds to focus more clearly on what we wish to achieve. Next time you feel as though you are being pushed to the brink and that you can't cope with one more crying child, one more demanding phone call, one more bill to pay, one more nerve wracking day at the office, I invite you to inhale, bathe or massage with the aid of some stress-reducing aromas listed below.

These combinations can refuel your body and mind.

Bath Blend 1

Bergamot – 2 drops
Lavender – 2 drops
Cedarwood – 1 drop

Bath Blend 2

Orange – 2 drops
Jasmine – 1 drop
Sandalwood – 2 drops

Bath Blend 3

Bergamot – 2 drops
Petitgrain – 1 drop
Geranium – 2 drops

DEPRESSION

Essential oils offer a source of assistance in dealing with depression. When we are sad and troubled we need a little something to make us feel better in ourselves. Grapefruit, Ylang Ylang and Clary Sage are some suggestions to leave you feeling more uplifted and resourceful.

Breathing in the aromas of nature connects us to the most simple qualities in life, makes us feel more tranquil and helps us to engage our inner strength to transform our lives.

Massage Blend 1

Bergamot – 20 drops
Lavender – 20 drops
Basil – 10 drops

Massage Blend 2

Lavender – 20 drops
Cedarwood – 20 drops
Jasmine – 10 drops

Massage Blend 3

Bergamot – 20 drops
Sandalwood – 20 drops
Geranium – 10 drops

STRESS RELEASE

As you become more proficient with essential oils, you can make your own synergistic blends to treat many ailments and emotional conditions.

For stress-related conditions, it is best to use the oils in a combination of three. As a general rule, it helps to have a basic understanding as to which oils act as stimulants, as sedatives or relaxants.

Stimulants

Basil, Clary Sage, Cypress, Eucalyptus, Fennel, Rose, Geranium, Juniper, Lemon, Lemongrass, Tea Tree, Neroli, Peppermint, Pine, Rosemary, Sage, Thyme, Ginger, Black Pepper, Cardamon, Petitgrain, Palmarosa, Grapefruit, Lime.

Sedatives / Relaxants

Roman Chamomile, German Chamomile, Cedarwood, Frankincense, Lavender, Geranium, Marjoram, Myrrh, Neroli, Orange, Patchouli, Rose, Sandalwood, Vetiver, Ylang Ylang, Jasmine, Mandarin.

You will notice that some oils appear in both lists. This is because of the phenomenon called "adoptogens". These are essential oils which act as natural balancers. They instigate a reaction in the body, that achieves a state of homeostasis or balance.

- ***To Release Anger***

  Roman Chamomile, Rose, Neroli, Ylang Ylang

- ***To Settle Anxiety***

  Basil, Bergamot, Cedarwood, Geranium, Lavender, Neroli

- ***To Relieve Boredom***

  Basil, Frankincense, Lime, Peppermint

- ***To Enhance Confidence***

  Jasmine, Myrrh, Rosewood, Sandalwood

- ***To Clarify Confusion***

  Cypress, Lemon, Petitgrain, Rose

- ***To Uplift Depression***

  Bergamot, Clary Sage, Patchouli, Ylang Ylang

- ***To Settle Emotional Instability***

  Bergamot, Geranium, Neroli, Myrrh, German Chamomile

- ***To Release Envy/Resentment/Jealousy***

  Rose, Juniper, Thyme, Roman Chamomile, Ylang Ylang

- ***To Disperse Fears***

  Frankincense, Lavender, Sandalwood, Petitgrain, Cedarwood

- ***To Release Frigidity***

  Clary Sage, Roman Chamomile, Ylang Ylang, Jasmine, Neroli

- ***To Soothe Grief***

  Marjoram, Rose, Cypress, Neroli, Rosewood

- ***To Relieve Insomnia***

  Bergamot, Lavender, Marjoram, Neroli, Orange

- ***To Settle Impatience/Irritability***

  Lavender, Neroli, Rose, Ylang Ylang, Palmarosa

- ***To Release Mental Fatigue/Poor Memory***

  Basil, Rosemary, Lemongrass, Pine, Cardamon, Grapefruit, Palmarosa

- ***To Calm Nightmares***

  Bergamot, Frankincense, Sage, Nightmares

- ***To Re-Balance feeling Disoriented***

  Sandalwood, Vetiver, Fennel

- ***To Release Stress***

  Bergamot, Lavender, Neroli, Rose, Sandalwood, Myrrh

- ***To Heal Emotional Wounds***

  Rose, Roman Chamomile, Frankincense, Palmarosa

– ***To Ponder***
Petitgrain, Orange, Cypress

To Reflect
Frankincense, Jasmine, Lavender

– ***To Inspire***
Pine, Lemon, Eucalyptus

– ***To Concentrate***
Lime, Rosemary, Petitgrain

– ***To Be Confident***
Myrrh, Mandarin, Lavender

– ***To Soothe***
Lavender, Neroli

– ***To Empower***
Rose, Cedarwood, Sandalwood

– ***To Be Creative***
Pine, Grapefruit, Lime

ACTIVE SPORT

Always warm up carefully before you exercise, especially if the surroundings are cold. Practise new movements slowly so as to avoid wrenching a muscle. Most importantly, set yourself realistic goals! Do not overdo it on your first few days. You may be discouraged to turn up next week. Remember, it is not how much exercise you do that really counts, but how regular and consistent you are. Once you build some aerobic fitness, you will be inspired to do a little more.

Studies at the Centre for Disease Control in Atlanta, USA, show that even 20 minutes of walking, three times a week, confers significant protection from heart disease and most cancers.

Also, exercise is valuable if you want clear vital skin and a healthy disposition. Exercise stimulates the lymphatic system, cleans the body of toxins, opens the pores, and clears the mind.

Remember to always balance the combination of regular exercise – toning exercise, strengthening exercise and aerobic exercise.

Regular exercise, combined with a well-balanced diet high in complex carbohydrates, low in fat, with adequate protein and fluid intake, will assist you to maintain peak expression of your physical body and support you to feel your most vital self.

Be kind to yourself with exercise. Learn to listen to your own body. Pace yourself, but be consistent. Make a commitment to yourself to exercise more frequently.

SPORTS BLENDS

Massage Blends for Motivation and Energy

Massage Blend 1 (Competition)

Bergamot – 30 drops *Basil – 5 drops*
Rosemary – 15 drops

Massage Blend 2 (Endurance)

Thyme – 10 drops *Rosemary – 10 drops*
Sandalwood – 30 drops

Massage Blend 3 (Motivation)

Eucalyptus – 15 drops *Lemongrass – 20 drops*
Basil – 15 drops

Caution: Citrus oils are photosensitive and are not to be used topically in the presence of ultra violet light.

Massage Blends for Physical Support

Massage Blend 1 (Respiratory)

Eucalyptus – 10 drops *Rosemary – 25 drops*
Peppermint – 15 drops

Massage Blend 2 (Circulatory)

Rosemary – 15 drops *Juniper – 20 drops*
Ginger – 15 drops

Massage Blend 3 (Muscle Tonic)

Eucalyptus – 10 drops *Rosemary – 25 drops*
Lemongrass – 15 drops

Massage Blend 4 (Joint Rub)

Chamomile (G) – 5 drops *Frankincense – 20 drops*
Juniper – 25 drops

Remember, the most effective and beneficial way to use essential oils is to massage them into the body. The more area covered the greater the benefit. I suggest you massage these blends into your body for special results.

Massage Blend 1 (Recovery)

Eucalyptus – 20 drops *Juniper – 20 drops*
Lemongrass – 10 drops

Massage Blend 2 (Fitness)

Eucalyptus – 20 drops *Petitgrain – 10 drops*
Black Pepper – 20 drops

Massage Blend 3 (Marathon)

Myrrh – 5 drops *Petitgrain – 15 drops*
Juniper – 10 drops *Eucalyptus – 20 drops*

Massage Blend 4 (Athletic)

Peppermint – 5 drops *Rosemary – 15 drops*
Eucalyptus – 30 drops

Massage Blend 5 (Weightlifting)

Frankincense – 20 drops *Ginger – 10 drops*
Juniper – 10 drops *Myrrh – 10 drops*

Use as a massage blend in 100mls of Jojoba and Sweet Almond oil combined.

You can also use the following blends on a wristband. Place 1 drop of one essential oil listed below onto the top of your wristband and allow it to penetrate the cloth for several minutes before wearing the band.

Massage Blend 1 (Energiser)

Eucalyptus – 15 drops *Sage – 20 drops*
Mandarin – 15 drops

Massage Blend 2 (Endurance)

Cardamon – 10 drops *Rosemary – 20 drops*
Sandalwood – 20 drops

Massage Blend 3 (Muscle Tonic)

Eucalyptus – 20 drops *Rosemary – 20 drops*
Lemongrass – 10 drops

Massage Blend 4 (Nervous Butterflies)

Berg*amot – 20 drops* *Basil – 10 drops*
Black Pepper – 20 drops

CHAPTER NINE

Natural Therapies

HEALING THE "WHOLE" IS BECOMING INCREASINGLY popular and more people are incorporating different natural therapies into their life. Natural healing isn't some trendy new notion; it has been employed by many indigenous cultures for thousands of years. Indigenous cultures have a strong connection to Mother Earth and an admirable understanding of natural health.

The Greek physician Hippocrates, known as the father of modern medicine, was insightful enough to realise that the elements needed to produce and maintain health were natural, and they included hygiene, a calm balanced mental state, proper diet, a sound work and home environment and physical exercise.

Today, natural therapies are recognised on the basis that they don't just observe the physical but also take into consideration the emotional and spiritual when it comes to health and healing.

I've included a run down of some of the most popular natural therapies available today.

ALEXANDER TECHNIQUE

The Alexander Technique is a method of re-educating the body and mind to overcome poor posture and movement, reducing physical and mental tension. It was created by Frederick Matthias Alexander, a Tasmanian actor born in 1869 who spent 10 years studying the movements of his body to formulate the technique. He noticed how essential neck, head and back alignment was for proper movement and functioning.

The technique helps to restore neuromuscular coordination as old, inhibiting patterns are replaced with free, more flexible movement. It's usually taught on a one-to-one basis with pupils being shown how to use muscles the way they were originally designed to work.

Recommended for: stress, anxiety, depression, breathing problems, neck and back pain, circulatory disorders, digestive disturbances and muscular aches and pains.

CHIROPRACTIC

Chiropractic was founded by Daniel David Palmer around the turn of this century. He became fascinated with the spine after he treated his office janitor for deafness by realigning bones in his spine.

Widely accepted in modern medicine, chiropractic regards the nervous system as central to good health. Pain and disease occurs when undue pressure is placed on the nervous system.

To maintain health and the normal functioning of the nervous system, chiropractors concentrate on realigning displaced bones, joints, muscles and ligaments, especially around the spine. Spinal adjustments are central to the therapy: the chiropractor concentrates on improving the movement of the spinal joints, and x-rays are used to determine the client's underlying bone structure. X-rays help to diagnose a problem and determine whether chiropractic treatment will be beneficial. If a subluxation is found then treatment is undertaken.

A subluxation refers to improper joint movement which in turn affects the nervous system and surrounding structures.

The chiropractor aims to bring health to the spine and musculo-skeletal system using specialised adjustment of the joints which may involve a number of different movements.

Recommended for: neck, back and shoulder pain, sciatica, stiff joints, sporting injuries and neuro-musculo-skeletal problems.

COLONIC HYDROTHERAPY

Colonic therapy promotes the healthy function of the colon. Its aim is to balance body chemistry, eliminate waste and restore proper tissue and organ function. This is achieved through placing a tube into the rectum and flushing water through it to remove toxic waste that is believed to be caked on the colon. It differs from an enema which uses water to clean the lower bowel, and not the colon, of built-up faeces.

The benefits of colonic hydrotherapy are often questioned. While some people report weight loss, increased energy and clearer, more vibrant skin, others have reported no such advantages. Furthermore, colonic hydrotherapy can strip the bowel of beneficial bacteria:

bacteria that is necessary for the healthy functioning of the gut.

Recommended for: only for special circumstances. Because of the negatives involved, practitioners avoid colonic hydrotherapy. If you were to get it done, make sure it's by a highly trained professional. It is important to follow through with the after care program that is recommended to rebalance the flora of the colon.

FELDENKRAIS

Israelis scientist Moshe Feldenkrais developed Feldenkrais based on the premise that improving posture can change inappropriate muscular and physiological function. It's similar to the Alexander Technique in that it concentrates on correct posture. From a deep desire to heal his own recurring knee injury, Feldenkrais went on to develop this system of healing. It can be applied in two ways.

A trained practitioner can gently manipulate the body in a one-on-one session that lasts 45-60 minutes. This encourages the body to adopt a new approach to movement. The idea is to reprogram the brain via information fed directly to the nervous system so movements are made more efficiently.

The second application is known as awareness through movement. This is taught in groups where students are shown a number of specific movements which they follow. The student is encouraged to remain focused on what the body is doing. Movements need not be exaggerated. With realisation, simply lifting the arm a few centimetres from the body can tell an individual whether they are moving their body correctly. If not, they can re-train it to move in a way that is not going to bring tension and pain.

Like the Alexander Technique, actors, dancers and performers find Feldenkrais beneficial.

Recommended for: conditions where movement has been lost, arthritis, pain, spinal problems and musculo-skeletal injuries.

HERBAL MEDICINE

Herbal medicine is the most ancient form of health care known to humankind; it involves the use of plants to bring about healing. The word "herb" comes from the Latin for grass and although, technically, herbs are seen as plants other than shrubs or trees, many shrubs and trees are used in herbal healing.

Herbs are considered to work by assisting the body's own ability to fight disease and are considered to act biochemically, triggering neurochemical responses in the body. Taken in moderate doses for long enough, the biochemical responses are said to become automatic, even after the herbs are no longer taken. Herbs can work in the body by improving the whole immune system. They work in synergy with the body and are very gentle. The properties of herbs have a powerful ability to draw out the body's toxins.

There are minimal side effects associated with herbal healing: herbs are more easily tolerated by the body. There is also minimal drug interaction, meaning that whereas for example alcohol or certain prescriptions cannot be used in conjunction with some Western drugs because of adverse reactions or counteractions, this is not the case with herbal medicine.

Recommended for: allergies, digestive concerns, headaches, respiratory problems, sleeping disorders, menstrual problems, menopausal concerns and skin diseases.

HOMEOPATHY

Developed in Germany by Samuel Hahnemann nearly 200 years ago, homeopathy is now widely accepted in Europe as a viable form of medicine. In Australia, it is slowly gaining greater acceptance as more people recognise its inherent power to heal.

Homeopathy is based on the principle of "like cures like", also known as the Law of Similars which states that a homeopathic remedy that produces a set of symptoms in a healthy person will relieve those symptoms in a sick person.

The philosophy of homeopathy is that symptoms are signs of the body's effort to throw off disease. Minute doses of biological substances are used to stimulate healing in the body. A professional homeopath can formulate homeopathic remedies which are individually tailored to the client's specific needs for maintaining health. Because homeopathic medicines are so highly diluted, there is little danger of toxicity or side-effects. As a result, they are considered safe to use in the home and are valuable in the treatment of domestic illnesses and for treating children.

Recommended for: colds and flu, allergies, catarrh, depression, stress, cold sores, travel sickness, and much else including acute, chronic, physical, emotional and inherited diseases. How effective treatment is will depend on the individual.

HYDROTHERAPY

Water has long been recognised for its healing benefits. Documented evidence suggests Hippocrates, the father of modern medicine, used water for healing purposes as far back as 460 BC. Since then many have benefited from the healing power of water whether it be by bathing in a natural spring nestled in the mountains or in the bath tub at home. Traditionally speaking, hydrotherapy can be employed in many different ways including compresses, enemas and steam inhalations, ie any treatment that involves the use of water.

Recommended for: relaxation, pain, muscle spasm, assisting joint movement, strengthening muscles and improving circulation.

KINESIOLOGY

Kinesiology, also known as "muscle testing", is the study of muscle movement. It uses gentle muscle testing to monitor information about a person's wellbeing and identifies blockages in the body's natural energy flow. According to kinesiology, muscles become monitors of stress and imbalance in the body. It was developed by chiropractors in the 1960s but unlike the chiropractor, a kinesiologist isn't trained to manipulate the body. A kinesiologist instead uses massage points, diet, nutrition and emotional healing to remedy diagnosed problems.

Kinesiology finds energy blockages in the body. It then concentrates on increasing energy so the body can heal itself.

Recommended for: allergies, stress, emotional disorders, bronchitis, breathing difficulties, PMS and psoriasis.

NATUROPATHY

Naturopathy acknowledges, as the name suggests, nature as the true and only healer – practitioners merely create the optimum conditions for this to occur. Developed in Europe in the late 18th century, naturopathy deals with internal health problems, metabolic disorders and imbalances through treatment of the whole person. Naturopathy addresses the underlying cause of illness, primarily unfavourable habits or lifestyles. It deals with restoring health rather than combating disease. In naturopathy, symptoms are viewed as signs that the body is trying to heal itself.

The aim is to induce health by making the individual more resilient, improving the strength of the immune system. Naturopaths are viewed as teachers rather than doctors, working with patients and educating them about good health practices. Treatment may involve dietary changes, herbal medicines, homeopathy, bodywork or nutritional supplementation. It is gentle and non-intrusive.

Some naturopaths will use iridology. Iridology means "a study of the eyes". The iris works as a display unit of everything that takes place in our bodies. Its various colours, tissues, fibre structure and patterns all correspond to specific organs and tissues in the body and an iridologist can tell through the changes in patterns and colours the state of health of each organ in a person. Iridology cannot tell the name of a disease, but it does show inflammation, toxicity, catarrh deposits, blood supply, and nerve condition, lesions or irritation. Often the cause of an ailment is found in a different location to the site of the symptom. Early indication of imminent conditions can be apparent so that appropriate treatment can be taken to prevent major ailments later in life.

Recommended for: all ailments and conditions.

OSTEOPATHY

Osteopathy is a bodywork therapy that combines a number of principles to help restore the structural balance of the musculo-skeletal system. It combines joint manipulation, physical therapy and postural re-education. It was developed prior to chiropractic and relies on stimulating the body's natural ability to self-heal. While the spine is central to the therapy, the diagnosis of structural problems within the musculo-skeletal system and the corresponding manipulative treatment are the most fundamental aspects of osteopathy.

An osteopath views the body as a complete unit made up of interconnective parts. When the body is healthy it is able to defend itself against injury and infection. It's also able to recover more readily from trauma. This ability to defend itself can only take place when the body is in peak condition, and according to osteopathy this can only occur when there is maximum health at a structural level. It therefore aims to correct any internal malfunctions, encouraging the body's ability to heal itself.

Osteopathy uses "hands on" techniques such as deep tactile pressure, stretching and gentle manipulation of muscles and joints.

Recommended for: back, neck and should pain, headaches, other bodily aches and pains, sprains, sinus problems, sciatica and repetitive strain injuries.

POLARITY THERAPY

Polarity Therapy is based on the premise that illnesses arise because of blockages in our energy flow. This view of energy is very much in line with Eastern thinking, ie the Chinese chi or Indian prana.

Dr Randolph Stone, a naturopath, chiropractor and osteopath, developed the therapy over a 50 year period. Polarity therapy employs a number of "hands on" techniques for healing including massage, breathing techniques, hydrotherapy, exercise and reflexology. All techniques employed are designed to restore a healthy energy flow through the body. These techniques are combined with dietary considerations and counselling to form a holistic approach to healing.

Recommended for: allergies, respiratory problems, headaches and migraines, back pain, digestive complaints, stress and anxiety.

POSTURAL INTEGRATION

Postural Integration is a slow and systematic way of loosening the deep tissue and muscles of the body. During the process, any distortion in posture is reduced and closer alignment with gravity is restored. Also, any repressed fears, needs and wants are expressed and released together with any childhood traumas. These are then integrated, helping the client towards a greater clarity of being, be it in relationships or career. A more vibrant and harmonious state of wellbeing is achieved.

This kind of bodywork is more closely associated with psychotherapy as it pays more attention to the psycho-emotional effects of physical restructuring.

Recommended for: stress, depression and anxiety.

REFLEXOLOGY

Reflexology is the specific bodywork technique of stroking or applying pressure to one part of the body to affect changes in another part of the body. It can be used to relax muscles and stimulate the body's own ability to heal itself. Reflexology works on the principle that the hands and feet are a map of the complete anatomy with reflex areas corresponding to every part of the body.

Reflexologists massage specific areas to relieve tension or blockages along energy meridians which can cause pain and disease. They often target the break-up of lactic acid and calcium crystals accumulated around the 7,200 nerve endings in each foot. The nerve endings found in the feet interconnect extensively through the spinal cord and brain to all areas of the body.

In a typical session, the reflexologist holds each foot, using mainly thumbs to stoke or press the bottom, top and sides. The bottom of the foot has the more effective reflex points but working the top and sides of the foot also has benefits. The treatment will be a combination of general foot massage and pressure on specific points which may correlate to specific problem areas.

Recommended for: stress, circulatory problems and release of toxins.

REIKI

Reiki (pronounced ray-kee) was developed by Dr Mikao Usui, a Japanese Christian. It is based on ancient Tibetan knowledge Usui rediscovered in the mid 1800s.

As a minister in Kyoto, Japan, Dr Usui began researching world religions for a description and understanding of Jesus' healing methods.

After learning Sanskrit, so he could read the ancient and esoteric sutras and after years of study and meditation, Dr Usui finally uncovered the healing knowledge he sought within the symbols of the sacred Tibetan texts. Dr Usui named this rediscovered healing system from the Japanese work rei meaning boundless and universal and ki- the vital life force energy flowing through all living beings.

In Reiki, a practitioner acts as a channel for the universal life force, which enters the body through the crown of the head, and is then experienced as a tingling sensation or warmth, heat, chills or tremors.

A typical treatment covering all the vital areas may take an hour and a half. After a full Reiki treatment clients report a lift in vitality and mental clarity.

Recommended for: stress, fatigue, aching muscles, headaches, colds and flu, cuts, burns, stomach upsets and sprains.

SHIATSU

Shiatsu is a Japanese massage technique that literally translates into "finger pressure". It incorporates a rhythmic series of finger pressures held between three and five seconds to awaken the acupuncture meridians. It also utilises a series of stretches, thus the treatment can be stimulating as well as relaxing.

The aim is to use pressure on the right points to induce the muscles to relax, allowing the chi to flow, and promoting the body's own recuperative abilities. Shiatsu practitioners need to have a good balance of energy themselves as a strict requirement of shiatsu is that the ki or chi of the therapist is in good shape.

Rather than using a massage table, a full shiatsu is usually carried out on a futon or on the floor.

Recommended for: headaches, asthma, constipation, menstrual problems, hay fever, circulatory concerns and tense muscles.

TRADITIONAL CHINESE MEDICINE (TMC)

Based on the principles of yin/yang, TMC embraces a wide range of time tested natural remedies that are thousands of years old. Diagnosis includes tongue, abdomen and pulse readings.

Medicines are used from the mineral, plant and animal kingdom. Some of the herbs used include licorice, mandarin skins, ginger, cardamon and ginseng. The herbs are usually made into special formulas. Traditionally, the herbs are simmered in a ceramic pot, but new methods of extraction have allowed them to be made into more convenient forms like granules and tablets.

Practitioners observe disharmony in the client's systems and then work to bring balance using different treatments. TMC today incorporates a wide range of treatments, including herbal medicine, acupuncture, dietary therapy and massage.

Each treatment is designed to keep a delicate balance of health, emphasising the prevention of disease rather than the masking of symptoms. TMC is a popular form of Eastern healing, practised commonly in the West.

Recommended for: all ailments and conditions.

YOGA

Yoga has been practised in Eastern nations for over 2,000 years and is known as the surest way to reach "the world of permanent happiness". It is derived from a set of 10 basic postures called asanas that go far beyond the famous lotus (sitting cross-legged) position. Each of the static poses focuses on a different area of the body, relaxing and stretching it to prevent injury.

Each posture acts as a counter balance to other postures to make certain balance is maintained. While some of the stretches require a degree of strength and flexibility, yoga is primarily a gentle art and is accessible to everyone. Attention is also paid to breathing exercises, meditation and relaxation.

Recommended for: circulatory problems, lower back pain, stress, asthma, respiratory problems, sleeping disorders, arthritis, anxiety, depression and digestive concerns,. Helps to promote general wellbeing.

Meridian Essential Oils

CENTRAL NERVOUS SYSTEM ***(Brain)***

Basil, Bergamot, Cypress, Frankincense, Geranium, Juniper, Lavender, Lemongrass, Myrrh, Neroli, Palmarosa, Petitgrain, Peppermint, Rosemary, Rosewood, Sandalwood, Tea Tree.

GOVERNING ***(Spine)***

Jasmine, Myrrh, Sage

STOMACH

Black Pepper, Basil, Cardamon, Lime, Bergamot, Tea Tree, Vetiver, German Chamomile, Clary Sage, Cypress, Eucalyptus, Fennel, Geranium, Juniper, Lavender, Lemongrass, Marjoram, Neroli, Orange, Peppermint, Rose, Rosemary, Sage, Sandalwood

HEART

Frankincense, Neroli, Petitgrain, Rose, Rosemary, Sandalwood, Ylang Ylang

SMALL INTESTINE

Basil, Cardamon, Fennel, Frankincense, Geranium, Juniper, Lavender, Marjoram

BLADDER

Clary Sage, Cypress, Frankincense, Juniper, Lavender, Rosemary, Rosewood

KIDNEY

Fennel, Ginger, Frankincense, Juniper, Rose, Sage, Sandalwood

CIRCULATION

Jasmine, Lime, Cardamon, Ginger, Grapefruit, German Chamomile, Roman Chamomile, Lavender, Vetiver, Mandarin, Marjoram, Neroli, Palmarosa, Patchouli, Petitgrain, Rose, Sandalwood, Ylang Ylang

TRIPLE WARMER ***(Thyroid)***

Bergamot, German Chamomile, Roman Chamomile, Frankincense, Jasmine, Lavender, Lemongrass, Marjoram, Patchouli, Peppermint, Pine

GALL BLADDER

Basil, Grapefruit, Rosemary

LIVER

Basil, German Chamomile, Clary Sage, Frankincense, Grapefruit, Lavender, Lemon, Marjoram, Orange, Pine, Rosemary

LUNG

Cedarwood, German Chamomile, Eucalyptus, Lavender, Lemon, Lemongrass, Lime, Marjoram, Peppermint, Pine, Rosemary, Rosewood, Thyme

LARGE INTESTINE

Black Pepper, Cardamon, Eucalyptus, Fennel, Mandarin, Neroli, Tea Tree

SPLEEN

Frankincense, Lavender, Neroli, Patchouli, Petitgrain, Rosemary, Sandalwood

TRIPLE WARMER ***(Adrenals)***

Black Pepper, Neroli, Patchouli, Sage, Thyme

CHAPTER TEN

Aromatherapy & Meditation

MEDITATION HAS BEEN REVERED FOR MANY thousands of years, especially in Eastern cultures. Although its introduction into the West has been met with some scepticism, emerging research has confirmed that through daily practice, meditation can rebalance and restore the mind/body connection. In time this practice translates into a whole new way of seeing and relating to life.

Meditation enables us to be aware of every part of our body. It is a powerful way of becoming more in touch with our essential nature. For centuries humans have recognised a struggle between the heart and the mind, and this struggle often leaves people distressed and confused. The mind can be busy, the body tired and emotions stretched to the limit. Meditation can be practised to provide an equilibrium. The beauty of meditation is its unique ability to centre a person. When you live in the "present moment" life becomes less of a struggle and you find yourself swimming contentedly upstream. Edgar Cayce, referred to as America's "Sleeping Prophet" because he did his best work while meditating, described meditation as "the attuning of the mental body and the physical body to its spiritual source". Meditation also brings a certain calm to that never-ending stream of thoughts.

Every minute of every day can be taken up with mind chatter. We have around sixty thousand thoughts each day of which many are simply recycled – that's a lot of mental activity. Wouldn't it be wonderful if we could be a casual observer to our thoughts rather than an active participant in them? When they provoke unnecessary emotion, worry and concern, to be able to, at any moment we choose, observe the "movie of our mind" and simply sit down to watch. With meditation this is possible.

With meditation instead of pursuing each thought, we simply become aware of its flow. That is, each thought forms and dissolves again, flowing into the consciousness from which it arose.

According to Deepak Chopra, a committed meditator, the ultimate purpose of meditation is to find out who we are "through the progressive settling of the mind". In other words, as the mind begins to settle we come to a greater understanding of who we are and what our life purpose is. It brings us closer to ourselves. In this quiet haven, answers we seek are spoken and desires are fulfilled. Meditating helps you connect with yourself. In our experience, meditators have a calm and self-assured nature. They usually find that everything can be accomplished with ease, fitting in countless activities effortlessly.

The positive physiological effects on the body include the relief from pain and physical discomfort. It can activate the immune system, normalise the heart rate, blood pressure and breathing. In addition to these benefits, the endocrine system (it regulates our hormones) is influenced. Edgar Cayce linked the endocrine glands to the chakras, or spiritual centres. Chakras are powerful energy points within the body located along the energy channel that leads from the bottom of the spine to the top of the head. Along this channel lie seven major chakras. The seven glands of the endocrine system are, according to Cayce, an integral part of the spiritual centres. Meditation helps to open these centres, establishing a connection between the lowest chakra (root chakra) and highest chakra (crown chakra). The book Meditation and the Mind of Man discusses these concepts in greater depth and is well worth reading if you're seeking a deeper understanding of how meditation affects the physiological body in relation to spirit.

Meditation often brings mental harmony and emotional balance. If practised regularly you may feel an even greater sense of wellbeing, increased energy, and enjoy a more restful sleep. Like a pebble dropped into a pond, whose rippling effect sweep out, so too these benefits will flow into other aspects of your life. Embracing meditation is a gentle process which can enhance the quality of your life.

Types of Meditation

GUIDED VISUALISATION

For those who are new to meditation, guided visualisation is a gentle but effective introduction. During this process a story is relayed which takes you on an inner visual journey. There are many cassette tapes and CDs on the market that combine guided visualisation with soothing music, assisting the mind to reach a meditative state. Guided visualisation can take you to many places. You may like to journey through Mother Nature's forests, to deep-sea realms and crystal caves full of wonder, or perhaps you'd like to go for a walk along a beach with your inner child.

Essential oils can enhance each of your visualisation meditations. If your visualisation exercise takes you into forests or calls for you to be inspired to create a new future, you may wish to anchor it by using Pine. Perhaps you want more joy and creativity? The sweet fragrance of Orange would be an ideal choice. If it is a journey where you desire strength, courage and emotional support, Sandalwood is recommended. Use your intuition to guide you and be confident that the oils' properties will safely enhance your quiet time.

ZAZEN

Zazen involves nothing more than being aware of your breath – a technique that is often more difficult to practise than it sounds. The idea of Zazen is to breathe normally, and with each "out" breath to count silently to yourself. Once you have counted to ten you start again from one. After you have established a rhythm you can then begin to count as you inhale and exhale. If you lose count half-way, start again from number one. The first few times you attempt this meditation you may find yourself losing count and being distracted by thoughts or noises. Each time your mind wanders, gently bring your attention back again to counting the breath. Breathing in the aromatic molecules of essential oils such as Eucalyptus will increase the uptake of oxygen in your body. Use Frankincense to connect with your higher self. Basil and Lemon will enhance focus and clarity.

MANTRA MEDITATION

Mantra meditation involves repeating a chosen word (mantra) over and over again while focusing on the sound of the word itself and involving yourself as much as you can in what you are doing.

When choosing a word for mantra meditation try to keep it to no more than two or three syllables. Anything longer can become uncomfortable to repeat during the exhalation of one breath.

While some philosophies maintain that it's the meaning of the chanted word or phrase that matters most, others focus on the vibrational quality of the sound itself. You may find using sounds like aah or mmm more to your liking than using a particular word. Resonance in the body has profound healing effect on organs and tissue.

A repeated sound focuses your awareness and lulls you into a peaceful state. If you find your mind wandering while meditating on a mantra, use the sound of the mantra as a gentle hook to bring your mind back into focus.

TRANSCENDENTAL MEDITATION

Transcendental Meditation (TM) is a simple, natural and effortless procedure. It is widely recognised for its simplicity and effectiveness, and a large body of research over the past thirty years verifies the physiological, psychological and sociological benefits of practising it daily. TM was introduced to the world in 1958 by Maharishi Mahesh Yogi.

During TM your thought processes become calm and the body gains deeper levels of rest. On this level, where the mind is quiet and physical activity is significantly lower, the body has the opportunity to rejuvenate.

TM is simple to practise and easy to learn, but it is best taught by a trained teacher. Generally, the training sessions last four-and-a-half hours and continue over four consecutive days. Rose is a beautiful oil to use during this meditation. I often make my own special massage blend and massage one drop into the centre of the forehead, temples, nape of the neck, and wrists. This anointing ritual is a perfect adjunct to this and other forms of meditation.

VIPASSANA

The basic premise of Vipassana meditation is passive observation to clear the mind. While some techniques utilising mantras or creative visualisation are effective in their own way, they do not address one of the principle objectives of traditional meditation – to clear the mind completely.

Clearing the mind totally so you experience a profound sense of your true self without the mind's constant chattering and interruption is not easy. A ten-day Vipassana retreat gives you the opportunity to learn the technique where you are removed from the distractions of the outside world while receiving guidance from experienced instructors.

The basic technique involves passing your awareness over every part of the body, observing its sensations and allowing thoughts to arise and pass until eventually your mind is cleared and you are at one with your spiritual self.

During this process you can become aware of the mind's constant activity and the power of the ego. However, once a Vipassana student learns to "be" with the mind, the real work begins. Emotions which may have been repressed for a lifetime can emerge.

It takes great courage and patience to remain emotionally objective. One of the most important aspects of Vipassana is to observe without attachment or aversion. If there are painful thoughts, feelings or sensations, the objective is to observe and let them pass. If you reach the blissful advanced stages, as many students do, the challenge is to remain free from attachment.

In some ways, resisting attachment is more difficult than resisting aversion. Imagine being free from the clutter of the mind, simply being you, a divine, infinite and eternal being without worries or restrictions.

Although the ten days seem to pass slowly, most people find by the end of the course they don't want to leave. The retreat takes them away from the worries of the world and puts them in touch with their true, inner selves. The best aspect of this experience is you leave the retreat equipped with a wonderful meditation technique. Jasmine can be used to assist in the process and practice of non-attachment.

PRIMORDIAL SOUND MEDITATION

Primordial Sound Meditation (PSM) originated in India and has been used for thousands of years. Deepak

Chopra recently re-introduced this ancient technique into the West. It does not relate to activity within the mind; its aim is to get to the level of the spirit.

PSM is said to help you get in touch with your essential nature. It is a technique that allows you to take your awareness from the level of activity to a level of silence within.

Deepak describes the silence as the spaces or "gap" between our thoughts. One thought is activity, the next thought is activity, and between these two thoughts is a space where you are having the thought. For example, you may be thinking about work, about what to buy for dinner, that you'd like to eat a chocolate bar – between each of these ideas/thoughts is you, the one who is having the idea/thought. In this silence, the Creator, the originator of the idea/thought, resides.

Sound is used to enter this state of silence. Each person using PSM is given an individual mantra which is based on the sound that was predominant in the universe when they were born. According to Deepak, ancient sages recorded the sounds and then employed the process of Vedic mathematics to actually calculate a person's individual sound. It was an in-depth process that took many hours to calculate. Today, thanks to modern technology, a person's individual mantra can be determined in minutes.

The mantra does not take you back to the moment of your birth, it takes you back to that point of awareness where you originally accessed universal consciousness rather than localised consciousness.

Ancient seers and modern scientists have described the universe as a field of energy and information. Before we are born everything is timeless and spaceless. We then enter a dimension that is defined in time and space. No longer essentially "one with all" we see ourselves as separate individuals and the silence that once reigned is stirred and primordial vibrations arise to structure the world. Vedic science describes this creative process as Nada Brahman – "the universe is sound".

As beings with physical bodies, we too are composed of vibrations. When we are living in balance with our environment our vibrations are in tune with natural rhythms – our individual song is in harmony with the music of the cosmos. The most direct means to create this resonance is to take time each day to quiet our minds through meditation. In this state of restful alertness we can easily access our creativity and energy.

It is believed that certain vibrations – certain sounds – are more conducive to creating this coherence and integrity than others. The most fundamental vibrations of nature – primordial sounds – connect us with the deepest aspect of our beings. We are then reminded that our essential nature is beyond the limitations of time and space, that we are ultimately spiritual beings.

There are many different primordial sounds. The sounds of nature can have a profoundly calming effect – the rhythmic breath of ocean waves, the flowing song of a river, the whisper of the wind through the leaves, the calls of morning birds welcoming the sun. Since the beginning of humankind we have sought connection with nature by producing our own primordial sounds through chanting, drumming and singing. Cultures around the world have developed systems using rhythms and harmonic sound to align individuals with their community and ancestral traditions.

Vedic science has explored the use of specific primordial sound vibrations/mantras. According to this science, the cosmos sings a repertoire of primary vibrations over cycles of time. Knowing the time and place of a person's birth allows the calculation of the appropriate mantra.

Birth is the process of transition from unmanifested universality to manifested individuality. The vibratory energy of the universe at the moment of your birth can service as the vehicle to take you back from individuality to universality. In PSM, your mantra is chosen from about 100 traditional bija or seed sounds which are the subtlest impulses of human language. These gentle vibrations are used mentally to carry your awareness to more refined levels of thinking until you slip into the silent space between thought.

PSM is a simple and direct way to go beyond time-bound individuality to the infinite, eternal realm of pure awareness – the abode of spirit. Regularly accessing this field of unbounded consciousness allows you to connect with the freedom and joy of your innermost being while experiencing the local challenges of daily life.

Once you have been given a mantra and are practising PSM the way you have been taught, you may find other mental activity going on at the same time, your attention going back and forth between the mantra and other thoughts. The idea is not to push the thoughts out. Any time you become aware that the thoughts are dominating, gently shift back to the mantra. As you proceed you'll find the thoughts will get fainter and fainter, then suddenly there comes a time when the mantra disappears altogether and so do the thoughts.

According to Deepak, when you slip into the gap you suddenly become aware of your own presence. With PSM you get to know the spirit as a real force – abstract, mysterious, incomprehensible, but real, more real than gravity, more real than time.

Meditation is a journey that takes us to our essential nature where we can experience this state undisturbed. An individual may only have brief glimpses of their essential state amidst continuing activity of the mind. If you sit down and close you eyes it doesn't matter what you do, it's highly unlikely that you are going to get rid of all your thoughts. Use your special meditation blend to deepen your PSM experience by rubbing a small drop to the centre of your forehead and under your nose. This action will assist you to quieten the inner chatter. By simply, effortlessly and spontaneously using the primordial sound given to you, you will, now and again, experience your true and essential nature.

AROMATHERAPY AND MEDITATION

Smell is interpreted by the right side of our brain, the creative side, therefore encouraging our intuitive response to life. In the process of enhancing our intuitive response, we become more conscious of both our external and internal world, more awake and actively engaged in life.

Our sense of smell plays an integral role in awakening our awareness to our external surroundings.

Practising meditation with aromatherapy will enhance awareness of our inner life.

Aromatherapy can be used in a number of ways to help heighten the meditative experience, and it is possible to create a specific fragrant ambience each time using the simple practice of vaporisation.

Using aromatherapy while meditating brings the revitalising quality of nature into our hearts and homes, awakening our senses and enabling us to engage more fully in life. It is not always possible to find a sanctuary among natural surroundings. With essential oils you can bring nature to you, which is especially beneficial for those living in the heart of the city.

Composing an harmonious meditation blend allows you to explore your own creativity as you experiment with different essential oil combinations. You can blend essential oils in many different ways. You can choose oils intuitively, being led by the fragrance itself, for their specific characteristics or different evaporative rates, for their odour intensity, or simply because they make you feel good.

It takes only a moment to prepare and create your own blend before each meditation session. I have included some of my favourites which you may like to try for yourself. Use a maximum combination of eight drops only.

Essential oils that complement meditation are:

Vaporisation Blend 1.

Geranium, Sandalwood, Mandarin

or

Vaporisation Blend 2.

Lemon, Black Pepper, Petitgrain

or

Vaporisation Blend 3.

Frankincense, Bergamot, Sandalwood

These particular blends can be used to centre the mind and body. As well as vaporising, apply 1 drop of the chosen essential oil combination to the centre of the forehead, the temples, the nape of the neck and the pulse points of the wrist.

GETTING STARTED

There are many ways to mediate. I have included an overview of several methods so you can choose the one that is the most appropriate for your lifestyle. Effective meditating opportunities are always available. You can meditate while sitting on your back verandah, walking, gardening, sitting in an aromatic bath or just before falling asleep. To make this quality time available, plan it in your day.

Responses to meditation vary. If your mind races, let it run. If your mind wanders, let it stroll; it is a time to observe. If you are focusing on a particular point or mantra then gently bring yourself back to it each time your mind wanders. When you observe the mind rather than attempting to control it, the chatter becomes quiet and the mind less cluttered. There are several essential oils which have properties that help to focus the mind and clarify thoughts. Blending these oils with others which have qualities you like will further enhance your meditative experience.

Vaporisation Blend 4.

Lemon, Basil, Ginger

or

Lime, Rosemary, Basil

Vaporisation Blend 5.

Lavender, Neroli

or

Jasmine, Cedarwood, Mandarn

PREPARING FOR THE DAY

You can welcome in a new day by meditating before sunrise. Before you sit down to meditate, be aware of what is present in the moment and what messages were revealed from sleep – you may like to write down your dreams. Then take a few minutes to think about what lies ahead. Once you have walked through the day in your mind, take twenty minutes to become the observer of your thoughts and allow body and mind to enter a deep, meditative space. This time of silence will provide a solid platform from which to begin your journey. You will come out of this meditation feeling alive, refreshed, alert and ready to take on any challenge that lies ahead.

Vaporisation Blend 6.
Lemon, Black Pepper, Petitgrain

Vaporisation Blend 7
Sandalwood, Cardamon, Frankincense

MIDDAY MEDITATION

Balance is not a static state. Your own internal barometer is constantly at work monitoring stress levels in the body and the mind. In order for the scales not to tip, we must continually fine tune and adjust as we meet our challenges, be it in the corporate world or as a busy parent. Taking time out during the day will ensure the scales are balanced, it will give you more energy and help you enjoy the challenges that lie ahead. If you're working under fluorescent lighting and in an air-conditioned office, a brisk walk in the sunshine will help to enliven your body. A twenty-minute doze in a nearby park will regenerate body and mind. On these occasions bring with you a handkerchief or tissue that has your favourite oil on it (you can choose from the oils below) and inhale the wonderful aromas. Some of the best oils to use in the middle of the day are:

Vaporisation Blend 8.
Peppermint, Fennel, Rosemary

or

Vaporisation Blend 9.
Ginger, Cardamon, Lime

EVENING MEDITATION

We can use this time to let go of our daily activities and concerns and prepare for the evening ahead. In ancient times an aromatic blend was used to do just this. It was known as Kyphi. Records of its ingredients were found written on Egyptian papyrus of Ebers, 1500BC. Susanne Fischer-Rizzi, author of the Complete Aromatherapy Handbook states it was originally burned as incense and is documented as the first commercial perfume recipe, marketed by the Greeks and Romans. The original Kyphi blend contained 16 fragrances yet only 12 were translated.

According to ancient historians (Plutarch and Dioscorides), this exotic mix of herbs and spices was burnt during the evening to honour the sun god Ra. It was said that Kyphi removed the worries of the day, relaxed and calmed fears and anxieties and brought about sweet dreams.

Vaporisation Blend 10.
Ginger, Myrrh, Frankincense

AYURVEDA

"Healing is a matter of unification" writes Dr Vasant Lad, an Ayurvedic doctor in the USA. We believe Ayurveda and aromatherapy can be a dynamic duo in enhancing the process of total wellbeing in a very gentle and natural manner.

To understand how we can benefit from this therapeutic union it is important to grasp the Ayurvedic approach to life, from its most primal to its most cosmic expression. The principles associated with Ayurveda have been developed by some of the most profound scientists, doctors, seers and sages in the world over thousands of years. Although relatively new in Western civilisation, its concepts are being hailed by institutions such as the World Health Organisation as the alternative medical kit for the nineties.

A large proportion of India's population has always been treated by Ayurvedic methods and still is because of the use of local products rather than dependence upon Western treatments. Herbs and essential oils are used in many of their treatment programs.

The ancient tradition of Ayurveda was originally cultivated by holy men (Rishis) in India approximately 5,000 years ago. It is claimed to be the oldest of all medical traditions and has impacted upon medical practices in the East including Tibet and China, the Middle East, Egypt and as far south as Indonesia. It was suppressed for a time during British colonisation of India and was brought to the West by holistic pioneers including Dr Vasant Lad and Dr Deepak Chopra.

Deepak describes Ayurveda as the "wisdom of life" whereby our bodies can be seen and treated "as unique expressions of nature's intelligence" as opposed to the Western way of isolating an area that is causing problems, pain or disease and alleviating the symptoms as quickly as possible, without dealing with the root cause of the problem. In the Western psyche, wellbeing is often evaluated primarily through the physical signals that a person carries: if everything looks good on the outside and we contain, hide or deny any neuroses such as stress, then we are considered well.

Ayurveda encompasses a holistic approach to healing and looks deeply and broadly, applying a "three-part harmony" (body, mind, spirit) to evaluate, establish and clarify a pattern of total health in the belief that physical ailments mostly result from a breakdown within the body's emotional, psychological and internal systems. It is the threefold aspect of essential oils (addressing mind, body and spirit) that makes aromatherapy such a powerful ally to Ayurveda.

The Sanskrit term for Ayurveda literally means "science of life". It relates to our body's unique interrelationship between physical experiences (including physiology, work or career path engaged in during a lifetime, diet, the surrounding environment and climate), the emotional equilibrium, and the cosmos which expands to include the realms of higher consciousness.

According to Ayurvedic philosophy, experiencing life is one of the most important qualities contributing to total health. If you lose all sense of time when you are engaged in an activity, this is a sure sign that you are on the right track to recognising where your spirit soars and where lies the potential to discover your ultimate purpose in life. From this place a wellspring of positive lifeforce or prana can be released, the desire for health is strong and a harmony can be encouraged naturally within the body. It is primarily an imbalance of prana that causes discomfort within a person leading to disharmony and disease.

AYURVEDIC PHILOSOPHY

To gain a greater insight into Ayurveda it is beneficial to comprehend its underlying philosophy. The Rishis spoke of two metaphysical principles behind existence – Purusha, the Primal Spirit, the principle of consciousness, and Prakruit or Great Nature, the principle of creativity. It is in the union of these two principles, Purusha representing the original male energy and Prakruti representing the original female energy, that everything in existence material and ethereal is produced. Ayurveda states that within all things dwells the essence of Purusha – consciousness and individuality, and the entity of Prakruti - creation and the power to create. Through the union of these great dynamics comes the birth of Cosmic Intelligence.

According to Ayurveda, this intelligence lies within every cell contained in each one of us and also abides in the ever-evolving, expanding cosmos. Inside every molecule of essential oil is the blue print to Mother Nature, whole and complex. What interrupts the continual process of prana is the ego, which produces a state of separation from this powerful union. It is our ego, both collective and individual, which can build conditioned mind-sets, limit our liberated state of consciousness and bind us to the limits of self-perpetuating misconceptions rather than continually evolving knowledge and life.

KNOW YOUR BODY TYPE

Ayurveda is a highly personalised therapy that embraces elements such as diet, meditation and yoga, herbal remedies, movement and exercise, mild sun exposure, breathing, and massage to restore balance. Aromatherapy is incorporated by using its powerful indications to bring harmony to what is called the doshas. There are three major doshas contained in Ayurveda; they represent the entire constitution of a person both physically and emotionally. To know your dosha is to gain an intimate understanding of yourself.

Deepak Chopra describes the doshas as an individual's blueprint which outlines all of the innate tendencies built into the human system. For example, a dosha can explain why one person reacts to particular food types, aromas or environmental conditions in a certain way while another reacts quite differently. The doshas do not only include the physique such as build, hair thickness, colour of eyes, shape and size of facial features, digestive qualities, skin texture, but also sexual tendencies, foods most often desired, fragrances most often preferred, emotional characteristics and the way a person is motivated to make decisions on their life's path.

According to Ayurveda there is a Five Element Theory which explains how each of the doshas has been derived. The Rishis believed that everything is made up of the five natural elements: space, air, fire, water and earth. It is the relationship between these elements which forms each of the doshas.

The first dosha, Vata, is composed from the first two elements in nature – space and air, which depicts freedom of movement. Many of the qualities of a Vata type express these characteristics. For instance, agile, cool, dry skin, thin build, tendency to be restless and so on. Pitta, the second principle, is derived from the elements fire and water and characterises transformation. You will note that Pitta types have fiery emotions, such as aggression and passion, and inflammatory qualities, i.e. prone to ulcers. Yet they also can have water or moist attributes including perspiring skin, excellent clarity and sharpness of mind, and a noticeable balance between both elements. Kapha is the third principle and is the combination of earth and water which characterises structure. Kapha types have solid builds, moist, cool skin and strong, definitive gestures and, similar to earthy qualities, are sturdy, patient and calm.

The Rishis also recognised that the three doshas are aligned to the three principles of nature which incorporate the elements mentioned above: Vata – movement, Pitta – transformation or metabolism, and Kapha – structure. These relate to specific physical components of the human body. Alternative Medicine – The Definitive Guide compiled by The Burton Goldberg Group explains that Vata activates the physical system and resides in circulation, breath and functions that involve motion. Pitta involves transformation and metabolism, therefore it is responsible for digestion and the intake of air and water that charge our enzymes. Kapha is located in the bone, muscle, and fat tissues that hold our body together. According to the vedas, when all elements and forces that structure our body are in complete harmony with the elements and the forces which structure the body of the universe, optimum health and wellbeing can be achieved.

I have listed the characteristics of each dosha. You will probably find you have qualities from all three but generally one dosha will dominate. It is very rare to have all three dominate equally. You may have a dominant physical Vata dosha but emotionally you are akin to Pitta qualities. This is not unusual. Sub-doshas are just as important in learning to understand exactly which dosha you are. Often people are dominant physically in one dosha and emotionally in another. When you become intimate with these qualities you can begin to meditate on the attributes of each, and learn to apply essential oils which bring balance and harmony. I also encourage you to further research each dosha.

VATA DOSHA TYPE

- *Light, thin build, unusually tall or short.*
- *Prominent joints.*
- *Agile and quick in movement.*
- *Olive complexion – tends to tan easily.*
- *Body hair light or excessive.*
- *Small eyes, usually brown/dark.*
- *Cold skin, particularly hands and feet.*
- *Dry, rough skin prone to premature wrinkling.*
- *Dislikes cold weather.*
- *Often has chapped, dry lips.*
- *Dry hair with a thick, rough texture, often wavy.*
- *Bowel movement often constipated or hard stools.*
- *Menstrual cycle light, irregular.*
- *Light sleeper; tendency toward insomnia.*
- *Eats at irregular intervals.*
- *Dislikes routine.*
- *Talkative.*
- *Enthusiastic, vivacious, imaginative.*
- *Excitable, mood swings.*
- *Has difficulty making decisions.*
- *Good short-term memory.*
- *Tendency to worry and become anxious.*
- *Imaginative, restless.*
- *Motivated creatively.*
- *Performs activity quickly.*

IT IS VERY VATA TO

- *Be hungry at any time of the day or night.*
- *Love excitement and constant change.*
- *Go to sleep at different times every night, skip meals, and keep irregular habits in general.*
- *Move quickly.*
- *Display bursts of emotion that are short-lived and quickly forgotten.*
- *Eat either raw or rich foods.*
- *Suffer insecurity, nervousness and flightiness.*

BALANCING EXCESS VATA

To return the body to a more mobile state, when lightness of being and a sense of warmth are needed to remove any obstacles, use the following essential oils: Black Pepper, Clary Sage, Fennel, Frankincense, Lemon, Lemongrass, Myrrh, Sandalwood, Ginger, Pine, Thyme.

PITTA DOSHA TYPE

- *Medium build.*
- *Medium bone structure.*
- *Moderate strength and endurance.*
- *Fair or ruddy skin, often freckled.*
- *Light, fine body hair.*
- *Light coloured eyes.*
- *Skin warm to touch.*

- *Oily skin.*
- *Aversion to the sun, hot weather.*
- *Lips red, prone to cold sores, blisters.*
- *Fine, oily, fair, red hair, tendency to greying.*
- *Regular bowel movement with loose, oily stools.*
- *Often heavy menstrual bleeding.*
- *Regular sleep patterns.*
- *Can't miss meals.*
- *Organised.*
- *Precise, articulate speech.*
- *Caring, intelligent, sharp.*
- *Enterprising character, likes challenges.*
- *Quickly makes decisions.*
- *Good long-term and short-term memory.*
- *Can become irritable under stress.*
- *Focused.*
- *Motivated intellectually.*
- *Performs activities meticulously.*

IT IS VERY PITTA TO

- *Feel ravenous if dinner is late.*
- *Take command of a situation.*
- *Wake up in the night thirsty.*
- *Have determined stride when you walk.*
- *Become sarcastic, or critical at times.*
- *Love spicy, stimulating foods.*

– *Become aggressive, irritable or jealous.*

BALANCING EXCESS PITTA

To return the body to a calm state, dispelling heat and providing nourishment to the whole organism are what is needed. Essential oils with cooling and astringent properties are: Bergamot, Cedarwood, German Chamomile, Cypress, Fennel, Lavender, Lime, Palmarosa, Peppermint, Neroli, Rose, Tea Tree, Vetiver, Ylang Ylang.

KAPHA DOSHA TYPE

– *Solid, powerful build; great physical strength and endurance.*
– *Big, heavy bones.*
– *Steady energy, slow and graceful in action.*
– *Tans easily.*
– *Moderate body hair.*
– *Big, often blue or liquid brown eyes.*
– *Skin cool but not cold to touch.*
– *Cool, smooth, thick, pale and often oily skin.*
– *Dislikes heat or humidity.*
– *Full lips.*
– *Thick, dark, lustrous hair.*
– *Full, healthy bowel movements.*
– *Often fluid retention accompanies menstruation.*

- *Loves sleep.*
- *Comfort eats.*
- *Likes routine.*
- *Slow in speech.*
- *Patient, compassionate, relaxed.*
- *Tendency towards obesity.*
- *Slow, steady decision maker.*
- *Good memory.*
- *Tendency to be possessive, complacent.*
- *Gentle, quiet, sweet nature.*
- *Like to follow plans.*
- *Performs activities at a steady pace.*

IT IS VERY KAPHA TO

- *Eat regular meals.*
- *Feel content.*
- *Wake up slowly, lie in bed a long time.*
- *Meander, walk gracefully.*
- *Hold grudges.*
- *Love, sweet, heavy foods.*
- *Become greedy or attached.*

BALANCING EXCESS KAPHA

To give the body a more light and refined state, movement and warmth are key factors in bringing balance. Essential oils with warming and stimulating qualities are:

Basil, Cardamon, Roman Chamomile, Eucalyptus, Fennel, Grapefruit, Jasmine, Juniper, Mandarin, Petitgrain, Rose, Rosemary, Sage.

Once you have established your dosha type you will open up a new understanding of the way you function naturally. This can be a very liberating experience, and the challenge of intimately knowing yourself and what works for you in life can be greatly illuminated.
Everything you eat, your actions, the exercise you partake in and the essential oils you use to enhance your wellbeing can be chosen with a new awareness that is in line with your individual needs.

When doshas are balanced you will experience a sense of effervescence of spirit that you may not have felt in years. You will begin to easily detect when you are not in balance, recognising symptoms such as stress, lethargy and physical ailments as signs that you need to realign yourself. Listen for the messages, as many internal and external causes can throw you off balance. Aromatherapy can assist in gently eliminating any internal turmoil which can be very powerful if it is an aggravated attribute within your dosha.

One guiding rule of thumb to remember when learning to balance your dosha is that like-increases-like. Dr Vasant Lad writes that it was the great Ayurvedic physician Charak who discovered that all organic and inorganic matter as well as thoughts and actions have definite attributes. If you are subject to too many attributes in any one dosha, imbalance, even derangement, can result. For instance, if you are Pitta dominant and eat loads of hot, spicy foods you will find that you become aggravated because of the fiery qualities in both. Similarly, if you are Vata dominant and live in a chilly, windy climate or in cold conditions e.g. air-conditioning which is too strong and cool, you will not be living in total harmony with your dosha.

Contrary to the rule of balance where applying an opposite attribute is necessary to bring balance, a natural rhythm and flow also has to be considered, especially when it comes to talents and abilities. By denying innate qualities within your character great imbalances can arise. For example, it's easy to imagine a slow, steady Kapha type thriving in a career where there is not too much pressure to perform quickly, and where steady, methodical talents are required. A Vata type would either go crazy with boredom, become anxious that there was something wrong with them for not being able to handle the job, or try to make the job right and eventually suffer from stress or even a nervous breakdown if the demand for performance was high. Alternatively, the

Kapha type would have a similar reaction if placed in a highly creative environment where there was a need for quick-witted action and little routine.

Blends that can bring balance and clarity to dosha attributes are:

Vaporisation Blend 11. (Vata)
Black Pepper, Lemon, Pine

or

Clary Sage, Lemongrass, Thyme

Vaporisation Blend 12. (Pitta)
Bergamot, Cedarwood, Lavender

or

Lime, Neroli, Vetiver

Vaporisation Blend 13. (Kapha)
Grapefruit, Petitgrain, Fennel

or

Jasmine, Mandarin, Cardamon

A PEACEFUL STATE OF MIND

In Ayurveda there are three states of mind or mental energies by which we are dominated. At the lower end is Tamas which basically brings out the worst expression of our dosha qualities. People dominated by Tamas are totally absorbed in themselves. A Vata type dominated by Tamas is characterised by insecurity, nervousness and depression. A Pitta type would be dominated by anger, aggression and destructive tendencies. Kapha characterised by Tamas would produce apathy, laziness and ignorance.

The second state of mind is called Rajas which still skirts around the lower state of mind but is more conscious of materialism whereas Tamas is ego-driven. Rajas temperaments are inspired by material attainment and possession, and are interested in prosperity, politics and prestige. The Vata mind dominated by a Rajas state brings anxiety, frenetic activity and indecision. A Pitta mind dominated by Rajas is critical, bossy and boastful. A Rajas-dominated Kapha is greedy, materialistic and overbearing.

The higher state is Satva which expresses the essence of purity, beauty, graciousness and love. The Vata type dominted by Satva will be a great communicator and vivacious with strong healing qualities. The Pitta type will be friendly, clearly focused and intelligent, and Kapha types will exhibit great compassion, loyalty and stability. Do any of these Satvas sound like you? Recognising where you stand with them can be a great indicator of your own growth, and at the same time be a guide to your state of balance.

Oil Blends to assist a Vata Satva state:

Orange, Frankincense

Oils to assist a Pitta Satva state:

Palmarosa, Lavender, Lime

Oils to assist a Kapha Satva state:

Rose, Roman Chamomile, Mandarin

DOSHA MEDITATION

Because Ayurveda embraces meditation as part of its treatment in promoting the highest state of wellbeing, it is also important to use oils that encourage the best qualities during meditation.

VATA MEDITATION BLEND

Vata types need to be calmed and relaxed. For Vatas, meditation is a time to slow down, to rest the mind and gain clarity and peace. Oils to use are Orange, Frankincense, Sandalwood.

PITTA MEDITATION BLEND

Pittas need to embrace love, joy and a cooling of the temperament. They also need to rebalance and regain focus. Oils to use are Bergamot, Clary Sage, Ylang Ylang.

KAPHA MEDITATION BLEND

Kaphas need to stimulate both the mind and body. They need to release emotions, gain inspiration and regain a sense of vitality and confidence, giving them even greater access to the fruits of life. Oils to use are Black Pepper, Mandarin, Sage.

The meditation blend of Lavender, Jasmine, Rose, Orange and Frankincense in Jojoba can be used for each of the doshas.

Pittas need a cooling oil such as coconut, and Kapha types who already have an oily constitution should need only a minimum amount of oil. Light oil such as sweet almond is best

If you are receiving a massage it is a good idea to discuss your dosha type with the therapist. Ask them to use smooth, relaxing strokes with lots of oil if you are a Vata-dominant. If you are Pitta-dominant ask that the massage promote deep peace with lots of variety in strokes. Kapha types need a more rough and tumble massage, using lots of firm, stimulating strokes that revitalise their slow system.

Learning the techniques of Ayurveda is not so much a complex task as a concentrated one. It does take time to become familiar with the principles involved, but once they are grasped they can initiate a speedy rejuvenation process. Just remember, if you are feeling unbalanced, use your intuition to guide you in your choice of essential oils. By trusting your own intuition you will bring about a renewal of spirit.

We offer these Ayurvedic principles coupled with aromatherapy so you may embrace a beautiful and natural approach to total wellbeing: body, mind and spirit.

APPENDIX

THE FOLLOWING APPENDIX IS A QUICK REFERENCE guide when considering which oils to use for different moods. The first graph refers to oils that help dissipate certain moods and emotions, while the second graph focuses on the moods you'd prefer to enhance. Use this guide with awareness as you develop your own unique relationship with oils. keep in mind that you need to experience each oil in order to gauge its effects.

I know that when I was starting out it made a big difference to be able to access oils for their noted strengths. enjoy and remember to experiment with caution as the oils are very potent and they impact uniquely on each individual.

Refer to the Methods of Use section in this book for creative, effective and safe methods of using the following oils.

TO DIMINISH

Anger	***Roman Chamomile, Rose, Ylang Ylang, Neroli***
Anxiety	***Basil, Bergamot, Geranium, Lavender, Neroli, Cedarwood***
Boredom	***Basil, Frankincense, Lime, Peppermint***
Confidence *(Lack of)*	***Cedarwood, Frankincense, Rosewood, Sandalwood, Myrrh, Jasmine, Vetiver***
Confusion	***Cypress, Lemon, Petitgrain, Rose***
Depression	***Bergamot, Clary Sage, Patchouli, Ylang Ylang***
Despondency	***Ginger, Lime, Lemon, Black Pepper***

Emotional Instability	*Bergamot, Geranium, Myrhh, Neroli, German Chamomile*
Envy/Resentment	*Rose, Roman Chamomile, Juniper, Rose, Thyme, Ylang Ylang*
Fatigue	*Thyme, Palmarosa, Black Pepper*
Fears	*Cedarwood, Frankincense, Sandalwood, Lavender, Petitgrain*
Festering upset	*Tea Tree, Rose, Thyme*
Frigidity	*Roman Chamomile, Clary Sage, Ylang Ylang, Jasmine, Neroli*
Grief	*Marjoram, Rose, Cypress, Rose, Rosewood*

Hysteria (during) (at the end)	*Roman Chamomile, Neroli, Orange, Petitgrain*
Impatience	*Lavender, Ylang Ylang, Rose, Neroli, Palmarosa*
Insomnia	*Bergamot, Lavender, Marjoram, Neroli, Orange*
Jealousy	*Rose, Roman Chamomile, Lime*
Low self-esteem	*Jasmine, Lavender, Grapefruit*
Memory *(Poor)*	*Basil, Rosemary, Lime, Lemon*
Mental Fatigue	*Basil, Cardamon, Pine, Grapefruit, Palmarosa, Lemongrass, Rosemary*

Over sensitivity	*Orange, Lavender, Mandarin*
Nervousness	*Ginger, Palmarosa*
Nightmares	*Bergamot, Frankincense, Mandarin, Sage*
Rage	*German Chamomile, Marjoram, Lavender*
Rigidity	*Peppermint, Sage, Mandarin*
Sadness	*Rosemary, Mandarin, Rosewood*
Spaced-out	*Sandalwood, Myrrh*
Stress	*Bergamot, Lavender, Rose, Myrrh, Sandalwood, Neroli*
Wounds *(Emotional)*	*Roman Chamomile, Frankincense, Rose, Palmarosa*

TO ENCOURAGE

Accepting *(of change)*	*Geranium, Lemon, Sandalwood, Petitgrain, Grapefruit*
Assertion	*Fennel, Basil, Cedarwood, Cypress, Patchouli, Jasmine, Ylang Ylang, Lime, Bergamot, Frankincense*
Assurance	*Geranium, Marjoram, Patchouli, Pine, Frankincense, Cedarwood*
Awakening	*Basil, Peppermint, Juniper, Frankincense, Rosemary, Neroli*
Awareness	*Roman Chamomile, Neroli, Juniper, Rose, Mandarin, Frankincense*

Balance	***Bergamot, Cedarwood, Clary Sage, Marjoram, Cypress, Geranium, Orange, Lavender, Thyme***
Calmness	***Roman Chamomile, Clary Sage, Lemon, Marjoram, Neroli, Ylang Ylang***
Caring	***Lavender, Rose, Roman Chamomile, Sandalwood***
Changeability	***Cypress, Cedarwood, Eucalyptus, Rosemary, Lemon, Myrrh***
Clearing	***Fennel, Juniper, Pine, Cypress, Lemongrass***
Cleansing	***Juniper, Cypress, Pine, Cedarwood, Neroli, Frankincense, Lemon***

Communication	*Orange, Geranium, German Chamomile, Clary Sage, Lemon, Grapefruit*
Concentration	*Basil, Bergamot, Peppermint, Thyme, Rosemary, Cedarwood, Lemon*
(Intellectual)	*Lemon, Basil, Bergamot, Lemongrass, Cedarwood, Peppermint, Eucalyptus, Rosemary, Frankincense*
(Spiritual)	*Frankincense, Neroli, Myrrh, Rose, Roman Chamomile*
Confidence	*Bergamot, Cedarwood, Clary Sage, Cypress, Fennel, Ylang Ylang, Jasmine Absolute, Orange, Pine, Rose, Rosemary, Sandalwood*

Contentment	*Cypress, Rose, Lavender, Bergamot, Orange, Ylang Ylang, Patchouli, Roman Chamomile, Neroli, Sandalwood*
Conscious	*Lemon, Rosemary, Basil, Bergamot, Lavender*
Courage	*Frankincense, Marjoram, Orange, Fennel, Thyme, Cedarwood, Sandalwood*
Creativity	*Bergamot, Lemon, Orange, Neroli, Geranium, Rosemary, Frankincense, Rose, Sandalwood, Cypress, Juniper, Black Pepper, Rosewood*
Decisiveness	*Basil, Lemon, Thyme, Cedarwood, Vetiver, Peppermint, Lime*

Emotionally Refreshing	*Peppermint, Lemon, Bergamot, Orange, Grapefruit, Palmarosa*
Empowerment	*Thyme, Sandalwood, Cedarwood, Frankincense, Jasmine*
Endurance	*Myrrh, Thyme, Pine, Sandalwood, Rosemary, Black Pepper*
Enthusiasm	*Orange, Lemon, Ylang Ylang, Basil, Lemongrass, Geranium, Mandarin, Clary Sage*
Expansiveness	*Orange, Clary Sage, Vetiver, Geranium, Lavender, Grapefruit*
Expressiveness	*Neroli, Sandalwood, Orange, Clary Sage, Mandarin*

Extroversion	*Patchouli, Rose, Sage, Eucalyptus*
Flexibility	*Geranium, Lavender, Clary Sage, Orange, Ylang Ylang*
Focus	*Cedarwood, Marjoram, Lemon, Bergamot, Basil, Cypress, Juniper, Lemongrass, Rosemary, Black Pepper*
Generosity	*Lemon, Sandalwood, Lavender, Geranium,*
Growth	*Vetiver, Fennel, Orange, Frankincense*
Groundedness	*Clary Sage, Patchouli, Vetiver, Sandalwood, Myrrh, Fennel, Ginger, Petitgrain*

Humility	*Juniper, Pine, Neroli, Roman Chamomile, German Chamomile*
Imagination	*Rose, Patchouli, Orange, Jasmine Absolute, Neroli, Ylang Ylang*
Intuition	*Sandalwood, Juniper, Clary Sage, Sage, Pine, Lavender, Frankincense*
Inspiration	*Thyme, Frankincense, Pine, Neroli, Rose, Bergamot, Lemon*
Integrity	*Basil, Orange, Marjoram, Vetiver, Lavender, Cedarwood*
Invigoration	*Thyme, Peppermint, Rosemary, Eucalyptus, Pine, Cedarwood, Lime, Lemongrass, Cardamon*

Joy	*Bergamot, Neroli, Orange, Fennel, Rose, Frankincense, Ylang Ylang*
Letting go	*Lemon, Peppermint, Pine, Rose, Marjoram*
Loving	*Rose, Neroli, Lavender, Ylang Ylang*
Meditative States	*Frankincense, Myrrh, Juniper, Lavender, Sandalwood*
Motivation	*Black Pepper, Basil*
Organisation	*Basil, Cedarwood, Lemon, German Chamomile, Peppermint, Eucalyptus*
Passion	*Patchouli, Ylang Ylang, Jasmine, Rose*

Positivity	*Basil, Lemon, Cedarwood, Bergamot, Pine, Vetiver, Patchouli, Juniper, Myrrh, Cypress, Orange, Rosemary, Geranium, Frankincense*
Powerfulness	*Cedarwood, Cypress, Thyme, Sandalwood, Patchouli*
Protectiveness	*Cypress, Frankincense, Cedarwood, Geranium, Roman Chamomile, Jasmine Absolute, Rose, Lavender, Sandalwood*
Purity of heart	*Cypress, Neroli, Rose, Roman Chamomile*
Purposefulness	*Basil, Cedarwood, Peppermint, Eucalyptus, Lemon, Grapefruit, Lime*

Regeneration	*Clary Sage, Geranium, Neroli, Orange, Lavender, Rose, Frankincense*
Relaxation	*German Chamomile, Roman Chamomile, Clary Sage, Lavender, Cedarwood*
Restorative	*Rosemary, Eucalyptus, Peppermint, Lavender, Pine, Clary Sage, Neroli*
Revitalising	*Orange, Peppermint, Rosemary, Clary Sage, Lavender, Neroli, Lemon*
Reviving	*Rose, Eucalyptus, Bergamot, Lavender, Rosemary, Geranium, Lemongrass*
Self-awareness	*Clary Sage, Ylang Ylang, Cypress, Geranium, Pine, Sandalwood*

Self-esteem	*Sandalwood, Vetiver, Ylang Ylang, Rose, Bergamot, Geranium, Cedarwood*
Self-image	*Orange, Lavender, Pine, Roman Chamomile, Ylang Ylang, Sandalwood, Jasmine, Cedarwood, Frankincense*
Sensuality	*Rose, Sandalwood, Ylang Ylang, Patchouli, Jasmine*
Spontaneity	*Lemon, Orange, Grapefruit, Neroli, Roman Chamomile*
Stability	*Roman Chamomile, Geranium, Myrrh, Sandalwood, Neroli, Rosemary, Cedarwood, Cypress*

Straight forwardness	*Peppermint, Frankincense, Basil, Cedarwood, Lemon*
Strengthening	*Cedarwood, Ginger, Marjoram, Rosemary, Sandalwood, Lavender, Jasmine, Petitgrain*
Sympathetic	*Orange, Lavender, Geranium, Neroli,*
Tenderness	*Neroli, Rose, Lavender, Jasmine, German Chamomile*
Transformation	*Frankincense, Myrrh, Patchouli, Petitgrain, Sandalwood*
Upliftment	*Lemon, Eucalyptus, Orange, Basil, Palmarosa, Rosemary, Bergamot*

Visualisation	*Lavender, Frankincense, Sandalwood, Myrrh, Fennel*
Warmth	*Ginger, Ylang Ylang, Sandalwood, Jasmine*
Wisdom	*Frankincense, Juniper, Rose, Vetiver*

BIBLIOGRAPHY

LITERATURE THAT I HAVE SCANNED OVER THE YEARS helped me considerably in the compilation of this book.

I extend my thanks and appreciation to the authors of these books and journals.

AROMATHERAPY

The Sense of Smell, Olfaction, Report by Dr Lewis Thomas,

Chancellor of Memorial Sloan-Kettering Cancer Centre, New York, and Chairman of *Monell Chemical Senses Centre,* Philadelphia.

The Book of Perfumes by Eugene Rimmel.

The Fragrant Pharmacy by Valerie Ann Worwood (Macmillan, London).

Aromatherapy for Women by Maggie Tisserand (Thorsons).

Using Essential Oils For Health and Beauty by Daniele Ryman (Century).

Scents and Scentuality by Judith White and Karen Downes (Nacson & Sons).

The Relationship Between Health and Outside Stimuli, Report by Arch Minchin, PhD, University of Wisconsin, USA (1986).

Aromatherapy – Therapy or Placebo by Arch Minchin, PhD, & Peter Young, PhD, University of Wisconsin, USA (1987).

The International Journal of Aromatherapy, Sussex, England.

The Complete Guide to Aromatherapy, Salvatore Battaglia

The Aromatherapy Practitioner Reference Manuals, Sylla Shepherd-Hanger

L'Ami des ingredients Naturels, Alban Muller International.

Essential Oil Safety, Robert Tisserand, Tony Balacs (Publisher Churchill Livingstone).

Aromatherapy for Scentual Awareness, Judith White and Karen Downes (Nacson & Sons)

Aromatherapy for Meditation & Contemplation, Judith White, Karen Downes and Leon Nacson (Nacson & Sons)

Aromatherapy for Lovers & Dreamers, Judith White, Karen Downes and Leon Nacson (Nacson & Sons)

Aromatherapy for Natural Health, Judith White and Karen Downes (Nacson & Sons)

Aromatherapy for Men, Judith White and Karen Downes (Nacson & Sons)

HEALTH AND FITNESS

The Biogenic Diet by Leslie Kenton (Arrow, London).

Peace Of Mind by Ian Gawler (Hill of Content Publishing, Melbourne).

The Health Revolution by Ross Horne (Southwood Press Pty Ltd).

Meditation by Judy Jacka (Lothian Publishing Company, Melbourne).

The Book Of Massage by Lucinda Lidell with Sara Thomas, Carola Beresford Cooke and Anthony Porter (Ebury Press).

The Family Book Of Homeopathy by Dr Andrew Lockie (Penguin Books, Australia).

Nature and Health Magazine, February 1992, Vol 13, No. 1.

Alternative Health Care For Women by Patsy Westcott (Collins Angus & Robertson Publishers)

Rudolf Hauschka Nutrition, Stuart & Watkins London

OTHERS

Blue Eyeshadow Should Still Be Illegal by Paula Begoun (Beginning Press, Seattle, Washington, USA).

Oxford Concise Medical Dictionary (Fifth Edition) Editor Elizabeth A Martin, Oxford Uni Press

MAKING THE RIGHT CHOICE

FOR EFFECTIVE THERAPEUTIC USE IT IS VITAL that only pure essential oils are used in aromatherapy. Do not fall into the trap of buying cheaper, impure oils. Often they do not work effectively on a therapeutic level and there may be bodily reactions to the additives.

Unscrupulous suppliers can and do dilute a pure essential oil into a massage base oil and pass it off as pure essential oil. For this reason it is advisable that you purchase your oils from a reputable company.

I recommend that you investigate the commitment and dedication your supplier has to the healing arts. Their intention and attention in this arena will greatly determine their choices in quality.

Remember these oils are digested by your body on many different levels!

TAKE GOOD CARE

Not all plants and plant products are beneficial to health. Some are poisonous and dangerous. The author encourages you to follow the guidelines in this book.

The material in this book is not meant to take the place of diagnosis and treatment by a qualified medical practitioner. The author's recommendations in this book is based on her own experiences and extensive personal research. However, a small number of people may react differently to certain oils due to biochemical individuality.

For this reason, the author and publisher make no guarantees as to the effects of their use and no liability will be accepted.

For more information

Freecall 1 800 802 036 or **Freefax 1 800 062 888**

Or write to:

Judith White, c/o 221 Kerr St, Fitzroy, VIC, 3065 Australia